The Individual and Society
A Cultural Integration

The Individual and Society
A Cultural Integration

Fathali M. Moghaddam

Georgetown University

Worth Publishers

To Mariam, Nikoo, and Guilan

The Individual and Society

© 2002 by Worth Publishers

All rights reserved.
Printed in the United States of America
ISBN: 0-7167-5222-0

First printing, 2002

Sponsoring Editor: Graig Donini
Executive Marketing Manager: Renee Altier
Associate Managing Editor: Tracey Kuehn
Production Manager: Sarah Segal
Art Director/Cover Designer: Barbara Reingold
Interior and Cover Designer: Lissi Sigillo
Cover Art: Andy Warhol, *Let Us Now Praise Famous Men,* The Andy Warhol
Foundation, Inc./Art Resource, NY
Composition: Compset, Inc.
Printing and Binding: R. R. Donnelley and Sons, Harrisonburg

Library of Congress Cataloging-in-Publication Data
Moghaddam, Fathali M.
    The individual and society / Fathali M. Moghaddam.
        p. cm.
    Includes bibliographical references and index.
    1. Social integration. 2. Individuation (Philosophy) 3. Social psychology.
I. Title.

    HM683 .M64 2002
    302.5'4—dc21

                                                2001046902

Worth Publishers
41 Madison Avenue
New York, New York 10010
www.worthpublishers.com

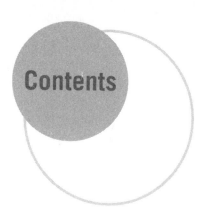

Contents

Chapter 3

Chapter 4

Chapter 5

Chapter 6

Chapter 7

Chapter 8

Chapter 9

Intelligence and the Social Order   128

PART 2 | THE INDIVIDUAL

Chapter 10

Memory as Carrier   149

Chapter 11

Chapter 12

Chapter 13

Foreword

All we know and can hope to know begins with our awareness, our personal conscious experience. Scientific knowing works in two ways: the first is the more common dissection of our experience into its parts. The other is by way of consensual validation, the idea that the socially valid meanings of symbols come from a consensus among the members of a community. *The Individual and Society* takes account of both approaches to knowing, though it emphasizes the less commonly acknowledged path through consensual validation.

I am pleased to find a text that takes this approach to the psychological disciplines and, perhaps surprising, given Moghaddam's cultural orientation, makes progress along a path I helped to innovate, but from a neuroscience perspective. Back in the mid 1960s, I drew this distinction between two ways of doing science: the downward-looking dissecting path is called reductive science; the upward-looking consensual path is called normative science.

Normative science has its beginnings early in experience. A baby is hungry, sees its mother, and hears her talking and singing. The mother picks up the baby, who feels the mother's skin and breast, then grasps the nipple, sucks, and tastes the milk. These many experiences are ordinarily seamlessly intertwined into a single experience, which later is called "Mama."

Somewhat later in life we obtain knowledge and a vocabulary to deal with knowledge through consensual validation provided by caretaking persons. When my older children pointed to a flying object, they were told that it was a bird. Bird, bird, bird. But occasionally the flying object was a plane, and they had to differentiate plane from bird. Not bird, plane, plane, plane. With my younger children, the course of validation was the opposite. They first encountered planes and then birds!

Reductive and normative approaches are used in both the natural and the social sciences. In physics, the theories of relativity of Einstein are not reductive: They are extremely context sensitive. Einstein imagined himself riding on a beam of light. He recognized the odd feeling one has when on a train or plane and there is relative movement. One does not know whether it is one's carriage or the surroundings that is moving.

On the other hand, in the social sciences, when an economist worries about the effect on inflation of adjusting the interest rate, he is selecting one particular variable to manipulate (experiment with) in a complex situation that is affected by many other variables.

As noted in *The Individual and Society,* context sensitivity brings up the problem of causality. Moghaddam argues that meaning, rather than cause, is central to understanding human behavior. Here, he is referring to what Aristotle called efficient causality: The cause precedes the effect it produces. Aristotle also discussed formal causality, understood as a more general explanation of the form or structure of a process which we ordinarily do not heed in science. Formal causality is the appropriate vehicle for understanding meaning.

Final causation, explained by Aristotle as an end or purpose of natural processes, is also to be reckoned with. Arnold Toynbee in *A Study of History* (Oxford University Press, 1946) notes that the effects of a cause are inevitable, invariable, and predictable. However, he also points out that the initiative that is taken by one or another of the live parties to an encounter is not a cause; it is a challenge. A challenge is to be understood in what we today call an "attractor" in nonlinear dynamics. The point is that final and formal "causality" can portray Toynbee's challenge and the meanings in *The Individual and Society.*

Both Toynbee and *The Individual and Society* make the point that as traditionally interpreted by social scientists, the natural sciences are essentially devoted to efficient causal explanations. But the theories of relativity do not fit this traditional mold nor does quantum field theory where observations differ depending on which experimental apparatus is being used.

The Individual and Society explores the point that the reductive approach deals with performance capacity while the normative approach deals with performance style. Further, it makes the point that performance capacity becomes meaningful only through performance style. One of my experimental observations supports the view that brain processes need to be considered in terms of performance style, not just performance capacity. I removed the amygdala on both sides of the brains of monkeys and showed that, as a rule, the monkeys were dramatically tamed. However, taming depended on the form or structure of the social colony from which and into which the monkeys were returned immediately after surgery. If the amygdalectomized monkey was not challenged by an aggressive cage mate, the amygdalectomized monkey became even more aggressive.

When, during the 1960s, the assistant attorney general of California entertained the idea that amygdalectomy might be used to "cure" violent prisoners, I called his attention to these results. The amygdala of the brain is not a "center," a reductive cause of aggression. Brain processes are much more subtle than that.

And so are social processes. Fathali Moghaddam has captured this subtlety in *The Individual and Society.*

Karl Pribram
Stanford University

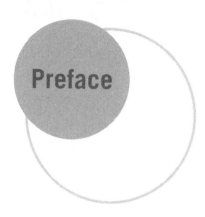

Preface

How is it that individuals grow up to be independent beings with private thoughts and feelings, yet also become integral parts of society? The mystery of our individuality and separateness from society, but at the same time our immersion in collective life, of the individual in society and society in the individual, continues to be central in understanding the human condition. Yet largely because of increasing specialization and fragmentation in research, the dynamic relationship between the individual and society, a very broad topic, does not receive the attention it deserves.

Each group of researchers tends to remain within the confines of their own narrow specialized territory, and in this way the larger picture is neglected. The behavior of individuals is taken to be the domain of psychology, but psychologists rarely give due attention to societal processes related to social class, revolution, war, and the like. Sociologists, political scientists, and others do attend to societal processes, but they rarely attend to intra-individual processes, such as those related to memory, intelligence, and cognitive development.

I wrote this book to show how, on the one hand, even the most micro and biologically based aspects of individual behavior, such as Alzheimer's disease and depression, are fundamentally influenced by the larger social context. Culture matters, even for biological processes. On the other hand, even the most macro features of social context are influenced by micro-level processes at the level of individual behavior. Individuals are not passive receivers of culture; they actively influence larger societal processes. We have no choice but to break out of disciplinary boundaries to better understand the interactive and dynamic relationship between individuals and society.

In line with a multidisciplinary ethos, I have drawn on research from a variety of different domains, including social psychology, sociology, political science, anthropology, cultural psychology, neuroscience, and cognitive psychology. To make the book more accessible, I have avoided unnecessary technical terminology and details and used an informal, often conversational style. The fifteen chapters are brief and structured by numerous headings. To encourage further reading, key references are provided at the end of each chapter.

Acknowledgments

If all the individuals who influenced this book were laid end to end, they would not lead to the concluding chapter. However, they would probably see some aspect of themselves in it, and hopefully would be pleased with what's new. The ideas of the following scholars were particularly influential: Rom Harré (Philosophy, Oxford University), Michael Cole (Psychology, University of California, San Diego), Anthony Giddens (Sociology, London School of Economics), Paul Ehrlich (Biology, Stanford University), Richard Shweder (Human Development, University of Chicago), Michael Billig (Social Sciences, Loughborough University), Don Taylor (Psychology, McGill University), Robert Putnam (Kennedy School of Government, Harvard University), and Karl Pribram (Psychology, Stanford University).

I am also indebted to a number of reviewers of earlier drafts, including Julie Allison (Pittsburg State University), Timothy Dowd (Miami University, Ohio), Yueh-Ting Lee (Minnesota State University), Connie Meinholdt (University of Missouri, Rolla), Philip Moore (George Washington University), Don Taylor (McGill University), Sheralee Tershner (Western New England College).

In writing chapter 6 I relied particularly on earlier research collaboratively undertaken with David Crystal, and similarly in writing chapter 14, I am indebted to the research of my colleague Steven Sabat.

I want to pay special tribute to Graig Donini, a truly inspired and insightful editor, who made substantial contributions to this book. It has been both a privilege and a pleasure to collaborate with Graig. My only complaint is that he tried to dispel the image we authors uphold of publishers and their four-hour lunches.

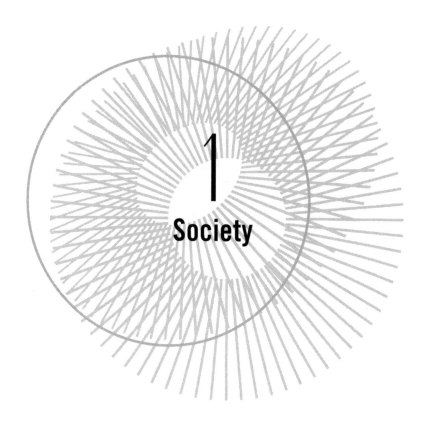

1

Society

1

Toward an Integrated Account of the Individual and Society

"This is the first day of your new lives," the master of ceremonies was announcing emphatically. "From this day on, you will be different people. You will join your fellow Americans in the land of opportunities."

I was seated in a crowd of about 3,000 people, looking up at a stage on which an exciting ceremony was unfolding.

"You are about to become Americans," exclaimed the master of ceremonies, "free Americans, proud Americans."

He paused and we followed his cue to applaud. The military regalia decorating the enormous hall we were in, the glorious fanfare music, the formal attire and respectful demeanor of our fellow would-be Americans, the example set by the master of ceremonies and the other dozen or so men and women standing to attention on stage—all moved us along with the mood of the event.

In case we had any doubts about what we were letting ourselves in for, the next speaker, introduced as an expert in motivation, cleared up matters.

"You can make it. *You* can make it. You *can* make it. You can *make* it," he exhorted in rhythmic style, "But you are asking how? How? *How* can I make it?"

I could feel all 3,000 would-be Americans leaning forward to catch every syllable of what was being passed on to us. The question "How?" was about to be answered. The Indian computer scientist sitting in front of me signaled to her two children to pay close attention. The Chinese family to my right sat even more upright.

"Next time you are walking through a city, an American city, or even a large city in some other part of the world, look around, look up: What do you see?"

I could almost hear 3,000 brains ticking faster, trying to think of the answer. "What do I see?" the Indian computer scientist asked herself. She urged her children to think about the question. "What do we see?" the Chinese children puzzled, frowning and scratching their heads.

"What are you absolutely sure to see?" Asked the speaker, trying to prod us in the right direction. But we proved to be dull pupils, so he jumped in with the answer himself.

"The Colonel!" he exclaimed, "Kentucky Fried Chicken! That's what you see."

I could sense that all 3,000 people in the audience were absolutely amazed by this answer.

"The Colonel started with nothing, with nothing!" To emphasize his words, the speaker pulled out his pockets to show nothing, threw his open hands up into the air to reveal nothing. "But the Colonel made it; he made it and so can you."

The speaker bounded across the stage, waving his arms in the air to inspire us. It was with his exhortations of "You can make it" ringing in my ears that I went through the rest of the ceremony lining up to receive my official papers and crossing the threshold from "resident alien" to American citizen.

In one instant, with that official change of status, so much had changed. Before that moment, I could not vote, but after that I had the right to vote. I could run for political office, for the senate or the House of Representatives. I would now be able to get a U.S. passport and travel as an American. All the rights of citizenship instantly became mine. It was like a revolution.

But something of fundamental importance had not changed. As the ceremony ended and I walked out onto the sunlit street, I did not think and behave any differently, certainly no more like an American than I had before I became a citizen. My own research on immigrants to North America shows that sometimes the longer people live in this part of the world, the less they feel they belong here, so that after a lifetime they feel more like outsiders than they did when they first arrived. But even for those who eventually do feel they belong and do become more American in thought and deed, the process is often a very long one, certainly much longer than the process of getting citizenship papers.

America is often described as a land of immigrants, and received wisdom tells us that it is also a land uniquely characterized by change. However, immigrants also experience America as a land that is in some ways resistant to change, forcing them to try to adapt themselves to their new conditions. Such adaptation is not easily achieved: Immigrants discover that while some of their individual characteristics can be changed fairly easily, others stay persistently stable. For example, while they might become functional in a new language fairly quickly, they cannot change their ethnicity. Similarly, American society changes rapidly in some respects but remains relatively stable in others. For example, laws regarding immigration can change overnight, but attitudes and everyday social practices toward ethnic minorities have generally proved to be far more resistant to change. The immigration experience, then, involves two interdependent processes: Immigrants change as they interact with their new surroundings, and the host society changes as it absorbs and accommodates new groups of immigrants.

The immigration experience acts as a mirror, reflecting the integration experiences of all individuals in society. Human infants eventually become integrated into the larger society into which they are born, while remaining independent individuals to some degree. Inherent in this gradual process is a tension between the rights of individuals to independence, self-expression, and so on, and the duty owed by individuals to the larger society to conform to certain norms, meet certain standards, and so on. At the same time that a sense of independence and free will prevails, so that individuals maintain some measure of separateness, society exerts a profound influence on individual behavior, so that people generally behave in line with *social norms*, ideas about correct behavior in particular contexts. As a consequence of this penetration of the social into the minutest detail of personal lives and the associated integration of individuals into society, we can identify certain regular patterns of behavior in populations. It is to this wider social world, collaboratively constructed but privately interpreted and appropriated, that we must look to explain a wide range of regularity and predictability in human individual behavior, although the subtlety of this influence means that it is easily overlooked.

Of course, individuals also actively and often intentionally influence the larger society; they are not just passive receivers of external influence. Through the countless choices they make in their everyday personal and professional lives, individuals have an impact on larger societal trends. By deciding to use one means of transportation rather than another (the bus rather than the car, for example), by voting for candidate X rather than candidate Y in an election for political office, by purchasing brand Z rather than the alternatives offered on the market, by deciding to attend one educational institution rather than another, individuals exert some influence on larger trends. The role of individual choice must not be overlooked; individuals actively make choices, sometimes with the explicit intention of influencing larger societal processes. This is often clear in elections for political office ("I am voting for this candidate because I want more government control in education and the economy") as well as in commerce ("I refuse to buy this brand because the company uses animals in their research").

Indeed, the argument has been made that in capitalist systems the masses do exert considerable influence on societal processes, including the economy, through their purchasing power. What they buy strongly influences the shape of the market, so it is not the case that the owners of capital have monopoly control. At the same time, the force exerted by "the masses" is made up of individual choices.

Here, then, we have a fundamental challenge for scientists: to provide an integrated account of individuals in society as each influences the other. My argument is that this challenge is best met through a two-pronged approach.

First, we begin by noting that neither the individual nor society is static; both are in a state of continuous change. Consequently, our focus is on an integration of *changing individuals in changing society*.

Second, the changes under consideration involve an enormous range. It is essential that we incorporate this broad range, *from micro-level biological processes to macro-level societal processes*.

Two Central Themes: Change and Micro–Macro Processes

You can't step twice into the same river, Heraclitus pointed out more than 2,500 years ago. Everything flows, everything changes. Our personal experiences, from birth till death, confirm this view of life as flux. We enter this world helpless but with enormous curiosity and potential, and in the blink of an eye we are adults with children and even grandchildren of our own. Change is integral to our lives and the key to understanding ourselves.

Yet in order for us to recognize change, some things must remain the same. Some things can change very quickly; others are relatively static. A law passed in one day can grant everyone equal rights, but it can take a much longer time before people come to treat one another as equals, as shown by the experiences of women, African Americans, and other minorities who still suffer discrimination. A change of government from dictatorship to "democracy" can come about in a matter of months, or even days or hours through revolution or coup d'état, but it takes a lot longer for people to learn behavior appropriate for democratic societies—as is painfully obvious, for example, from the experiences of former communist societies since the early 1990s. Such differences in the speed at which change takes place play an important role in relationships between the individual and society.

It is sociologists, political scientists, and social psychologists who historically have paid closest attention to the relationship between the individual and society. From the time of Charles Montesquieu (1689–1755) and the beginnings of modern sociology, a major challenge has been to fill in the gap between the macrosociology level of major institutions and the microsociology level of individual actors. Macrosociology seems to leave little room for human agency, depicting individuals as controlled by societal forces; microsociology seems unable to account for the stability and seeming independence of social structures.

Anthony Giddens is perhaps the most influential modern sociologist to have taken up the challenge of filling in this gap. Interestingly, he depicts individuals as actively engaged in changing the world around them. How much they can change that world, however, is restricted by aspects of the macrosociety that are beyond the scope of individual influence, aspects that he refers to as rules and resources. Just as individuals are active agents who can bring about change, they are in turn influenced by larger societal processes. Thus Giddens sees individuals and society in a continual process of mutual influence and change.

One of the limitations of the approach adopted by Giddens and others in the sociological tradition is that they do not give adequate attention to individual-level processes, where biological and psychological factors interact. Although a few theorists, such as Talcott Parsons, have discussed a role for "physic–chemical" subsystems in human behavior, this has not led to individual-level processes being seriously considered in sociological theories. Even microsociologists do not adequately attend to intelligence, depression, memory, and similar fundamentally important aspects of individual behavior. It may be argued that such behaviors are influenced by biological processes and therefore outside the scope of sociology, social psychology, and other such "more macro" social science disciplines. However, a counterargument, which I support, is that intelligence and other such individual-level behaviors are also fundamentally influenced by social and cultural processes and thus should not be treated as the sole territory of biologically oriented researchers. *The social penetrates each and every aspect of human behavior.* Consequently, in moving toward a theory that integrates the individual and society, I discuss both macro-level topics, such as class, gender, and race, and micro-level topics, such as depression, memory, and intelligence.

Just as sociologists have failed to give adequate attention to behavior at the micro level, psychologists have failed to pay adequate attention to macro processes. Psychologists have tended to treat individuals as isolated beings who are in possession of intelligence, memory, and other such characteristics that can be studied as if they were completely unaffected by social interactions. As a step toward remedying this situation, I emphasize psychological characteristics of individuals, such as memory and intelligence, as imbedded in social relationships. I do not view memory or other such aspects of thinking as private and taking place within isolated individuals or isolated brains. Rather, I emphasize the collaborative social processes involved in constructing what we take to be memories. For example, Alice remembers her high school graduation not as a laboratory-dwelling hermit who never communicates with others about such matters but as an active participant in a social world, where the story of high school graduation, with its many funny incidents, dramas, and triumphs, is collaboratively constructed and reconstructed, changing over the years in key respects with each act of telling.

At the heart of the integration I develop is the issue of change. Quite apart from the theoretical reasons for attending to change, there are practical ones. If we better understand why some things are more difficult to change and others easier, we can apply this knowledge to improve our personal and professional lives as well as the lives of those around us.

Through understanding why some things change and others are stable, we can develop more appropriate *expectations* of what should and what should not change. This fit between expectations of change and actual possibilities for change is at the heart of so much human success as well as failure. Human rights groups encouraging governments to live up to human rights declarations, members of different ethnic groups learning to interact with one another in changed circumstances, the student wanting to improve her study habits, the middle-aged person trying to lose weight through a diet program, the CEO with a "revolutionary" plan for how the organization should work, the depressed person going through therapy, political elites adjusting their policies to the needs of constituents, women and men trying to adapt to new laws that bear on gender relations—in these and most other cases involving attempts to achieve change, we discover varying degrees of resistance to change. Everything is in flux, but some things change faster than others, and to be successful in our plans we need to match our expectations to actual possibilities for change.

Carriers

Carriers and Continuity

As I sat through the ceremony to become a citizen, I went through several different moods—I laughed, became anxious, sad, then joyous again—but I could not change my height or skin color or body shape. I changed what I thought about and I tried different tactics to answer questions in the citizenship test, but I could not change the size or structure of my brain. We all recognize *physical barriers* to change fairly easily, these being material characteristics of ourselves and the environment.

While we tend to be highly conscious of such physical barriers to change, we rarely notice continuity created by *carriers*, the means by which styles of social thinking and doing are sustained and passed on from generation to generation. Carriers are of two basic types. *Symbolic carriers* stand for something, usually values and beliefs. They can be physical objects, such as a flag, or they can be conceptual constructs, such as "nationalism" and "American exceptionalism," the belief that the United States is different from other industrialized societies with respect to its experiences with social class. The U.S. flags hanging all around the hall we were in represented the nation we were about to join as citizens.

"Look at the *beautiful* American flag," the master of ceremonies was urging us. "Look at it and *love* it. That flag stands for freedom. That flag stands for opportunity. That flag stands for your nation, my nation, our nation."

The master of ceremonies was also evoking nationalism, a conceptual rather than physical symbolic carrier.

"Throughout the history of this greatest of nations," he proclaimed, "brave men and women have proved that Americans are patriotic. They have proved that Americans love liberty."

Thus symbolic carriers support continuity in behavior by using physical symbols, such as a flag, and conceptual constructs, such as "nationalism," to pass on key parts of a culture.

Even more detailed instructions about how to behave are passed on by *control carriers*, which include both formal laws and informal rules regulating behavior. An example of a formal carrier is immigration laws, which control the types and numbers of immigrants allowed into the United States. A change in immigration laws, allowing more of some groups to enter and fewer of other groups, would eventually change the social fabric of the United States. Informal control carriers include *social norms*, prescriptions for correct behavior in different contexts; *social rules*, prescriptions for correct behavior between people in different role relationships (doctor/patient, lawyer/client, parent/child, and so on); and *social roles*, expectations based on norms and rules about how a person in a given position (such as woman, man, mother, father, child) ought to behave.

The influence of carriers in support of continuity is particularly resilient, in part because it is seldom noticed. The Berlin Wall was a physical barrier to change, and when it came crashing down East and West Germany were physically united. But symbolic and control carriers proved much more resilient, so that culturally East and West Germany are still worlds apart after so many years of physical unity.

Carriers gain their great resilience and power from being social, shared, and mutually upheld. They exist in the public domain and are part of the fabric of ongoing social relationships. For example, the American flag is an important carrier in the United States, and "becoming an American" involves taking on certain attitudes, values, and behaviors in relation to Old Glory. Through this collective, public, and pervasive feature, carriers such as the U.S. flag become appropriated by individuals as part of the toolkit needed for persons to "belong" and to function effectively in society. Thus carriers also come to have a role in the private cognitions and emotions of individuals.

All carriers involve cognitive and affective components, knowledge and feelings. For example, consider a national flag, such as the U.S. national flag, as a carrier. Children are taught certain things about the U.S. flag ("the 50 stars represent the 50 states, the 13 stripes represent the 13 original colonies," and so on), and most adults at least know that the term "Old Glory" refers to the U.S. flag. In addition to this knowledge component, which may actually be minimal, people come to have feelings, sometimes extremely strong ones, associated with the flag. The army veteran saluting the Stars and Stripes may not know much about the details of the symbolism on the flag, but when he makes his salute he experiences deep, sincere, and strong feelings of nationalism, pride, honor, and the like. In practice, the emotional components of carriers are often the most important.

In just over two hours, about 3,000 immigrants from scores of different countries around the world completed the citizenship ceremony and became Americans, as I did that day. All of us held citizenship certificates in our hands, and in this way we had all become the same. But the vast hall also housed countless differences, sustained by carriers, that were far more resistant to change, including norms, rules, roles, values, beliefs, political ideas, religious and moral systems, and languages. Even during the brief time we spent together, I could clearly see these important social characteristics being passed on to the next generation, as the new Americans instructed their children on how they ought to behave. The Italian families, the Greek families, the Chinese families, the Arab families, the German families, the Nigerian families, the French families—all the families in that hall were effortlessly and for the most part unconsciously using carriers to pass on their ideas and ideals to their children. Mothers and fathers were training their children to do the right thing according to the traditions they knew best, just as their parents had taught them.

Carriers and the Active Individual

Carriers are already present when an individual arrives in society, and they continue to exist after an individual has exited. The existence of carriers out there in the larger society is not dependent on any individual; carriers transcend individual lives, are part of the cultural fabric into which individual lives become woven. Flags, the crucifix, sports club emblems, the mullah's turban, the business suit and tie, the judge's formal robe, the scientist's white laboratory coat, national anthems—like a caravan that has its source in some mysterious distant time and place, such carriers combine to weave the individual into an intricate fabric of meanings and to enable the individual to join the caravan on the next part of the journey.

Carriers are central to the two-way process leading to the integration of the individual into society—but also the integration of society into the individual.

On the one hand, the individual becomes a participant in social interactions that collaboratively uphold carriers and sustain and continue the construction of meanings. By singing the national anthem and paying homage to the national flag, for example, an individual endorses, sustains, and continues the meanings ascribed to the anthem and the flag. This participation serves to integrate the individual into the fabric of social interactions and shared cultural systems. At the same time, through this participation the individual comes to appropriate the meaning systems of the larger society, and in this sense society becomes integrated within individuals. The individual is by no means passive in this process.

Individual experiences lead to the active appropriation of carriers, but in a personalized way. First, not all available carriers are appropriated to the same degree; some are barely noticed, while others are deeply absorbed. For example, while Mahmood, a fundamentalist Muslim, takes little notice of the national flag, he is completely alert to the Islamic veil worn by women and takes every step possible to enforce the wearing of the veil, thus upholding the values he associates with this carrier. Second, appropriated carriers are ascribed new meanings through personal experiences. This personalized construction of meaning takes place even in the case of widely shared carriers. For example, even a national anthem, familiar to millions of people, has some meanings that are personal to particular individuals. Third, personal experiences lead to the construction of some personal carriers that are not necessarily shared by others. For example, Paula, an 89-year-old widow, has kept the gloves she wore on her first date with her late husband, and only for her do the gloves carry significant meanings associated with her past.

Thus, through active and intentional participation in social life, individuals come to uphold and sustain particular carriers and to pay less attention to others. In some cases, individuals will oppose and try to dismantle particular carriers. For example, some people would rather burn the American flag than salute it. In order to better understand the meaning of such behavior, it is useful to attend to two meanings of the term *performance*.

Varieties of Performance

Two Meanings of *Performance*

"Shhh! Sit still and listen," the Indian computer scientist was telling her children.

"I can't hear him, mummy," protested her smallest.

The sound system became fully functional again after a momentary break-down, so the master of ceremonies became audible again to the audience of aspiring Americans.

"Now listen," commanded the Indian computer scientist. In following her instructions, her children were showing several different types of performance. *Performance capacity* refers to how well human beings can do things: how well people can hear and see, how sensitive are they to touch, and so on. The study of this kind of performance is central to the most scientifically rigorous branch of psychology, the study of perception. Tests developed to check auditory abilities and eyesight are among many practical benefits of perception research. They help to determine whether a person needs a hearing aid, eyeglasses, or other such helpful devices.

Measurement of performance capacity gives us a clear picture of the range of human abilities, such as sensory capacities. Young adults can hear tones down to about 20 hertz and up to about 20,000 hertz, can see light waves ranging from about 360 to 700 nanometers, and can smell foul substances such as ethyl mercapton in concentrations as low as 1 part in 50 billion parts of air.

Performance capacity can be measured accurately under laboratory conditions. The classic laboratory study on performance capacity examines causal relations between independent and dependent variables, such as noise level and auditory perception. Experimenters control all factors in the environment, then manipulate one variable, the *independent variable*, in order to measure the impact of this manipulation on a *dependent variable*. Noise level (independent variable) is increased until it reaches threshold level and the participant in a study reports hearing the noise (dependent variable). The increase in noise level can accurately be described as having caused a change in sensation, from not hearing to hearing something. When the sound system failed during our citizenship ceremonies, the master of ceremonies was no longer audible to us. When the sound system was fixed, it enabled us to hear his voice.

But performance capacity tells us only about the range of human physical abilities, how well a person could perform on visual, auditory, and other such tasks; it does not tell us anything about the meaning of what is seen or heard. Meaning is fundamentally important; it may be that a person does not want to hear or see certain things, even though they fall well within the range of the audible and visible. This leads to consideration of another type of performance, *performance style,* referring to the way in which behavior is carried out and the meaning it is given. While performance capacity is akin to what the neuroscientist Karl Pribram refers to as a deterministic structure, performance style is akin to dynamic processes with greater degrees of freedom.

Consider the case of memory, discussed in Chapter 10. A study of performance capacity would lead us to research such questions as: How many bits of information can people remember? How quickly do they forget? This is like asking: How much water can a sponge soak up and keep? It is to treat human beings as purely physical entities, so that hearing, seeing, remembering, and so on can be measured in the same way as weight, height, and other physical features.

Performance capacity provides only a description of the range of human abilities in limited domains. It informs us about highs and lows in abilities, but it informs us neither about how people behave *within this range* in everyday life nor about how people do things or the meanings events have for people. What people actually remember about past events is influenced by what others have told them, what they think others want to hear, what their situation is now, and numerous other such factors. In other words, memory in everyday life involves reconstruction of the past through the active collaboration of others rather than just reproduction by an isolated individual. Reconstruction is influenced by numerous biases; it is like a jointly produced impressionistic painting of events. Reproduction, on the other hand, is more like a photograph, an identical image of the original produced by one person acting alone.

Traditionally it has been performance capacity that has changed more slowly. Sometime around 4.5 million years ago, our ancestors starting walking on two feet in Africa. Thus began a very long journey, eventually leading to the development of humans with larger brains and elaborate language skills around 150,000 years ago. The enormous length of time it took for our physical characteristics to evolve certainly suggests that performance capacity can change only very slowly, much more slowly than performance style. The sensory abilities that allowed me to see and to hear the Indian computer scientist on that April day would seem to change much more slowly than the meanings involved in our interaction—meanings associated with how we said hello, shook hands, exchanged pleasantries, told each other our experiences as immigrants, wished each other luck in our adopted country, and said goodbye.

But technology has dramatically altered the situation, now making it possible to change performance capacity much faster than performance style. From eyeglasses and hearing aids to laser surgery that can make eyesight better than 20/20, heart pacemakers, memory-enhancing drugs, and a whole variety of new possibilities opened up by pharmaceutical and other research, new tools are increasingly available to quickly and radically change performance capacity. Technology has altered the traditional relationship between performance capacity and performance style, so that it is now social barriers that often hold up change.

Modern technology, driven by rapid advances in biochemistry, microbiology, biotechnology, and other hybrid sciences, is fast pushing back the limitations set by performance capacity. Physical barriers to change are being manipulated and dramatically different possibilities are developing as our control over the material world increases. We are increasingly capable of changing our physical selves in fundamental ways, through surgery for instance. Current research on stem cells, "undifferentiated cells," suggests enormous possibilities for developing cell-replacement therapies, suggesting that more physical barriers to change could be overcome. However, very little attention is being given to social barriers to change, and so they persist and continue to block progress.

War and violent intergroup conflicts, extreme poverty, illiteracy, continuing discrimination against minorities, violent crime—the challenges confronting human societies are enormous. At the personal level, too, major challenges remain, from loneliness, depression, weight and substance-abuse problems to failures in marital, family, and community relations. Despite the trend to try to find purely technical solutions to moral and social problems, such major challenges will not be successfully met only through improved technology; they also require changes in performance style and thus a manipulation of the carriers that sustain continuity in human life.

Because carriers work in such subtle and often unnoticed ways to sustain continuity, attempts to achieve change often fail. This process is often baffling; it leaves us wondering why things do not change as expected. One of the people I met at the citizenship ceremony was a Congolese supporter of the revolutionary leader Laurent Kabila, who had ruled the Congo since the demise of the former Congolese dictator, Mobutu Sese Seko, in 1997. (Kabila was subsequently assassinated in early 2001.) My Congolese acquaintance was bitterly disappointed with how things had not changed. The whole story was captured by a newspaper headline: ONLY THE FACES CHANGE: KABILA'S 1ST YEAR RESEMBLES CONGO'S FORMER 30-YEAR DICTATORSHIP. Again and again, revolutions have raised expectations and social barriers to change have dashed hopes. As a first step to understanding this cycle of change and continuity, we need to distinguish between two types of accounts, one appropriate for performance capacity and the other for performance style.

Performances and Causes

In 1890 the great psychologist William James reported the case of a blind woman who worked in the laundry of an asylum. She was able to sort the inmates' clothes using smell only, even after the clothes had been washed. No doubt the sense of smell was particularly enhanced in this woman, but more recent research has shown that people can identify their own clothes, as well as tell the gender of other individuals, using only the sense of smell. Women and younger people tend to be more sensitive to smells than men and older people. Such sensory abilities have developed over very long time periods in our evolutionary history.

Because performance capacity in humans changes very slowly, it is not possible to change how sharp our sense of smell is over a matter of decades or even centuries. We can adapt to odors, as we adapt to our own perfumes and bodily smells, so that we notice them less. We can practice and become better at describing smells in words, and it is interesting to note that women benefit more from such practice than men. But the basics of the range of human sensory abilities, such as smell, sight, and hearing, can only change over the very long term.

In addition to being relatively stable, performance capacity has a causal relation to human behavior. Changes in performance capacity cause changes in behavior. If a person suffers serious injury to his eardrum as a result of prolonged exposure to loud noise, such as that produced by heavy metal bands, this will cause hearing impairment, just as a serious leg injury will cause a runner to be unable to run as fast as before.

During the last few decades of the twentieth century, neuroscientists made exciting discoveries about the relationship between different parts of the human brain and various types of behavior. We now have the beginnings of a map of the brain, in terms of which parts are responsible for at least some types of memory.

This is an important example of research on performance capacity. In the case of a patient widely known as H. M., neurosurgery intended to minimize epileptic seizures had the side effect of destroying parts of the temporal lobe of his brain. This caused H. M. to suffer from anterograde amnesia, meaning he could remember events before the operation but had difficulty learning anything new after the operation.

While a *causal account*, which stipulates cause–effect relations, is appropriate for explaining changes in performance capacity, it will not do for explaining changes in *performance style*, the meaning of behavior. Performance style requires a *normative account,* which assumes that human beings have some measure of freedom in using social norms, rules, roles, and other aspects of culture as guides to correct behavior in given contexts. When a driver is coming up to a red light, his ability to see the light is a necessary *but not sufficient* factor leading him to stop. Seeing the red light per se does not cause a change in his behavior; drivers can, and sometimes do, choose to drive through red lights. Most people choose to do the right thing and change their behavior in the appropriate way: They come to a stop.

Of course, the argument could be made that if we ever come to know everything there is to know about factors that influence human behavior, then we would be able to identify a cause for every human act. There would be nothing left unknown and no room for "woolly" concepts such as free will. The proponents of this view consider themselves closer to the hard sciences, more "empirical," compared to proponents of normative explanations. Ironically, however, this "more scientific" viewpoint fails a crucial test: The main hypothesis it puts forward is not testable, or "nonfalsifiable" as the philosopher of science Karl Popper might have described it. That fateful day when we "know everything about factors influencing human behavior" has not arrived, and we have no way of predicting if or when it will ever arrive. Consequently, we are asked to have faith that the promised day will arrive, and this makes the entire proposition closer to religion than to science.

When the master of ceremonies told us we could emulate the Colonel and become successes in the style of Kentucky Fried Chicken, we would-be Americans clapped our hands because we thought it was the correct thing to do in that context. But he did not causally determine our behavior—some of us actually chose not to clap. Most of us conformed to social expectations by clapping, and such conformity shows itself in the patterns and predictability in human behavior often discerned by psychologists and others. It is easy to mistake normative regularities for causal ones.

Performances, Carriers, and Continuity

It was one of those encounters that make one believe it really is a small world. I was walking along M Street in Georgetown, enjoying the crisp, sunny April weather, when the Indian computer scientist I had met at the citizenship ceremony stepped out of a shop onto the pavement in front of me. We immediately recognized each other and began to reminisce about the citizenship ceremony.

"My family is under tremendous pressure," she explained. Before I had time to ask for elaboration, she rushed through an account of her troubles.

"My children are in danger of changing in ways that I do not like, of losing the best part of their own heritage and copying the worst habits of their American classmates." She was in a serious and determined mood as she added, "But my husband and I are resisting."

She went on to tell me that as part of her "program of resistance," her children were attending Indian dance classes and learning about traditional Indian clothes, food, and music.

"Even clothes help," she added. "This sari is a symbol of our values, and my daughter is relearning how to wear a sari."

After listening for some time, I asked her how things were progressing at the computer services company she had founded.

"I expected the company to turn around and perform according to the new plans sooner. It is all taking far too long for the employees to change over to the new system. Some of them cling to the past too much."

Strange, I thought, how some things changed too quickly for her and others, too slowly.

"Individually they can all do the work, they are great at their jobs," she added as an afterthought, "but together they are not the new company I wanted us to become. Perhaps I am expecting too much, but I did not move my business all the way from India to fail. I came to change my life and to get things around me changed. You know what it's like, you are an immigrant."

After twelve years in the United States, six years in Canada, nineteen years in England, and other periods spent in different countries around the world, I had encountered many immigrants similarly baffled and disappointed with how things had changed for them in some ways and how there was a lack of change in other ways. I was also aware that, irrespective of whether or not they are immigrants, people actively try to cope with change, rather than just passively accepting what happens to them.

Plan of This Book

The integrated view of the individual and society presented in this book has three distinct features. First, both the individual and society are envisaged as being in a process of continual change. Thus the integration we are considering has at its heart processes of change. Consequently, explorations of types of change constitute a major theme in the discussions to come.

Second, attention is given to a wide range of processes, from intraindividual processes at the micro level to societal ones at the macro level. In doing so, we touch on topics that are considered the proper domains of a wide range of disciplines, from neuroscience and cognitive psychology to social psychology and sociology. In this exploration, I have seen it as both necessary and useful to break out of traditional disciplinary boundaries. My justification is that the integration of the individual into society takes place through *the penetration of the social into every level of human behavior*, including the microlevel of intrapersonal experiences involving depression, memory, and the like. Culture is no less relevant to understanding such micro-level aspects of behavior than it is to macro-level aspects such as gender, social class, and other phenomena traditionally taken to be within the orbit of discussions about the integration of the individual into society.

Third, I formulate a cultural integration of the individual and society, giving particular importance to what I have termed *carriers,* things "out there" in the social arena that perpetuate particular behavioral styles, and their role in regulating social behavior. The concept of carriers becomes particularly powerful in explaining continuity when it is coupled with a distinction between two types of performance: performance capacity, continuities arising from physical barriers to change, and performance style, continuities in the ways in which people do things and the meaning they give to events. My purpose is to highlight the importance of carriers that perpetuate performance style, leading to continuities in the way things are done and meanings are ascribed.

All human behavior involves both types of performance, but the relative importance of performance capacity and performance style varies across types of behavior and thus across the chapters in this book. The chapter topics are organized from macro-level processes involving revolutions, social class, race and ethnicity, gender, war and peace, and rights and duties, to micro-level processes involving personality, intelligence, and remembering. The final chapters focus on practical challenges—eating disorders, Alzheimer's disease, and depression. Throughout, I point out how even processes that seem to be biologically "determined" can be, and generally are, greatly influenced by sociocultural factors. At the same time, micro-level processes at the individual level can, and generally do, influence larger societal processes.

In Chapter 2, we see how the mundane practices of everyday life, and the choices individuals make in relation to carriers, can influence even revolutionary politicoeconomic change. This is part of the explanation for one of the paradoxes of revolutions—that in many ways fundamental political changes fail to bring about other changes, particularly in the informal sphere of social relationships. The persistence of inequalities, injustices, and other things as they have always been is explained through the role of carriers and the behaviors they sustain. One should not be deceived by changes in formal life, in the formal system of governments and organizations, into imagining that the informal realm has also changed along the same lines.

In Chapter 3 we see that informal or commonsense justice precedes and gives shape to the formal. Rights and duties, it is argued, are first psychological and integral to social life and only afterward become formalized in law. Similarly, in Chapter 4 the discussion of social class highlights the role of certain micro-level cognitive processes within individuals to show that the perception of social classes and of conflicts of interest across those classes is not inevitable. American exceptionalism, the idea that, unlike the Old World of Europe, America is classless, is treated as an important carrier, supporting continuities in American society.

Chapter 5 turns the traditional way of viewing conflict on its head by asking "Why peace?" rather than "Why war?" and focusing on the everyday activities and carriers, particularly among individuals in military cultures, that perpetuate war. Continuity in styles of gender relations is the focus of Chapter 6, which again highlights how macro-level changes in the economy and legal system do not necessarily translate to parallel changes for individuals in their everyday lives. Not only can everyday practices of individuals remain immune to the transforming influence of macro-level changes, but in some instances they can sustain continuity and stability at the societal level. An example is the role played by romantic love, discussed in Chapter 7, which leads individuals to seek fulfilment through personal relationships rather than through social change.

Chapters 8, 9, 10, and 11 discuss personality, intelligence, memory, and human development respectively, in each case revealing the flexible, social, culture-based nature of individual characteristics. Traditional research has highlighted performance capacities associated with personality, intelligence, memory, and development, resulting in the spotlight being cast on the assumed fixed, inborn features of individual behavior. But more careful scrutiny reveals that personality, intelligence, memory, and development are highly malleable and strongly influenced by culture, in practice arising from collaborative constructions of individuals in interaction. They are social and collective, and they are sustained and perpetuated through carriers.

Chapters 12, 13, and 14 discuss eating disorders, depression, and Alzheimer's disease, all at one level problems afflicting individuals. One could, and many have, examined these as purely biological or psychological problems related to individual-level functioning. But, at the same time, we see that the larger social context shapes individual experiences in these areas in important ways. The final chapter presents an integrated account of the individual and society, looking ahead to challenges and opportunities presented by the concept of carriers in particular.

Thus the earlier chapters in the book explore how societal changes involving large collectivities—related to revolutions, rights and duties, social class, peace and conflict, and gender relations and romantic love—are also influenced by micro-level processes at the individual level. In particular, by adopting or opposing particular carriers, such as the "Red Flag" in Russia or "Old Glory" in the United States, individuals support or oppose particular values and behavior styles. In the second half of the book, the chapters explore how personality, intelligence, memory, human development, eating disorders, depression, and Alzheimer's disease are fundamentally influenced by the larger social context. In this perspective, the individual is not a separate entity but rather is enmeshed in social relationships and a product of collaborative construction through social processes.

Suggested Readings

Brewer, J. B., Zhao, Z., Desmond, J. E., Clover, G. H., & Gabrieli, J. D. E. (1998). Making memories: Brain activity that predicts how well visual experience will be remembered. *Science*, 281, 1185–1187.

Duke, L. (1998, May 17). Only the faces change: Kabila's 1st year resembles Congo's former 30-year dictatorship. *Washington Post*, p. A22.

Giddens, A. (1984). *The constitution of society: Outline of the theory of structuration.* Oxford: Polity.

Lewin, K. (1943). Forces behind food habits and methods of change. *Bulletin of the National Research Council, 108,* 35–65.

Moghaddam, F. M. (1990). Modulative and generative orientations in psychology: Implications for psychology in the Three Worlds. *Journal of Social Issues, 46,* 21–41.

Moghaddam, F. M., & Crystal, D. (1997). Revolutions, Samurai, and reductons: Change and continuity in Iran and Japan. *Journal of Political Psychology, 18,* 355–384.

Moghaddam, F. M., & Harré, R. (1996). Psychological limits to political revolution: An application of social reducton theory. In E. Hasselberg, L. Martienssen, & F. Radtke (Eds.), The concept of dialogue at the end of the 20th century (pp. 230–240). Berlin, Germany: Hegel Institute.

Posner, M. I., & Raichle, M. E. (1997). *Images of mind.* New York: Freeman/Scientific American Library.

Pribram, K. H. (1991). *Brain and perception: Holonomy and structure in figural processing.* Mahwah, NJ: Erlbaum.

Sekuler, R., & Blake, R. (1994). *Perception* (3rd. ed.). New York: McGraw-Hill.

Stevens, S. S. (1975). *Psychophysics: Introduction to its perceptual, neural, and social prospects.* New York: Wiley.

Turner, J. H., Beeghley, L., & Powers, C. H. (1998). *The emergence of sociological theory* (4th ed.). Belmont, CA: Wadsworth.

2 The King Is Dead; Long Live the King

HAFEZ ASSAD'S SON, BASHAR ASSAD, TO TAKE OVER IN SYRIA announced the newspaper headlines in early June 2000. Hafez Assad had seized power in 1970 and ruled Syria with an iron fist for almost 30 years. Although on paper Syria is a multiparty republic, not a hereditary monarchy, the actual course of events in that country reminds one of the phrase "The King Is Dead; Long Live the King." The system of dictatorial rule continues, with a strong tendency to pass power from father to son, as in "ancient" hereditary monarchies. But it is not just in Syria that such continuity of leadership style exists; we can witness the same continuity in other societies. Let me begin by recounting some of my personal experiences that relate to this.

I was born in Iran and educated from the age of 8 in England. I returned to Iran in the "Spring of Revolution" in 1979, immediately after the collapse of the shah's regime. This was a very exciting time. I arrived in Tehran, the capital, to find the population jubilant and the atmosphere optimistic. The monarchy, which claimed a 2,500-year-long history, had been smashed, and now, perhaps for the first time ever, Iranians had a real opportunity to build a democratic society. As I drove through the streets, I found jubilant crowds chanting and cheering. Shopkeepers were handing out flowers, cakes, sweets, drinks, and greeting newcomers with happy faces.

My first desire was to serve, to become useful, to do something good for the country. One possibility was presented, oddly enough, by service in the military. Iranians were supposed to complete 2 years of national service in the military, and individuals with a university education were usually assigned to jobs in which they could use their expertise in some useful way. I was going to try to teach in a village during my national service, so that I might help eradicate illiteracy. But when I went to report for duty, I found that there was no military to join. Army posts and barracks had been attacked during the revolution, and there was not an officer to be found.

Every day for several weeks I rose at dawn, prepared myself for national service, and joined thousands of others who also came to report to the military. But the chaotic state of the military was not improving quickly enough, so the "temporary" government in power decided that we would all be issued certificates of exemption. So I never got my chance to serve by joining the army and tried to find other avenues for making myself useful.

However, I soon discovered that the disarray and confusion of the military were shared by just about every major sector of the Iranian economy, both public and private. Many senior and even middle-level managers in most private corporations had either left or been pushed aside, while most company owners and major stockholders had fled the country; likewise for most senior and middle-level government officials. An enormous change took place in ownership of banks and major corporations, with the government taking over many of them. The economy became even more state controlled and centralized. Both private and government sectors were in turmoil, and nobody was hiring.

Still full of enthusiasm, I found opportunities to teach at several universities. However, the situation in academia was just as chaotic. Many university administrators, from presidents down to department chairs, had left their positions, sometimes voluntarily. Traditional curricula, courses, and books were under attack as "Western" and sometimes abandoned for alternatives, often poorly conceived ones. Professors were under pressure to change themselves in line with the revolution. The presence on campus of dozens of different politically active, and sometimes armed, groups, often with opposing ideologies, added to the feeling of instability and change. Every morning when I went to teach my class, I had a sense that more change would come by the end of the day. Within another year, the universities were in the grip of a "cultural revolution" modeled, implicitly at least, on Mao's Cultural Revolution in China in the 1960s.

The "cultural revolution" launched in Iranian universities put an end to regular academic classes for about 2 years. Students and professors were literally thrown out into the streets by mobs of club-carrying "soldiers of Islam." Academics were encouraged to reeducate themselves so as to move closer to the "Islamic masses" and to abandon Western ways. Those who failed to become "politically correct" according to the new norms were not allowed to return to the universities when they reopened.

As if all these political, economic, educational, and social changes were not enough, in 1980 a full-scale war started between Iran and Iraq. This resulted in the mobilization of millions of Iranian men to the front as well as the migration of millions of refugees trying to escape the fighting. Refugees poured into every major city, including Tehran. If any corner of Iranian society had somehow evaded the effects of the revolution, it did not remain unaffected by the bloody 8-year war with Iraq.

Thus anyone looking at Iranian society in the early 1980s would have been struck by the changes that had come about in just a few years since the revolution of 1979. The monarchy was replaced by a republic, pro-Western policies were replaced by anti-Western ones, many major private corporations changed hands, a larger sector of the economy was taken over by the government or by quasi-governmental organizations, and there were many changes in leadership at the top and even middle-levels in just about every sector of society. The revolution seemed to have transformed everything.

Of course, Iranian society had also been changing before the revolution, but the revolution seemed to represent a different type of change altogether, a "change of change." Paul Watzlawick and others of the Palo Alto School have compared this kind of transformation to a person getting out of a bad dream by waking up, as opposed to screaming, hiding, running, or fighting while still in the dream. This represents one of the very few attempts by psychologists to seriously distinguish between different types of change. Although the distinction will be shown to be problematic, it does serve as a point of departure for a broader distinction between three types of change that I introduce later in this chapter.

Carriers and Revolutions

Continuity Within a Revolution

The term *revolution* indicates a break from the past and an attempt to begin anew. The success of a revolution is often judged according to how much the ways of the past have been put aside and been replaced by new ways of doing things. But what is it that prevents revolutionaries from completely changing everything? For instance, in 1979 Iranian revolutionaries had seized control, the foundations of Iranian society had been shaken, a lot had changed, and opportunities were there to rebuild a very different, democratic society.

Symbolic of the success of the revolutionaries in seizing power, the prerevolution flag of Iran, with its historical association with monarchy, was cast aside, and a new flag was created to represent the new Islamic Republic of Iran. The new flag was to serve as a carrier of values upheld by the revolutionary regime. Anyone caught honoring the old flag or dishonoring the new one was severely punished. Everything seemed to have changed.

But yet, in hindsight, I can recognize that not everything had changed: We were still in the same dream and had not awakened into a completely different

state. In fact, some things, ranging from the trivial to the fundamentally important, had stayed the same, as if they existed on a plane apart from everything
else. Let me begin by recounting an incident, comical and at first glance unimportant. Several months after the universities had been forced to close, at the
time of the "cultural revolution," I went back to clear out my office and tie up
some financial loose ends with the university administration. I had decided
that since the universities were not allowed to fulfill their academic mission, I
should resign my faculty position. The campus looked dismal. There were no
students or professors there, only university administrators. I thought it would
be an easy task to find the relevant administrators, get the paperwork completed, and leave campus. After all, there were no classes or research activities
on campus, so the administrators would have nothing to do. To my amazement,
when I went to the central administration building I found everyone busy. The
academic life of the university was at a standstill, so what were all these administrators doing? The officials I needed to see were all in meetings. What were
they meeting about? It turned out that with nothing to do, the university administrators had created work for themselves, reorganizing everything in sight
and holding meetings to discuss and reconsider each former decision.

I discovered that in the details of how the administrators in universities and
other organizations worked, a lot remained the same. For example, both before
and after the revolution administrators would leave a few signs on their desks,
such as a pair of glasses or a jacket, to show that they had arrived at work but
were temporarily away from their desks. In this way some administrators could
hold more than one job and be in two or more places at once. The society in
which they lived, and the university they were part of, had experienced up-
heavals, but they kept doing the same old things. This reminded me of Burn's
law of social change: It usually takes about a century or three generations after
a far-reaching social change for a people to drop habits that are no longer
really relevant.

I eventually did get an appointment with the appropriate administrator and
I did finish the paperwork I had come to do, but it actually took no less time
than when the university had been officially open and fully functioning with
students and professors on campus.

But continuity was also suggested by far more serious and sinister signs, ones
that, incredible as it may seem, proved to be difficult to recognize, or at least act
on, at the time. Iranian society had traditionally been closed rather than open,
particularly in the sense that the people were not given opportunities to
choose between alternative political ideas. In the decades prior to the revolution, hereditary monarchy was the only choice presented to the people, and
the only political party allowed to function was the so-called Resurrection
party, which endorsed the monarchy and the status quo. After the revolution, a
referendum was implemented with only one choice presented to the people:

Say "yes" or "no" to the establishment of an Islamic Republic. No alternative was explicitly presented, but the implied alternative seemed to be anarchy or a return to monarchy. Everyone was strongly advised to vote "yes," and having no alternative, it seems they did. This "one-road" approach was strongly endorsed by chants taken up in the streets by Islamic fundamentalists, which sum up as: "Only one party, only one leader." The party they had in mind was the "party of God," and the leader was, of course, the Ayatollah Khomeini. This leads me to another major continuity, style of leadership. Events showed that continuity in leadership style is not limited to Syria.

Constructing the Leader

Leadership is one of the most important continuities in human social life. Although a few groups have experimentally functioned without leaders, most human societies and groups, particularly more complex ones and those with longer histories, continue to have leaders. Freud believed that leaders are absolutely essential to group life and that only through effective leadership can a group attain high levels of cohesion and efficiency. The roots of leadership probably lie in early human evolution, so that we can envisage groups of hunter-gatherers hundreds of thousands of years ago having leaders. Leadership and status hierarchies are well demarcated in groups of monkeys and apes, our closest animal relatives.

Although modern societies continue to be characterized by leadership, style of leadership has become more varied over time and across cultures. Most importantly, in modern democratic societies it is understood that political leaders can be criticized for wrongdoing, actively opposed, and even replaced before completing their terms of office, as in the case of Richard Nixon. Leadership in Iran represents a sharp contrast to this. In Iran prior to the revolution, the shah could not be publicly criticized or challenged. This tradition continued after the revolution, with the Ayatollah Khomeini in the leadership position. To publicly criticize Khomeini in postrevolution Iran was to risk probable imprisonment and even execution.

The similarity of the leadership role attained by Khomeini and by the shah is remarkable. Both held positions of absolute infallibility, so that the opinion they expressed on any subject (and they expressed opinions on just about every aspect of life) was treated as the final authoritative word, not to be questioned under any circumstances. It was as if these leaders had risen above the level of mere mortals. To criticize them was not just wrong; it was to commit sacrilege.

This infallibility was in both of their cases associated with lifelong supreme power. These were not leaders who would be replaced peacefully. These were not Nelson Mandelas who would voluntarily step aside for democratically elected Thabo Mbekis to replace them. The only possible way of ending their reigns, everyone understood, was by death or force, an assassins's bullet or a bloody revolution.

As long as the regime supporting the shah or Khomeini remained in power, the leader could not be criticized even after his death. The shah's father, Reza Shah, who ruled from 1926 until 1941, was treated as a glorious hero after he died, and his grave was treated as a national shrine—as long as his heir was in power. However, as soon as his heirs lost power, everything associated with Reza Shah was publicly condemned, and even his grave was physically attacked. I witnessed a bizarre scene during which Islamic fundamentalists attacked Reza Shah's enormous grave monument with sticks, shovels, pickaxes, and even bullets and grenades. Similarly, as long as the Islamic Republic survives, to criticize Khomeini is to risk life and limb. Even his more outrageous acts, such as the *fatwa* against the writer Salman Rushdie, have not been publicly condemned within Iran. But if the past is any indicator of future behavior, then we can expect Khomeini to be vilified publicly as soon as the Islamic Republic collapses.

This process of absolute obedience to a supreme leader, as long as he or his heirs remain in power, is not unique to Iran. Nor is it unique that one supreme authoritarian leader should be overthrown through revolution, only to be replaced by another very similar leader, now using a different title and "front." Just as Khomeini replaced the shah, so Lenin and his successors (including Stalin) replaced the tsar, "Emperor" Napoleon soon after replaced the king executed during the French Revolution, and Chairman Mao and the so-called New Emperors replaced the old prerevolution emperors in China. In numerous developing countries, revolutions against colonial powers have given rise to equally or even more harsh dictatorships under "elected" leaders, such as Saddam Hussein of Iraq, who cling to power for as long as they live. In North Korea, a supposedly communist society, the current dictator has an "heir apparent"—his son.

Traditional explanations of leadership have been of three types. First, the "great man" theories have explained leadership in terms of special characteristics of the leader. Terms such as *charisma, magnetism, mass appeal,* and *evil genius* are often used as a part of such explanations. Second, a smaller set of explanations focus on the context and ask, for example: What was it about the situation that resulted in a man such as Hitler rising to power? A third type of explanation looks at the interaction between type of person and type of situation. This is a more difficult approach, and a satisfying explanation is rarely achieved.

All three of these approaches have some merit, but they all miss an essential point: Leadership style is mutually constructed and is sustained by certain carriers that are part of collective life. A more effective alternative to these three types of explanations is to focus on the nature of the *collaboratively constructed ongoing relationships* between leaders and followers. These relationships are sustained by carriers, often woven subtly and intricately into the fabric of everyday social life.

Carriers and Authority Relations

From as far back as I can remember in my childhood, visiting my great-grandfather's house was a particularly joyous event. He lived in an old house near the Grand Bazaar of Tehran. To get to the house, one has to walk through a very old neighborhood of narrow, winding lanes surrounded by high walls, designed to protect pedestrians from the intense heat that engulfs that part of the world in the summer months. The house itself is built around two adjoining courtyards. Each courtyard has at its center a shallow pool and a few trees, surrounded by two-story buildings that look inward. Visitors are confined to the smaller courtyard, while family members enjoy privacy in the larger courtyard.

Coming in from the dusty streets, visitors take off their shoes and step into a calm, peaceful atmosphere, with one serene room leading to another. There is almost no Western furniture to be seen in the house, but all the rooms are covered with Persian carpets, and everyone sits on the floor. The house was a weekly gathering place for all my extended family, and in such gatherings enormous emphasis was placed on teaching children correct behavior. From the earliest age I followed the example of others, standing up when my elders entered a room and sitting closer than my elders to the entrance to a room. Later, I came to understand that such behavior indicates respect for elders. I came to see the room as having a "top" (*ballaa*) and a "bottom" (*paa-een*). The top of the room is away from the entrance and toward the center of the room; the bottom is at the entrance. High-status persons sit at the top. How one sits is also dictated by status. In the presence of those with higher status, one sits with feet neatly tucked under. The soles of feet are never shown. In the presence of lower-status persons, one can sit any way one wants.

My great-grandfather's house is now considered impractical and uncomfortable by younger generations. Those members of my family who still reside in Tehran now live in Western-style houses. In many ways their homes seem similar to middle-class homes in the West. They have modern electronic equipment and their rooms are filled with Western furniture, either imported or directly copied from originals commonly used in New York, London, and Paris. On the surface, then, it appears that these modern homes are very different from my great-grandfather's.

At a deeper level, however, there is continuity in behavior from my great-grandfather's home to these new Western-style homes in Tehran. People in the modern homes sit on chairs and couches instead of on the floor, but *where* they sit is still determined by traditional norms: The lower the status, the closer the person sits to the entrance. Of course, persons of lower status stand up when a person of higher status enters a room. Such features of social behavior are important because they reflect continuity in essential aspects of social relationships and social organization in society. The continuity of norms concerning seating arrangements is apparent not only in the privacy of homes but also in public places, such as mosques and offices.

It is to this kind of subtle continuity that one must look in order to recognize and make sense of continuity in leadership style before and after the 1979 revolution in Iran. Just as there has been continuity in the most important person's being seated far from the door and in a central location in a room, there has been continuity in absolute authority and power being concentrated in the most important person in a group. Just as changes in furniture and household gadgets should not distract us from recognizing continuity in seating arrangements, similarly changes in surface characteristics, such as clothing and titles, should not distract us from recognizing continuity in leadership style. Before the revolution the leader, the shah, appeared in Western clothing and tried to present the world with the image of a technologically up-to-date leader. After the revolution the leader, the Ayotollah Khomeini, appeared in traditional clothing and tried to present the world with the image of a spiritual leader. In both cases, however, control carriers sustained a leader–follower relationship that *concentrated absolute power in the hands of this single male.*

The control carriers relevant to leader–follower relations map out in detail the kinds of behavior that is correct for leaders and followers. I am not referring here to abstract ideas about how to behave but rather to concrete social skills that are imbedded in mutually upheld social activities *shared* by a collectivity. Control carriers in such settings rely on behaviors that arise *only* in collective life, through mutually constructed activities and meanings passed on from generation to generation and group to group. Much of this is integrated into religious ceremonies. For example, Muslims are required to pray five times each day. Daily prayers said as part of a collectivity and with an imam as leader have greater value (more *savaab*) than prayers said by an individual in isolation. Thus individuals are encouraged to participate in group prayer, and in this way they come under the influence of the leader. In Iran after the revolution, exhaustive efforts were made to strengthen this tradition; for example, by televising and glorifying group prayer meetings. In this way, the act of gathering daily and saying prayers in a collectivity with a leader has been sustained. The same local leader (imam) often also organizes political marches and rallies support for the supreme national spiritual/political leader.

The ritual of collective prayer, with followers standing behind an imam, is not taught to Iranians as an abstract idea. Rather, it is learned by children as an everyday social skill through their interactions with others and participation in collective social life. This process begins before children even know what prayer means. I have witnessed 2- and 3-year-old Iranian children imitating their parents at prayer, going through the ritual washing and the other various actions, as they might imitate their parents reading a book or cooking a meal.

Most of the individuals participating in such collective prayers do not know how to read a written version of the Arabic prayer they are reciting, nor even what the prayer means exactly. The vast majority of Iranians do not understand Arabic, but the Koran and the daily Islamic prayers are still in Arabic. They know the daily prayers by heart, as Catholics knew prayers in Latin by heart before services were translated into English and other local languages. Of course, some individuals do know the meaning of the daily prayers they recite in Arabic. But knowing or not knowing the exact translations of Arabic prayers is of no consequence for the actions of worshipers, because the act of following an imam in prayer emerges first and foremost as a shared activity, a mutually upheld social practice that strengthens a certain style of leader–follower relationship.

It is, then, through mutually constructed everyday collective life that individuals become skilled participants in daily prayers and learn to behave correctly in their following of the imam in group prayers. Similarly, it is through the details of mutually constructed collective life at the micro level that individuals learn to behave correctly in leader–follower relationships at the macro national level. Rather than being just a top-down or just a bottom-up process, the leader–follower relationship is at the same time dependent on macro and micro events.

Micro/Macro Social Relations

Revolutionaries and Collective Life

If the above analysis is on track, then those who want to change things must also attend to the details of mutually constructed social life. Surely I am not the first to have discovered this, and surely those who have wanted to achieve change, including revolutionaries, have tried to put this insight into practice? Indeed they have.

An intriguing aspect of major revolutions is that, from the outside at least, radical revolutionaries often appear to be obsessively concerned with changing even the details of everyday life, down to the names and images associated with everyday objects. Thus, following the French Revolution, images on playing cards were changed; for example, the queen of hearts became the "liberty of the arts." A revolutionary calendar replaced the traditional Gregorian calendar, with the days of the month renamed and each month divided into three 10-day periods with new names for days. Names of places were changed, such as the town of Lyon becoming Ville-Affranchie (Liberated Town) and the street Montmartre becoming Mont-Marat. Marseille suffered the ignominy of being renamed Ville-Sans-Nom (Town-without-Name).

Similarly, following the 1917 Russian Revolution traditional deferential titles ("your honor," "your excellency," and so on) were replaced by "comrade," the *Marseillaise* became the national anthem, the Red Flag became the national flag, red ribbons and all kinds of red markers were used to show support for the revolution, the double-headed eagle and other symbols of tsarist power were abandoned, and all names associated with the tsar were changed. For example, all place names associated with the former regime were changed, so that Palace Bridge became Freedom Bridge, Palace Embankment became The Embankment of Freedom, and so on. The names of naval ships were also changed, so that the *Empress Catherine* became *Free Russia* and the *Grand Duke Nikolaevich* became *Revival*. Personal names also underwent a change; for example, the name Nikolai, the most commonly used male name in the prerevolutionary era, now became rare.

If those who want to change things have found it useful to attend to the role of carriers at the micro level, so have those who want to keep things the way they are. As I write, there is a heated debate going on at Georgetown University, where I am a professor, between those who want crucifixes placed on the walls of all classrooms and those who oppose such a move. At one level, a crucifix might be seen as just a wooden cross, two pieces of wood nailed together. But from another perspective, a crucifix is a fundamentally important carrier of Christian (in this case Catholic) values; for some people it is the most important carrier, and as such it must be promoted at all costs. Thus, when "traditional" Catholics at Georgetown and other Catholic institutions fight vehemently to put crucifixes in classrooms and other prominent places, they are attending to such "details" because they recognize the central role of a crucifix as a carrier, just as those who adamantly oppose placing crucifixes in classrooms recognize the same.

The cross and other religious carriers were also a focus of attention during the French Revolution. Crucifixes were removed, replaced by "liberty hats," or paraded upside down and denigrated. Churches were desecrated, statues of saints and angels were smashed, mannequins of the pope were burned, and donkeys were dressed in a bishop's robes and paraded through the streets. But these attacks on the cross and other symbolic carriers were not as fine-grained and concerned with detail as were attempts to alter control carriers. Revolutionaries tried to change almost every detail of rules about behavior, from the way in which people were supposed to greet one another, to dress codes and outward appearance, to songs and poems taught to children, to gender roles and relations between generations. Citizens were to be "reconstructed" from head to toe.

Such concern with the details of behavior is also evident among more recent radical revolutionaries intending to change society. A massively orchestrated example that has deservedly received much critical attention is the Chinese Cultural Revolution of the late 1960s. This involved serious attempts at "reeducating" the population, particularly by turning on their head traditional intergenerational relationships. Schoolchildren and university students attacked teachers and professors, sometimes physically and with great ferocity, and gangs of Red Guards brandishing Mao's Little Red Book harangued and beat up "traditionalists" and "backsliders" who were accused of standing in the way of revolutionary change. The terms *cultural revolution* and *reeducation* were not used lightly in this context, since the idea was to change all important aspects of behavior in line with the requirements of a revolutionary Chinese society. The smallest details of behavior, including forms of address and dress, were targeted for change.

Remarkable similarities exist between the circumstances of the cultural revolution in China in the late 1960s and the one in Iran in the early 1980s. In both cases an aged leader, Mao in China and Khomeini in Iran, manipulated a situation in which young students spearheaded radical change, bringing to a standstill, in some cases for years, the normal functioning of schools, universities, government institutions, and other organs of "the establishment." In both cases the goal was not only to reeducate educators, bureaucrats, "experts," and the masses in an intellectual sense but to change even the most minute details of everyday behaviors, such as how two persons should talk with each other. For example, in Iran people were forbidden to look into the eyes of, or shake hands with, the opposite sex (except for husbands interacting with wives). All forms of contact and intimacy between the sexes in public, including hand holding, became taboo (even between married couples). Revolutionary zeal even entered the washroom: All toilets that allowed men to relieve themselves in a standing position were systematically smashed. Only the seated position was acceptable (the sight of washrooms with all the "stand-up" toilets smashed was both comical and grotesque).

Despite these kinds of efforts, which appear exhaustive and extreme, revolutionary movements almost always fail to bring about fundamental change. What is most apparent after revolutionary fervor has subsided, in just about every case, is a strong theme of continuity, not only in the domain of everyday social life but also at the macro level of the centralization of power and distribution of wealth. In most cases, the situation of the poor did not improve as a consequence of revolution, and when redistribution of wealth came about, it was between members of the relatively affluent classes. To put it succinctly, as did Simon Schama in his brilliant analysis of the French Revolution, "Fat cats got fatter."

But revolutions and collective movements generally do change some things rapidly, and it is instructive to pay attention to what changes and what does not. From this analysis there emerges a universal law of change.

The Maximum Speed of Change: A Micro/Macro Universal Law

The citizenship ceremony (mentioned in Chapter 1) had instantly made me an American, with all the legal rights that citizens enjoy. It felt wonderful to have such rights. I thought back to the situation of African Americans and other minorities several decades ago: There was a time when civil rights legislation instantly made them equal in the eyes of the law. In a sense, they became U.S. citizens for the first time then, despite having been born in the United States. It had been an uphill battle, but they made it; they got the laws reformed. How wonderful those minorities must have felt, and what a great achievement for the citizens of a country to be able to say that they truly enjoy equal rights in the eyes of the law.

But critics have pointed out that disparities continue to exist in the United States between the law and actual behavior. By law everyone has equal rights, but clearly some people are more equal than others. Studies of the U.S. legal system reveal that even the law is applied differently to different individuals depending on their ethnicity: African Americans receive harsher treatment than whites for the same crimes. It goes without saying that the rich enjoy more "equal rights" than the poor; this is one lesson that the "trial of the century," the O. J. Simpson case, effectively highlighted. Clearly, there is still a disparity between formal law, how it is "supposed to be," and how people actually behave.

A pattern emerges when we look at experiences with change at the level of legal and other macro systems, and change at the micro level of everyday behavior. Change at the macro level can come about very quickly: A law can be changed overnight, whole legal systems can be overturned, governments can topple, and economic policies and even political systems can be transformed through revolution, as in the case of systems changing from communism to capitalism in the later 1980s and early 1990s. Such changes can be very rapid: Many people who never dreamed they would see the collapse of the Berlin Wall woke up one morning to witness the entire Soviet communist empire come crashing down. However, the "end of communism" at the macro levels has not necessarily been matched by the speed of change in everyday behavior. The legal, political, and economic systems in the former Soviet Union changed much more quickly than did micro-level behavior, just as the citizenship ceremony made me a U.S. citizen much more quickly than I could change myself to "become" American.

To sum up, the maximum speed of change at the macro level of legal, political, and economic systems is faster than the maximum speed of change at the micro level of everyday behavior.

This simple insight can help us understand why the normal trend for revolutions involves a paradox. On the one hand, a government is overthrown, and rapid and dramatic changes are made in the laws of the land and the economy. On the other hand, an invisible hand seems to pull things back to the way they were, so that soon people feel that nothing has changed. How people actually behave seems to remain the same. Like anchors that refuse to allow a ship to move far from a particular location, carriers sustain old ways of doing things, even though "by law" behavior should have changed.

My analysis leads to a reconceptualization of types of change in human social life. Such changes are usefully conceptualized as involving first-, second-, and third-order change, where the fundamental difference between the three levels concerns the context in which change takes place. The type of change possible is circumscribed by the characteristics of the context, ranging from a context that fully supports inequalities to a context that fully supports equalities. The context of *first-order change* is one in which intergroup inequalities are justified by both formal law and the informal normative system. For example, in pre-apartheid South Africa inequalities were justified both by written, formal law and by the prevailing normative system of the country.

The context of *second-order change* is one in which formal law has been reformed to ban unequal treatment on the basis of group membership, but the informal normative system still allows unequal treatment. In books such as *Driving While Black*, critics argue that even advanced industrial societies, such as the United States, have not fully experienced this type of change. Thus, in first- and second-order change, there are changes in the relative positions of groups in society, but intergroup inequalities continue in practice.

The context of *third-order change* is one in which equal treatment is supported in both formal law and the informal normative system, and a true meritocracy is thus encouraged. That is, individuals are treated on the basis of individual characteristics rather than group membership. This sets the conditions for the realization of Plato's Republic, where circulation of talent takes place freely lest the Republic face the danger of collapse. Unfortunately, the democratic conditions of Plato's Republic have not been emulated successfully by any large modern society.

I have pointed to the powerful effect of carriers on continuities, making it difficult for societies to successfuly complete each of the three types of change, particularly the third type. Throughout much of the last 2,500 years, a major theme in Western civilization has been the idea of progress, the assumption that change toward a better condition of human life is taking place. But since the mid-nineteenth century, this assumption has been challenged more seriously. That is, it is seen as questionable whether we are moving toward third-order change.

Do Societies Evolve in Cyclical or Progressive Ways?

I have placed considerable emphasis on continuity in behavior and have proposed that everyday social practices can limit and even put a break on societal change. But what kind of societal change does come about in the long term?

Students of revolutions are presented with two very different pictures of the evolution of society by Karl Marx (1818–1883) and Vilfredo Pareto (1984–1923), two theorists who profoundly influenced the fields of sociology and economics, and indirectly psychology. Both Marx and Pareto adopted a conspiratorial model, proposing that in all societies real power rests in the hands of elites, who control all important resources, including education and the media, and rule over the nonelite. Marx argued that the nonelite (what he called the "proletariate") would eventually come to see themselves as a distinct group with interests that conflict with those of the elite (the "capitalists"). This "class consciousness" would emerge gradually through repeated clashes between the elite and the nonelite: Practices, everyday experiences, would lead to a change in worldview. Eventually, the nonelite would rebel, take over from the elite, and establish a dictatorship of the nonelite masses. Such a dictatorship would lead to a classless society; and since, according to Marx, government exists to protect class interests, there would eventually be no need for a central government. Everyone would have the same class interests because there would be only one class. (Interestingly, on this point Marx and radical libertarians agree: The ideal society has no government.) Thus, according to Marx, societal changes are "progressive," in that they lead inevitably through a succession of revolutions to a classless society.

Pareto's description of the evolution of society is seen as more "realistic" or "pessimistic," depending on one's politics. Pareto agrees with Marx that society is ruled by an elite and that eventually the nonelite would manage to revolt and topple the current regime. This would be achieved through the leadership of very talented nonelite members who had been prevented from rising to the top and joining the elite. In other words, when an elite makes the mistake of acting as a closed system, talented individuals who on the basis of merit should be part of the elite are kept out and untalented individuals who on the basis of merit should be part of the nonelite are retained as part of the elite. When talented individuals trying to rise up into the elite hit a "glass ceiling," they would mobilize and lead the nonelite to revolt against the system. So far, then, Marx and Pareto march in step, predicting the same events: the mobilization of the masses, led by a talented vanguard, to eventually overthrow the rulers. However, at this stage they part company in a dramatic manner: While Marx sees a final revolution leading to a proletariat dictatorship and eventually a classless society, Pareto sees the revolution as simply replacing one elite with another.

Marx, then, sees society as evolving through a series of revolutions bringing about real changes of systems, moving from first-, to second-, to third-order change; for example, a change from feudalism to capitalism, and then to the classless society (in which group membership becomes unimportant). Pareto, on the other hand, argues that so-called "revolutionary" changes would be only surface level, and at a deeper level the fundamental characteristic that matters would not have changed: An elite would still rule in all societies. Irrespective of the slogans and labels used, whether it is "democracy," "socialism," "capitalism," "Islamic Republic," or whatever, the fact remains, Pareto argues, that an elite will always rule over a nonelite.

Most critics would agree that the predictions of Pareto and Marx represent two extreme scenarios at opposite ends of a continuum (see Figure 2.1), with an outcome of classless society at one extreme (Marx) and the inevitability of elite rule at the other extreme (Pareto). Neither of these scenarios seems inevitable, and the reason may be in an important similarity shared by Pareto and Marx: a lack of sufficient importance being given to the role of individuals and to personal initiative or free will in individual styles of behavior. Both Pareto and Marx see individual behavior as determined by larger social and economic forces: For Pareto, individuals who become members of the elite inevitably become power hungry and determine to rule over the nonelite; while for Marx, the individuals' positions in the production process and class system shape their consciousness—how they think and feel about the world and their position in it.

Despite their limitations, the views of Pareto and Marx do alert us to an important point: that in order to understand individuals and society, we must look beneath the surface and "given" explanations. When we adopt such a critical approach, we find that despite changing rhetoric across regimes and revolutions, there is a strong continuity in the styles of leader–follower relations in many different societies.

FIGURE 2.1

The two extreme scenarios of societal change depicted by Marx and Pareto

End point: Third-order change	End point: First- and second-order change
Marx: Structural changes take place, so that class conflict eventually leads to a classless society	Pareto: The structure of society remains static, with elites always ruling over non-elites

Concluding Comment

Surveying the rest of the world from North America, it is sometimes tempting to assume that democratic capitalism is exempt from the trends I have identified. In dictatorial countries, such as Iran and China, or in revolutions of the past, such as the French Revolution, the cult of powerful individuals and dynasties has been perpetuated, but surely a very different situation exists in the United States, where people vote their political leaders into office? A hard-headed look at the American scene reveals that things here are different in some respects, but in some other ways they are remarkably similar.

I wrote the first draft of this chapter in the final days of 1999, a year in which John Kennedy Jr. died in a plane crash and the American public went through another phase in its relationship with the Kennedy family, dubbed the "royals of America." As I revise this chapter early in 2001, the front-runner for the Republican nomination for president of the United States, George W. Bush, the son of the former president, has beaten out the front-runner for the Democratic nomination, Al Gore, a descendant of another political dynasty, to become the 43rd U.S. president.

Perhaps America is different with respect to women leaders? In "traditional" societies, a "widow's mandate" seems to exist, whereby women gain political power by having close blood relationships with a former leader. Examples are Indira Gandhi, who became the prime minister of India, following in the footsteps of her father (Jawaharlal Nehru); Benazir Bhutto, who became the prime minister of Pakistan, as was her father (Z. A. Bhutto); and Corazon Aquino and Violeta Chamorro, who became presidents, respectively, of the Philippines and Nicaragua, as the widows of assassinated opposition leaders. But how different is it really in the United States? As 1999 came to a close, the two women political candidates who received the most national attention were the wife of the Republican party's last presidential candidate (Elizabeth Dole) and the wife of the sitting president (Hillary Clinton). In the final days of 2000, two newly elected females to the United States Senate were making a lot of news, one the widow of a former senator (Jean Carnahan) and the other the wife of the sitting U.S. president (Hillary Clinton). It was not until 1979 that a woman, Nancy L. Kassebaum, was elected to the U.S. Senate without being preceded in office by her husband.

The strong influence of dynastic families and the persistence of continuity in leadership is perhaps best highlighted by focusing on India and the United States, the largest and the richest democracies respectively. Both of these countries have "royal" families that have enjoyed continued power and influence in the way monarchies once enjoyed in Europe. The Kennedy clan are already well known, but consider a less publicized lineage of recent rulers in the world's most populous democracy: In India, the prime minister, Nehru, had a daughter (Indira) who became prime minister, who had a son (Rajiv) who became prime minister, who was slain and had a widow who became head of the Congress party and candidate for prime minister. Such a continuous lineage is the envy of many monarchists.

But the concept of carriers allows us to do more than just point to such revealing continuities; we can be more precise in identifying the particular mechanisms through which continuities are sustained. One such mechanism is the practice of rights and duties in human social life—what individuals demand from others and what they believe they owe others. Particular interpretations and implementations of rights and practices persist across generations and serve as important carriers, as we see in the next chapter.

Suggested Readings

Arjomand, A. A. (1988). *The turban for the crown.* New York: Oxford University Press.

Curtis, R. L., & Aguirre, B. E. (Eds). (1993). *Collective behavior and social movements.* Boston: Allyn & Bacon.

Figes, O., & Kolonitskii, B. (1999). *Interpreting the Russian revolution: The language and symbols of 1917.* New Haven, CT: Yale University Press.

Marx, K. (1964). *Karl Marx: Selected writings in sociology and social psychology* (T. B. Bottomore, Trans.). New York: McGraw-Hill.

Meeks, K. (2000). *Driving while black: What to do if you are a victim of racial profiling.* New York: Broadway Books.

Meyer, J., & Jesilow, P. (1996). Research on bias in judicial sentencing. *New Mexico Law Review, 26,* 107–131.

Middlebrook, K. J. (1995). *The paradox of revolution: Labor, state, and authoritarianism in Mexico.* Baltimore: Johns Hopkins University Press.

Miller, D. L. (2000). *Introduction to collective behavior and collective action.* Second Ed. Prospect Heights, Illinois: Waveland.

Nisbet, R. (1969). *History of the idea of progress.* New York: Basic Books.

Pareto, V. (1935). *The mind and society* (Vols. 1–4). New York: Dover.

Salisbury, H. E. (1992). *The new emperors: China in the era of Mao and Deng.* New York: Avon.

Schama, S. (1989). *Citizens: A chronicle of the French Revolution.* New York: Vintage.

Watzlawick, P., Weakland, J. H., & Fisch, R. (1974). *Change: Principles of problem formation and problem resolution.* New York: Norton.

3 Rights and Duties

"... a butler's duty is to provide good service. It is not to meddle in the
great affairs of the nation. The fact is, such great affairs will always be beyond the understanding of those such as you and I, and those of us who
wish to make our mark must realize that we best do so by concentrating
on what *is* within our realm; that is to say, by devoting our attention to
providing the best possible service to those gentlemen in whose hands the
destiny of civilization truly lies."

—KAMUO ISHIGURO, *The Remains of the Day*

In his insightful novel *The Remains of the Day*, Kazuo Ishiguro portrays the
character of Mr. Stevens, a butler who feels duty-bound to serve his master,
Lord Darlington, without ever developing and expressing his own feelings and
opinions. Mr. Stevens is strongly bound by traditional duties and, on the surface at least, he stands in sharp contrast to how most people in North America,
as well as in Europe, feel about rights and duties. Whereas Mr. Stevens emphasizes his duty to serve in an almost unquestioning way, most citizens of Western societies, at least now, highlight their *right* to question authority and to
express their own opinions.

Although there is some variation across cultures as to the level of emphasis
placed on rights, what is *demanded of others*, relative to duties, what is *owed to
others*, there is constancy in the pivotal role played by rights and duties in link-
ing individuals and society. Rights and duties are among the most powerful
and pervasive mechanisms bindings individuals and society. From their earliest
years, children enter social relationships that involve rights and duties. These
relationships begin with primary caretakers, typically the mother and father,
and soon expand to larger social networks, including siblings, more distant relatives, and others in the community. By the age of 2, and perhaps even earlier,

children are capable of carrying out specific behaviors that in particular cultures can be interpreted as involving rights and/or duties; for example, the duty to "share toys with friends" and the right to "have your turn on the swings in the public playground."

Of the two, rights strike us as being more in keeping with contemporary values, whereas the idea of duties seems to reflect more archaic values. The concept of human rights seems to be part and parcel of twenty-first-century living. Progress in human rights, it seems, has been sudden and rapid. When people speak of "rights," the implication is that only we in the modern world "possess" such a thing and that rights did not play a role in premodern societies. A focus on human rights is assumed to be associated with the rise of formal international and national legal institutions, such as the World Court at the Hague and the Supreme Court of the United States. The Universal Declaration of Human Rights was adopted in only 1948 (with Eleanor Roosevelt as chair of the United Nations Human Rights Commission), and civil rights legislation in the United States is even more recent.

This view of human rights, as something associated with developments in formal law that emerged in modern times, has some validity, but I want to present an alternative view, one that depicts both human rights and duties as being rooted in human social relations that predate the emergence of formal law by eons. Thus, instead of viewing human rights and duties as being part of rapid and recent changes, I argue that human rights and duties actually evolved very slowly, probably over a period of hundreds of thousands of years. This long time frame and slow evolution, I propose, are still characteristic of rights and duties outside formal law, and this helps explain why informal rights and duties often prove so resilient and obstinate in the face of efforts to influence them.

Primitive Social Relations

Human Rights and Formal Law

Received wisdom tells us that human rights are associated with developments in formal law, and of course there is merit to this view. From this perspective, in the West the doctrine that there are human rights originates in the ideas of thinkers associated with the Renaissance and the Reformation from the fourteenth to the sixteenth centuries, and later the Enlightenment of the eighteenth century. From the fourteenth century onwards, a succession of changes, nourished by ideas expressed earlier in the Magna Carta (1215) and, later, by reforms in the Christian church sparked by Calvin and others, allowed greater freedom of expression. Galileo's ultimately successful advocacy of the Copernican view of planetary movements and Darwin's articulation of the theory of evolution gave center stage to science and loosened religious and political shackles.

These progressive movements looked back to certain traditions of ancient Greece and Rome but were more directly and practically linked to modern liberal political thought. An important example of such thought is the idea of the social contract articulated by John Locke and others and already reflected in the English Bill of Rights (1688), central to which is the notion that although individuals necessarily sacrifice certain freedoms in order to enjoy protection from the state, there are certain rights, such as the rights to life and freedom from oppression, that are inalienable. The idea of inalienable rights is found in the writings of those associated with the two most important early revolutions and republics, the American and the French, as reflected, for example, in Thomas Paine's *The Rights of Man*, Jean-Jacques Rousseau's *The Social Contract*, and *The Federalist Papers* by James Madison and others. The U.S. Constitution (1787) and the Declaration of the Rights of Man and Citizen from the French National Assembly (1789) are perhaps the most well known early written embodiments of the idea that human beings have inalienable rights.

Although this view, which links human rights to formal law and legal reforms in modern times, is useful, it is too limited and fails to take into account a long evolutionary history of rights and duties as embedded in everyday social practices. When we step back and review this evolutionary picture, it becomes clear that changes in attitudes toward human rights and duties started much earlier than traditionally conceived and took place very, very slowly.

The Evolutionary Roots of Rights and Duties: Primitive Social Relations

Sometime around 4.5 million years ago, our ancestors began to walk on two feet, starting along the long evolutionary road that would eventually lead to tool use about half a million years ago and elementary language skills about 150,000 years ago. Our ancestors migrated enormous distances and colonized vast territories, living as hunter-gatherers in small groups. On this long evolutionary journey, behavioral characteristics could help, or hinder, or be neutral to human survival. Certain essential behaviors, which I refer to as *primitive social relations,* came to play a particularly important role in survival, in the sense that groups that had these characteristics were more likely to survive.

I should point out that in this context survival does not necessarily imply progress. The survival of politicians who use pollsters to make decisions, TV evangelists, and sellers of junk bonds does not represent progress; it simply means that they have managed to adapt to the demands of modern societies.

Four examples of primitive social relations are turn-taking, leadership, reciprocity, and trust. In each case, these primitive social relations are sustained by carriers associated with them.

■ Turn-Taking
Turn-taking is integral to much of human social behavior and probably appeared very early in human evolution, just as it appears early in the individual life cycle. Nursing infants learn turn-taking while resting and sucking during the first few weeks of life, guided by the mother, who also needs rest periods during feeding. As infants learn to communicate more effectively, they come to take turns in listening and expressing themselves, both verbally and nonverbally. By age 4 or 5, children practice turn-taking more or less effectively and often recognize when a violation of turn-taking practices occurs. They already have at least a rough idea of when it is appropriate to talk and when someone has spoken out of turn.

Turn-taking must have played an essential role in human communications at a very early stage in human evolution. For communications to be effective, person A must listen while person B speaks, and person B must in turn listen while person A speaks. If either person constantly interrupts the other and does not take turns, then communications breaks down. This is not to say that turn-taking is synonymous with democratic procedures. Individuals who enjoy higher status are more likely to start and finish conversations, as well as determine the subject matter discussed and make any decisions required. However, even a dictator has to engage in a minimum of turn-taking in order to get information from others, give orders, check that they are carried out, and so on.

Turn-taking is sustained by a vast network of carriers. Some such carriers are formal and dominate in formal settings, such as courts of law and official meetings. For example, in most courts of law, at least in Western societies, there are formal rules about who may speak and when, such as during cross-examination of witnesses by prosecution and defense lawyers. During official business meetings, there are elaborate rules about how a person can gain the right to speak, as well as when those present have a duty to listen to a speaker. Such procedures are taken to be a sign of civilization. In William Golding's brilliant novel *Lord of the Flies*, a group of boys stranded on a desert island devise a formal rule that whoever is holding a particular shell, "the conch," has the right to speak and be listened to. As the boys descend from their civilized state to savagery, the conch is smashed and turn-taking ends.

Carriers that sustain turn-taking in informal settings are no less numerous or elaborate. They are reflected in various handbooks on politeness and etiquette, guides for correct behavior for persons in particular social roles. A fundamentally important rule in politeness across cultures and across time continues to be turn-taking, as indicated by edicts such as "do not interrupt others."

■ **Leadership** Leadership is another important example of primitive social relations. Over the course of early human evolution, effective leadership provided some groups of hunter-gatherers with an advantage, enabling them to meet ecological challenges more successfully. Such leadership arose in part because of cultural characteristics of a group that made it more likely for potentially effective leaders to achieve recognition and power. We must not jump to the conclusion that a form of "meritocracy" was in place or that such leaders acted democratically. In most cases they probably ruled with dictatorial ruthlessness and their leadership may have been based in large part on physical strength and size.

As generation after generation of leaders emerged and functioned within a group, there developed basic patterns of social relations between leaders and followers. For example, a leader would expect to be obeyed when he gave a command (my assumption is that leaders tended to be men rather than women). On the other hand, followers would expect the group to benefit from certain protections through the special characteristics of the leader (e.g., cunning, superior physical strength and size). Such expectations were not necessarily verbalized in any detail but were nonetheless integrated as norms and rules and became part and parcel of collective life. In essence, these formed the rudimentary beginnings for the idea of the social contract articulated and formalized by social philosophers thousands of years later, in the middle of the second millennium A.D.

I am not suggesting that all groups must have leaders. Under certain circumstances groups and even entire societies can survive, at least in the short term, without effective leadership. In contemporary societies, there are examples of orchestras that perform at a very high standard without conductors, work groups in organizations that carry out tasks efficiently without a formal hierarchy and management, and even small tribal societies that function without centralized leadership. However, although such examples exist, they tend to be the exception rather than the rule. For the most part groups and societies in almost all regions of the world do have leaders. Also, as far as I am aware there are no examples of larger and more complex societies functioning effectively for long periods of time without leadership.

Leadership is sustained by numerous carriers, some of them explicit. For example, the king's crown serves as an explicit carrier, as does the swearing-in ceremony of the U.S. president. More subtle, implicit carriers sustain styles of leadership, including norms and rules about the nature of leader–follower relationships, an example being "unquestioning obedience" as the correct rule for followers in some societies.

To sum up, leadership is common to human groups and societies, just as are the expectations that have evolved on the part of leaders and followers with respect to their interdependent roles. Such expectations began as informal and rudimentary, later became articulated, and more recently have been formalized as rights and duties.

■ Reciprocity

Reciprocity, "give-and-take," is another example of primitive social relations that enabled some individuals and groups to enjoy an edge in the struggle for survival. The exact level of reciprocity that would be most advantageous for survival varies across ecological conditions. In any given context, the optimum level of reciprocity could be strategically calculated. Simply put, how many resources should person A put into a relationship in order to maximize outcome? A person who gives everything to others would end up with nothing for the self, and a person who gives nothing to others would run the danger of becoming an outcast and receiving no help from others when in real need.

It is likely that a link between reciprocity and turn-taking developed early in human evolution. The very idea of give-and-take suggests turn-taking. Person A does something for person B; then, in return, person B does something for person A.

Reciprocity is sustained by carriers that function in both formal and informal settings. In formal settings, contracts and written documents are drawn up to specify exactly how exchanges will take place—that is, to specify the terms of reciprocity—as in a business partnership (and increasingly in marriage partnerships in the West, following practices still in place in some Eastern societies). In informal contexts, carriers sustaining reciprocity include roles such as "host" and "guest," as well as norms regulating alternation of roles, so that the person who is the host this week becomes the guest the following week.

■ Trust

An example of primitive social relations that seems less concrete is trust. Particularly from the perspective of twenty-first-century urban dwellers, it may seem surprising to suggest that trust has been an essential feature of human social relations from our very earliest days, one that was imperative to survival. In the modern world, we are inclined to believe that distrust rather than trust characterizes human life. However, despite the pessimistic assumptions found in the modern media, my contention is that even in modern societies most people trust one another most of the time. If it were otherwise, life in the industrial world would quickly come to a standstill. Almost all business transactions and organizational work would end. Consider the following examples.

A man rushes to the airport in Hong Kong to catch a 2:00 flight to California. He is acting on the assumption that the airport information desk can be trusted and that his flight did not depart an hour earlier. When the captain announces "We will be landing in Los Angeles in another 10 minutes," the passengers generally trust the captain to have taken them to the correct destination.

A job applicant spends days completing application forms and preparing for a job interview, trusting that the job really is available and her application really will be considered. A tourist asks the way to a train station, trusting that the person she has asked will not purposely mislead her.

We routinely trust that others, often complete strangers to us, will tell the truth and act honestly, and as a general rule we are proved right. Of course, some individuals turn out to be exceptions, but eventually they tend to be recognized as untrustworthy.

Trust must have played an equally important role in early human evolution. Individuals and groups often needed to rely on one another for information about the location of water, animals, shelter, and other things important for survival. Is this berry edible? Will we find water in this valley? Are there any dangerous animals nearby?

Carriers that sustain trust include official roles, as indicated by uniforms and special emblems, such as a police officer's uniform and a priest's collar. Such carriers also include special ethical rules, such as the Hippocratic oath for physicians, which underlines the position of trust. In essence, others have a right to expect that a person in this position will fulfill a duty to behave in a way that justifies the trust others have in the position.

Let us now turn to the issue of how particular social relations came to be interpreted with respect to rights and duties, depending on cultural conditions.

Carriers, Culture, and Normative Rights/Duties

The Interpretation of Primitive Social Relations as Rights/Duties

Primitive social relations, then, are universal features of social behavior that arose out of the common ecological challenges faced by humans. The evolution of primitive social relations, such as turn-taking, leadership, reciprocity, and trust, took place over hundreds of thousands of years, even before the emergence of sophisticated language skills. That features of culture could be transmitted from generation to generation without the benefit of human language is suggested by the case of chimpanzees. Research has shown that certain styles of behavior, such as particular types of hunting skills and the use of tools unique to specific populations of chimpanzees in specific regions of the world, are passed on across generations of chimpanzees. Obviously chimpanzees do communicate with one another, but their linguistic capabilities are extremely limited. Nevertheless, they successfully transmit aspects of culture.

Similarly, early humans passed on cultural characteristics despite limited language skills.

Primitive social relations were passed on from generation to generation and came to be interpreted as rights or duties, depending on the particular biases of local cultures. For instance, turn-taking in communications could be interpreted as involving the right of individuals to practice free speech. Alternatively, it could be interpreted as involving a *duty* to *enable* others to enjoy free speech, rather than one's own right to practice free speech. Also, the focus could be on collectivities, rather than the current U.S. focus on individuals. Such an interpretation might lead to a focus on achieving equality of access for collectivities (ethnic and gender groups, social classes) to the means of mass communications, such as radio and television as well as more recent computer technologies. After all, what good is free speech if minority groups do not have a significant measure of control over television and other powerful means of communications? It is useful to step back and consider how the cultural interpretation of primitive social relations evolved.

In the human evolutionary process, primitive social relations such as turn-taking and reciprocity involved patterns of behavior and created expectations about "what should happen next." For example, turn-taking in communications created expectations that when person A has spoken to person B, person B will get a turn to respond to person A. Reciprocity created expectations that when person A has given food to person B, person B will return the favor when the opportunity arises. Such expected patterns of behavior were sometimes violated, such as when person A would not allow person B to have a turn to speak, or when person A had received food from person B but refused to return the favor even though the need and opportunity had arisen. In such cases, pressure was no doubt put on the transgressor to get back in line and do as expected. Again, research on apes and monkeys shows that this kind of group pressure can be brought to bear on transgressors in the absence of linguistic skills.

However, with the development of language there arose a new ability to articulate and interpret primitive social relations in an increasingly sophisticated manner. Turn-taking, reciprocity, and other primitive social relations that had evolved primarily as functional responses to ecological demands were now interpreted as rights and/or duties. Expectations and patterns already integral to collective life were now recognized. A person now had a "right" to a turn to speak and a "duty" to let others have turns, just as a person had a "right" to receive something in return for giving something of value to another and a "duty" to return favors. The language of rights and duties gradually crept into everyday life.

Early notions of rights and duties were first reflected in "commonsense justice," or how people think about justice in everyday life. Formal law, or legislated written law, with its associated national and international declarations of human rights, is much more recent. Also recent is the emphasis on the individual rather than the collectivity and the priority of rights rather than duties. The contemporary focus on individual rights in the United States reflects biases in recent American culture.

Carriers, Rights, and Duties

The Supreme Court justices in the photograph stared straight back at the onlooker with serious, unswerving eyes. The solemnity and power of the group was underlined by their dark robes and by the U.S. flag unfurled behind them. Each of the justices was seated or standing at an angle, tilted toward some invisible center of gravity in the group. Despite their gray hair and frail bodies, the photograph showed this group of old men and women as powerful, solid beings and as representing something permanent. Underneath the photograph was written in bold letters: "Upholders of the United States Constitution."

In a real sense the U.S. Supreme Court is a carrier of the U.S. Constitution. This does not mean that when I look at the justices of the Supreme Court, I see the U.S. Constitution in their faces. They do not literally carry the U.S. Constitution on their bodies. They do something much more important and subtle. Collectively they interpret the U.S. Constitution, keeping it alive by making sure that current legislation does not stray from the spirit and letter of the original document. In this way the U.S. Supreme Court acts as a control carrier, influencing limits to and guidelines for how people can behave.

But the U.S. Supreme Court is also a symbolic carrier, with its robes and formal ceremonies serving to represent authority and to help sustain the power of authority. No doubt these ceremonies were influenced by justices in Europe, who for centuries have had the trappings that help them serve the role of symbolic carriers, such as the traditional silk robes and horsehair wigs worn by judges in British high courts, the judge's mallet, and the ushers who ceremoniously announce their arrival and departure. The pomp and tradition of the British House of Lords well illustrates the power of such symbolic carriers when the Lords sit in judgment in important cases, often serving as a final authority of appeal, as in the case of General Augusto Pinochet's appeal to avoid extradition from the United Kingdom to Spain to face charges of human rights violations in Chile.

North Americans visiting British courts often note the "ancient" traditions still upheld there and express envy at the sense of history that still lingers. However, formal law in Europe is very young compared to the far longer history of the informal rule systems and the carriers that support them. Just as the roots of modern systems of justice go back to much earlier times, even prior to the development of human language, so do the carriers that sustain and help to transmit such justice systems. Control carriers, in the form of collective expectations about patterns of behavior and "what should happen next," probably emerged hand in hand with symbolic carriers, which may have consisted of special stones, sticks, animal hides, or other simple artifacts that served to symbolize authority. For example, certain individuals may have had special leadership roles, particularly during hunts, during fighting, or at the death of a group member, and their rights to command, take priority in speech, and so on may have been signified by their carrying or wearing particular symbolic carriers. This may explain the important role of ceremonial spears and other artifacts for various traditional tribal groups, such as the Tiwi of northern Australia. A Tiwi male might be wearing almost nothing that we would recognize as clothing, but he would consider himself "undressed" only if he were not carrying his ceremonial spears, indicating his status and rights and duties in traditional Tiwi society.

Initiation ceremonies are an important category of carriers associated with rights and duties that have both a very long history and a wide prevalence in modern societies. Initiation ceremonies mark transition points, after which individuals are accepted as members of particular groups, such as becoming an adult in a tribal society or a member of a college fraternity or sorority. Most discussions of initiation ceremonies focus on the physical and mental hardships individuals have to suffer in order to successfully "pass" from one stage to another, and the modern media often report stories of hazing and other physical abuse inflicted on new recruits undergoing initiation ceremonies in the military, college fraternities, and so on. But little attention is paid to the more important role of such ceremonies, which concern the rights and duties that new members take on and that initiation ceremonies help sustain. Such rights and duties are often spelled out in detail in oaths and other official declarations that new recruits recite.

An example of this is the oath of allegiance of the Klu Klux Klan, with its focus on "obedience," "secrecy," "fidelity," and "Klansmanship." This is a particularly interesting example, because it shows how a group can take positive carriers that people are familiar with, such as the Constitution and the Christian cross, and use them to serve its own devious purposes. An important duty of all Klan members is to uphold the Klan constitution, with its stipulation "to maintain forever the God-given supremacy of the white race." The Klan constitution serves as a control carrier, stipulating how Klan members can behave. For example, one of the punishable offenses is "being responsible for the polluting of Caucasian blood through miscegenation." A host of symbolic carriers—such as the sword, the burning cross, the robe, and the mask—are also used to support and transmit the value system of the Klan, particularly through the force of group conformity and anonymity. For instance, referring to the use of what I have termed a symbolic carrier, *The Klansman's Manual* states, "With the mask we hide our individuality and sink ourselves into the great sea of Klankraft."

Change in Formal Law and Change in Behavior

One of the most profoundly disturbing experiences for me in the 1970s was confronting human rights problems during my regular trips to Iran. I was studying in England at the time, and in some ways it was wonderful to go back to my family and friends and the rich Persian culture of my ancestors. The colorful bazaars, the exquisite artistry of traditional Persian artisans, the stupendous diversity of the land and its cultures—it was all a feast for my senses. At the same time, however, I was painfully aware that thousands of Iranians were in prison because of their political views and that many were being tortured in the notorious Evin prison in north Tehran. Like any other human being disturbed by the plight of those languishing in torture chambers, I looked forward to a day when people would not be imprisoned, tortured, or executed for their political beliefs.

During the struggle to topple the shah, one of the challenges was to free all political prisoners. This goal was gradually achieved during 1978 and 1979. Evin prison was finally taken over by revolutionaries, and for Iranians this was symbolically like the fall of the Bastille during the French Revolution. At last, political prisoners were freed! Jubilant crowds greeted the freed prisoners with flowers. They were carried on shoulders like heroes. Parts of the infamous Evin prison were opened to visitors for a brief spell, and newspapers ran long articles with pictures of torture chambers and stories of prisoners and their experiences. Former prisoners at Evin, including the Ayatollah Montazeri, who for a while was touted as the Ayatollah Khomeini's likely successor, recounted how they had been tortured at Evin (as with many "children of the revolution," Montazeri later found himself persecuted by a new wave of revolutionaries and his title changed from "Ayatollah" to plain "Mr.").

It had been a nightmare, but we seemed to have awakened. We imagined that the notorious Evin prison would be demolished or converted to something useful, such as a hospital. The thought did not occur to us that, within a very short time, Evin prison would once again be full of political prisoners and that the same torturers would be employed to carry on their work—but now with an even greater number of victims. Ironically, true to the dictum of revolutions eating their own children, wave after wave of revolutionaries found themselves persecuted, imprisoned, and tortured by agents of the new "revolutionary" regime.

Both before and after the revolution, formal law outlawed torture in Iran, and both the government of the shah before the revolution and that of the Islamic Republic after the revolution denied that torture was practiced. However, the weight of evidence clearly shows that political prisoners were tortured both before and after the revolution and that the torture and execution of political prisoners increased rather than decreased after the revolution. As reports from Amnesty International and other credible organizations make clear, torture of political prisoners continues in Iran in the twenty-first century. Why is it that the revolution did not bring about a positive change? Why is it that torture continued and even increased after the revolution?

To say that the torture of political prisoners continues because Iran remains a dictatorship does not explain much. A better and fuller explanation is to highlight the style of political behavior pervasive in Iran and the carriers that support this style. In order to prevent the imprisonment and torture of people for their political beliefs, there would need to be a weakening and eventual end to these carriers. This could not be achieved by changes in formal law alone, because the carriers in question operate for the most part outside the formal legal system.

Among the carriers that play an important role in this context are control carriers that influence the behavior of professional administrators, security officers, prison guards, torturers, and others who take part in the identification, capture, imprisonment, torture, and sometimes execution of members of the political opposition. It is instructive that the core band of professionals who fit this category in Iran remained the same after the revolution. Many of them were called back to do their old jobs after a brief time gap during the chaotic days of the revolution. They could do this—switching from serving in the shah's regime to serving the government of the Islamic Republic—in part because control carriers sustained the same role for them in the two regimes.

Central to these control carriers are rules and norms that articulate a *professional role* for torturers, administrators, and others involved in the mistreatment of prisoners of conscience. Like medical doctors, engineers, scientists, and others who also have professional roles, these torturers and administrators try to maintain a detached, objective manner, one that allows them to focus on achieving technical efficiency. Just as a medical doctors should not allow personal sentiments to bias their treatment of patients, in the same way torturers, administrators, and others involved in the "treatment" of political prisoners in Iran have tried to remain detached in applying their technical expertise. Thus we have detailed accounts of torturers forcing their victims to address them as "doctor" and using pseudo-technical language as one means of sustaining a detached, professional role. This "professional" role is also supported by sophisticated technology, drugs, and paraphernalia that create a distance between torturer and victim. The power of control carriers in this arena is such that they have allowed torturers to imagine themselves as surgeons in operating rooms, ignoring the fact that medical surgeons enter operating rooms to end suffering and save lives, whereas torturers enter torture chambers to inflict suffering and death.

As "professionals," torturers, administrators, and others involved in the "treatment" of prisoners of conscience in Iran and in many other countries are first and foremost concerned with professional allegiances and roles. They remain detached from ideology, just as they remain detached from and impersonal toward the prisoners they torture. This explains why they were able to make the switch from working for the shah's regime to working for the Islamic Republic. In essence, they do not owe allegiance to either regime. Ironically, unlike many academics, scientists, and other experts who were expelled from their jobs because they were not seen as committed enough to the new Islamic Republic, torturers and secret service agents who had worked for the shah were not required to pass a test of commitment to the new regime after the revolution. As is still the case in many parts of the world, in Iran even dramatic changes of government have not destroyed job security for torturers of political prisoners.

Rights, Duties, and Individualism

So far I have emphasized that rights and duties are learned as part of the process through which the integration of individuals into society takes place and that certain rights and duties, such as turn-taking, are inherent in all human relationships, while others, such as political freedoms, are more dependent on culture. I now want to turn to a fundamentally important cultural difference in the ways in which rights and duties are interpreted, and this relates to the nature of individualism in a society.

There has accumulated a vast array of evidence, much of its gathered since the 1980s, suggesting that there are cross-cultural differences in the emphasis placed on individualism versus collectivism. The research on individualism has gathered momentum, making it a major theme, directly or indirectly, in the work of leading psychologists such as Michael Cole, political scientists such as Robert Putnam, and sociologists such as Anthony Giddens. Individualism refers to a tendency to focus on self-help, individual responsibility, individual freedoms (including the freedom to move geographically), duty to the self, and the rights of the self. Collectivism, on the other hand, refers to a tendency to emphasize collective responsibility ("It takes a village"), duty to the community, group effort, collective rights, and community needs.

Recent findings caution against a simplistic dichotomy, because a society can be highly individualistic in some respects and highly collectivistic in others. For example, a group might emphasize both family ties (a collectivistic characteristic) and entrepreneurial spirit (an individualistic characteristic), as seems to be the case in Japanese society, for example. It is popular to make the point that a society need not be thought of as being on one end or the other of an individualism–collectivism continuum but, rather, as being multidimensional. Despite this complexity, it is still useful to describe very broad cross-cultural differences. For example, the United States is more individualistic and less collectivisitic compared to Russia, India, and China. This tendency has fundamental implications for the interpretation of rights and duties in these societies.

In the United States the individual person remains the main unit in relation to which rights and duties are defined. This tendency may even have been accentuated in recent years; there is some evidence that people are in certain respects becoming more individualistic, as suggested by Robert Putnam's controversial "bowling alone" thesis. In addition to a possibly greater focus on the individual rather than the collective, some have argued that there is also an increased focus on rights rather than duties. In my own research, I have found that it is not so much a case of young Americans neglecting duties as of reinterpreting the meaning of duties in line with individualism. For example, when I asked young Americans to complete the sentence "My most important duty is . . ." 10 times, they tended to focus on personal duties (such as "fulfill my potential," "do well at school," "make the most of my opportunities") and give less emphasis to duties in relation to community (such as "contribute to community efforts," "be a good citizen"). My interpretation is that the central place of duties in social life has not necessarily declined in the United States but that there has been a shift to a greater emphasis on duties to self compared to duties to the larger community and society.

Concluding Comment

A popular image of the United States is that it is the land of the self-made person, in contrast to the Old World of Europe and particularly England, where, according to popular belief, society is much more class based and individuals' opportunities are determined largely by the social class of their parents. John Cawelti has insightfully commented on this contrast and the role of immigrants in its creation:

Immigration, too, helped make America a country of devotees of success by sending to her shores men who believed in their rights and their need to better their condition. The ideal of rising in society was never subjected to the continual and devastating criticism of exponents of a traditional ideal of culture as it was in England.

—Apostles of the self-made man, p. 3

Very early in its history, the United States developed a particularly individualistic vision of rights and duties, and this served as a powerful carrier, sustaining continuity in social life across generations. In the next chapter, we shall see how another powerful carrier, the idea that America is exceptional in respect to its experiences with social class, sustained continuity in certain aspects of social life across generations in the United States.

But in discussing rights and duties, I have not focused solely on cross-cultural differences. Rather, I have argued that what we now call rights and duties have their origins in certain social-psychological aspects of human life—primitive social relations—that emerged early in human evolution. These primitive social relations, inherent in all forms of life we recognize as human, were sustained across generations by social practices that served as carriers. When a primitive right/duty such as turn-taking is violated, we all know something has gone wrong, irrespective of our culture and language. Thus, in addition to the modern, formal declarations of human rights, there are practices supporting certain rights and duties that developed over the course of evolution. This is surely a promising and hopeful feature of the human experience.

Suggested Readings

Amnesty International. (1999). *Amnesty International Report.* New York: Author.

Cawelti, J. G. (1972). *Apostles of the self-made man: Changing concepts of success in America.* Chicago: University of Chicago Press.

Finkel, N. (2001). *Not fair! The typology of commonsense unfairness.* Washington, DC: American Psychological Association Press.

Glendon, M. A. (2001). *A world made new: Eleanor Roosevelt and the Universal Declaration of Human Rights.* Random House.

Golding, W. (1962). *Lord of the flies.* New York: Roverhead.

Hart, C. W. M., Pilling, A. R., & Goodale, J. C. (1988). *The Tiwi of north Australia* (3rd. ed.). New York: Holt, Rinehart & Winston.

Ishiguro, K. (1990). *The remains of the day.* New York: Vintage.

Kasson, J. F. (1990). *Rudeness & civility.* New York: Noonday Press.

Lauren, P. G. (1998). *The evolution of international human rights: Visions seen.* Philadelphia: University of Pennsylvania Press.

Moghaddam, F. M. (2000). Toward a cultural theory of human rights. *Theory & Psychology, 10,* 291–312.

Moghaddam, F. M., Slocum, N., Finkel, N., More, Z., & Harre, R. (2000). Toward a cultural theory of duties. *Culture & Psychology, 6,* 275–302.

Rothman, D. J., & Rothman, S. M. (Eds.). (1975). *Sources of the American social tradition: Vol. 2. 1865 to the present.* New York: Basic Books.

Wrightsman, L. S., Nietzel, M. T., & Fortune, W. H. (1994). *Psychology and the legal system* (3rd ed.). Pacific Grove, CA.: Brooks/Cole.

4 Social Class and American Exceptionalism

> It was strange to read about the people he knew in New York, Ed and
> Lorraine, the newt-brained girl who had tried to stow herself away in
> his cabin the day he sailed from New York. It was strange and not at all
> attractive. What a dismal life they led, creeping around New York, in and
> out of subways, standing in some dingy bar on Third Avenue for their en-
> tertainment . . . how dull it was compared to the worst little trattoria in
> Venice with its tables of green salads, trays of wonderful cheeses, and its
> friendly waiters bringing you the best wine in the world! . . . It was not so
> much Europe itself as the evenings he had spent alone. . . . Evenings
> looking at his clothes—his clothes and Dickie's—and feeling Dickie's
> rings between his palms, and running his fingers over the antelope suit-
> case he had bought at Gucci's. . . . He loved possessions, not masses of
> them, but a select few he did not part with. They gave a man self-respect.
> —PATRICIA HIGHSMITH, *The Talented Mr. Ripley*

Tom Ripley, the central character in Patricia Highsmith's thriller, has his nose
pressed hard against thick glass, on the other side of which is a world of affluent
"somebodies" enjoying a life from which "nobodies" like himself are excluded.
But Tom Ripley has some extraordinary talents, and they help him seize an unexpected opportunity to escape from his lower-class life in New York and
enter an enchanted realm of opulence in Italy, first with Dickie Greenfield
from the fabulously rich Greenfield family, then *as* Dickie Greenfield. He
eventually cheats and kills, repeatedly, in order to be able to continue his new
life as a "fake somebody," a supposed member of the upper class, rather than a
"real nobody," an actual member of the lower class.

In the final section of the novel, Tom Ripley is described as ecstatic with the
freedom that wealth has bought him and the power he now has to affect oth-

ers. He looks ahead to his travels, most immediately to landing on the island of Crete, to the excitement that his arrival would cause among "the small-boy porters, avid for his luggage and tips, and he would have plenty to tip them with, plenty for everything and everybody" (pp. 289–290). The reader is left with an image of a huge gulf separating the rich and the poor, with the "talented" Mr. Ripley having joined the rich.

Although the depiction of rich and poor in the United States is not unusual in novels, films, and art generally, academic and mass media discussions have been strongly influenced by *American exceptionalism*, the idea that United States is different from other industrialized nations in terms of its experiences with social class (my use of the term *American exceptionalism* is narrower than found in discussions by Seymour Martin Lipset, among others). American exceptionalism implies that, unlike supposedly "class-ridden" societies such as that of England, the United States is classless. I shall argue that at least some of the assumptions underlying American exceptionalism are flawed but that being flawed does not prevent it from being influential in society. Indeed, American exceptionalism is pervasive and highly influential; *it functions as a very powerful carrier, perpetuating across generations certain styles of behavior with respect to social class*. American exceptionalism serves to sustain continuity in the way different generations of Americans behave in relation to social class.

Just as individuals come to take on different roles, such as gender roles, according to the normative systems of their societies, they also come to take their place in the social-class system of their societies. Children learn as they grow up that the districts and houses they live in, the schools they attend, the clubs they join, the vacations they go on, the clothes, food, and toys they have, the transportation they use, among many other things, all depend partly or wholly on how much money their parents have. All kids at one time or another hear the phrase "No, that costs too much" when they make requests, but some kids get this reaction when a toy costs $5, while others only hear it when a toy costs $50, and a very few hear it only when a toy costs $50,000. Along with an awareness of their purchasing power and the kinds of options available to them generally, children also learn about the correct way to think about social class in their society. American exceptionalism is central to the correct way of thinking about social class in the United States, and it plays a pivotal role in the integration of individuals into American society.

Associated with American exceptionalism is an interpretation of rights and duties that emphasizes the individual rather than the collectivity, the self rather than society. As discussed in Chapter 3, this individualistic interpretation places emphasis on the duty of individuals to help themselves and their right to an open society—to "bowl alone" in a world where traditional Old World barriers to social mobility have been put aside. This focus on individual rights and duties is associated with less importance being given to social class, something that is clearly reflected in the persistence and power of American exceptionalism in the United States.

In order to better understand the integration of the individual into society with respect to social class, I shall broaden the range of issues to include micro-level processes not traditionally considered in discussions about social class. At the heart of these micro-level processes are those that enable us to selectively process a potentially infinite amount of information in the environment. In particular, I focus on certain principles of perceptual organization and the role that categorization plays in information processing. Next, I discuss some consequences of social categorization. My argument is that humans are predisposed to categorize the social world and that categorization has behavioral consequences, such as an exaggeration of between-group differences. However, *the basis of social categorization varies in important ways across cultures*, so that in some cultures race serves as the most important basis for categorization, in others gender serves this purpose, and in a few others social class plays this role. These cultural traditions are sustained by carriers, and in the United States carriers such as American exceptionalism function to make social class less important as a basis for social categorization. However, there is nothing inevitable in this situation; cultures can and do change, and during certain periods in U.S. history, such as the 1920s and early 1930s, social class gained greater prominence as a basis for social categorization.

Cognition and Categorization

"Us" and "Them": A Universal Feature of Cognition?

"Not far now, our antique shop is just around another couple of corners," said my guide, a young man descended from merchants and now training to be a merchant in the grand bazaar in Istanbul. I had met him by chance while sitting in a café in Istanbul, and he told me about a number of apparently ancient manuscripts that had been smuggled out of Iran after the revolution and were now on sale in his shop. The grand bazaar of Istanbul is probably the most airy, modernized, and "user-friendly" of all the grand bazaars in the Near and Middle East, but it is still a formidable maze in which visitors can easily get lost. Upon stepping into the grand bazaar, one is immediately bombarded with a multiplicity of luxurious sights and sounds, with extraordinary colors and fragrances that wrap the mind. We passed mountains of spices, rows and rows of sheepskin coats, endless rainbows of silk scarves, leather hides and shoes and hats of all shapes, sizes, and colors, and, finally, piles and piles of carpets—so many that I was feeling overwhelmed just looking around.

"We are almost there," repeated my guide, adding "if you try to look at everything, you will get giddy."

He was right, I was feeling giddy. There was just too much to hear and see; I was finding it difficult to sift through all the information. In contrast to my confusion and experience of information overload, my guide was perfectly in control and able to maneuver us through the crowds with ease. While I had difficulty picking out particular things in the confusion, he could find just what he wanted effortlessly. "Look at that rusty red carpet with the cloud-band design; it's a Tabriz, but that pattern is originally from China," he said, pointing in the direction of a carpet shop. But no matter how hard I looked, I could not spot the one he was pointing to. Separating figure from ground was a skill that I had not yet acquired in this context.

Like most people who find themselves in a new environment extraordinarily rich with all kinds of information, I tried to cope by organizing the sounds, sights, touches, and smells that filled my senses. The ways in which people organize perceptions was demonstrated particularly well by Gestalt psychologists, who proposed that certain ways of perceiving the world are hard-wired into all humans. The leaders of Gestalt psychology were Germans, but their ideas spread to the United States fairly quickly because many of them immigrated to America early in the twentieth century. Among the most important principles of perceptual organization are closure (or completion), proximity, and similarity.

I experienced the principle of **closure** when I looked at the ceiling of the grand bazaar in Istanbul. I saw a pattern of lines that looked like an incomplete triangle, but I instantly completed the pattern in my own mind and saw it as a triangle. According to Gestalt psychologists, this is an automatic process.

The **proximity** principle revealed itself when I saw six stacks of bowls, some of which had been placed closer together than others. The proximity of the stacks led me to see them as three groups of two (see top of page 58).

Most importantly, I tried to group everything I saw in the bazaar in terms of **similarity.** For example, even though clothing can come in many varieties, such as shirts, skirts, pants, and jackets, in my efforts to simplify the environment I saw them all as one group. In the same way I put all shoes in one category, all dishes in one category, all spices in one category and so on. The symbols below show how we automatically group similar elements; in this case seeing vertical rather than horizontal patterns.

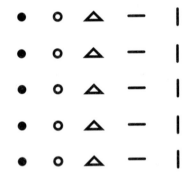

There is now solid physiological evidence suggesting that in some respects the way we see things is predetermined by built-in reactions of various cells to particular features of the environment. That is, certain cells are specialized to react to particular features of the external world. A very broad example is rods and cones, two types of receptor cells in the retina. Rods have developed to lead to colorless sensations, and cones specialize in color sensations. Other cells specialize in directional movement, so that they fire if an object moves in one direction but do not fire if movement is in the opposite direction. The specialization of cells may explain why certain features of objects, shape in particular, seem to be dominant in object perceptions. Children as young as 3 have been shown to give priority to shape—more than to size, color, or texture—in object-recognition tasks. The shape of things certainly seemed to guide me a great deal as I tried to make sense of the enormous variety of fascinating objects around the bazaar.

But it was not just merchandise that I grouped: All the while, I was seeing new people and placing them in different groups. There were men, women, Western tourists, Turks who worked in the grand bazaar, Turks who were there to shop, children, mothers, and so on. I was simplifying my task of making sense of the environment by chunking individuals as "types" of people, as members of categories rather than unique persons.

Just as continuity, proximity, and similarity influenced the way I grouped clothes, carpets, spices, and other things in the grand bazaar, they also influenced how I grouped people. This raises questions about the kinds of similarities there might be between the way we group nonsocial phenomena, such as carpets and clothes, and the way we group people.

Continuities Between How We Group Things and How We Group People

Henri Tajfel used to like to play a game in which each person involved would explain how many steps it would take them to reach the president, king, prime minister, or other most important figure in a country. Henri invariably won. He was a wonderfully colorful character who seemed to know everyone, everywhere. I met him in the early 1970s, when he was in his heyday as a researcher and spearheading the movement toward a distinct European social psychology. Henri had come to England as a refugee after the Second World War, but through a combination of talent and luck, he had landed important academic positions at Oxford and other illustrious institutions. Perhaps his greatest contribution, one that is often overlooked, is his demonstration of continuities between the way people categorize nonsocial and social phenomena.

Imagine you are looking at eight lines, such as those shown in Figure 4.1 on page 60, the lengths of which differ from one another by a constant ratio. Tajfel presented such a set of lines to participants in his research study in three different ways. In condition 1, the four shorter lines were labeled A and the four longer ones were labeled B. In condition 2, the lines were randomly labeled either A or B. In condition 3, the lines were presented without labels. What do you think he found?

Tajfel's study showed that participants in condition 1, who saw the shorter and longer lines grouped as A and B, showed between-group differentiation, meaning they exaggerated the difference between the length of lines in group A and group B. They also showed within-group minimization, meaning they estimated the differences in length between the lines within each group to be less than they actually were.

A lot of experience and experimental evidence suggests that similar processes are at work in the way we perceive people. Consider how we use color, particularly the black–white spectrum, to group people. Take the case of eight individuals, whose shades of color differ from one another by a constant ratio. At one extreme is the person closest to black and at the other, the person closest to white. In everyday life we tend to group people in such a way that one group is

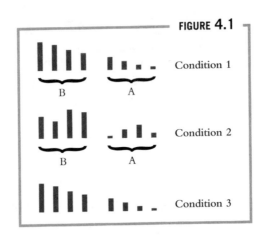

FIGURE **4.1**

Condition 1

B   A

Condition 2

B   A

Condition 3

lumped into the white category and the other into the black category. How we divide up the population into black and white is obviously determined by local rules and conventions rather than objective criteria. In the era of apartheid in South Africa, there were complex legal procedures for actually determining the category membership of individuals who disputed their racial classification. Through the courts, the racial category of an individual might be changed, so that an individual in the black category might be reassigned to the white category.

Evidence suggests that even though the categorization rules we use are arbitrary, once people are grouped, certain consequences follow: (1) intergroup differentiation, whereby differences between, for example, blacks and whites are exaggerated, and (2) within-group minimization, whereby differences within the black and within the white groups are minimized. In other words, after eight individuals are placed into group A and group B, we tend to exaggerate the difference between the people in these two groups and minimize the differences between the people within each group.

In categorizing the social world, we also group ourselves. Consequently, each of us has a number of *in-groups,* the groups we belong to, and *out-groups,* the groups we do not belong to. Research suggests that we are more likely to see in-group members as different individuals, all with their own special personality and unique characteristics, but to see out-group members as more similar to one another, a homogeneous mass. Westerners are used to hearing one another say things such as, "Chinese people all look alike to me," but they may be surprised to learn that to the Chinese, Westerners also tend to look very similar to one another.

From this analysis we would expect that a categorization of the social world into "rich" and "poor," or "upper class" and "working class" could lead to between-group differentiation and within-group minimization, so that the upper and working classes appear even more different than they are, and within each group people appear even more similar than they are. However, this would only take place in a culture where social class is an important basis for social categorization. We return to this issue later in this chapter.

The next question that arises concerns the possible *behavioral* consequences of grouping people into categories. So far we have considered ways in which grouping things and people leads to biases in our perceptions. But can it also influence actions?

The Big-Endiens and the Little-Endiens

Imagine a war between two nations that has been going on for generations, with thousands of people killed on either side. It all began by one side breaking their eggs at the bigger end and the other side insisting on breaking their eggs at the smaller end. Just such a long and bitter war fought on trivial grounds is described by Gulliver during his voyage to Lilliput, an imaginary land depicted in Jonathan Swift's classic novel *Gulliver's Travels*. In the same land of Lilliput, Gulliver learns that there are two political parties locked in a bitter struggle for power, distinguishable from each other only by the high heels versus the low heels on their shoes. The emperor is known to favor the low heels, as indicated by the fact that the heels on his shoes are at least one-fourteenth of an inch lower than the heels of anyone else at the royal court. But Lilluput is an imaginary land, and surely in real human societies such momentous divisions could not possibly come about based on such trivial differences as breaking one's egg at one end or the other or wearing shoes with very slightly higher or lower heels? Unfortunately, both experimental evidence and everyday life experience show they can and do, with consequences that are even more horrendous than those depicted in imaginary lands.

One line of experimental evidence comes from research spearheaded by Henri Tajfel and his students, Mick Billig and John Turner, at Bristol University in England, starting back in the late 1960s. As a first step, these researchers attempted to create what they called "minimal" groups by eliminating all the usual factors that are known to be associated with intergroup conflict. Such factors include similarity, familiarity, and cohesion. In other words, we have known for some time that when you think people in the in-group are similar to you and those in the out-group are dissimilar, when you are personally more familiar with in-group members than with out-group members, and when you have opportunities to develop strong in-group cohesion, then there is more likelihood for intergroup conflict to arise. The "minimal" groups created by Tajfel and his colleagues were designed to eliminate all such preconditions for conflict. How did these researchers go about creating "minimal" groups?

Imagine I tap my pen on the table twice and ask you which was louder, the sound made by the first tap on the table or the second. You guess that the first sound was louder. Next, I tell you that you have been placed in group X, along with all the other participants who also thought the first sound was louder. Group Y is made up of those participants who thought the second sound was louder. Thus you have been placed in group X or Y on the basis of what is clearly a trivial basis for group formation—whether you estimated the first or second tap on the table to be louder.

In the second part of the study, I ask you to allocate points to the members of group X and group Y. I also let you know that you yourself will not be getting any of the points that you allocate to members of groups X and Y. At this stage in the proceedings, you are very likely to ask, "How should I allocate points?" As the experimenter I respond, "In any way you want."

So as a participant in this study you are faced with the task of allocating points to anonymous others. You have never met them and will never know who they are. Your only information about them is that they are in group X or group Y. How do you think most people allocate points in this situation? Well, a small number allocate points randomly to groups X and Y, another small number allocate points equally, and even fewer give more points to "the other group"; the vast majority allocate more points to "their group." This basic experiment, referred to as the "minimal group paradigm," has been replicated hundreds of times with the same result: The in-group is favored, at least in Western societies.

In order to better appreciate the results of the minimal group study in context, let us review some basic issues. First, I pointed out that given a potentially infinite amount of information available in the environment, one way in which humans try to cope better is to categorize the world. Second, I suggested that there is evidence from both experimental research and everyday life that categorization has several consequences, two being the exaggeration of differences between groups and the minimization of differences within each group. Thus differences between groups are seen as being greater than they actually are, while differences within groups are seen as being less than they actually are. But so far we are dealing simply with perceptions. What about behavior? At this stage the minimal group studies become particularly relevant, because they demonstrate that as soon as people perceive others as members of groups X and Y, even anonymous others whom they will never meet, they tend to show a *behavioral* bias in favor of those particular others who are in their in-group.

But the minimal group studies were conducted in controlled laboratory conditions, typically with schoolchildren or college students as participants. Do we have any evidence to suggest the same things happen among ordinary people in everyday life outside the laboratory? Yes, there is plenty of research evidence and everyday experience to show just this. For example, anthropological studies have shown how otherwise objectively trivial differences between ethnic groups have been exaggerated and given importance as part of a justification for intergroup bias. An example is the supposedly considerable height difference between the Tutsi and the Hutu in Rwanda, which had traditionally been used to strengthen the stereotype of Tutsi superiority. In actuality, the height difference between the groups has been exaggerated.

I came across a fascinating example of this phenomenon in Islamic societies, where some males wear a black article of clothing, such as a turban, to indicate their being *sayyeds,* or direct descendants of the Prophet. These individuals have a privileged status in Islamic societies, and all kinds of positive characteristics are attributed to them. As soon as two males walk into a room, one wearing a white turban and the other a black turban, even when they are both complete strangers they will be attributed different characteristics on the basis of the color of their turbans. In essence, Islamic onlookers categorize the social world into black-turban and white-turban and attribute more positive characteristics to the black-turban group (this is obviously not what would be expected from a Western perspective, where everything positive is associated with white rather than black). What in other contexts would be a trivial difference, the black or white color of a turban, is given high importance.

There are also plenty of examples in modern Western societies of apparently trivial intergroup differences being given considerable importance and coming to play a central role in intergroup conflict. For instance, soccer might be considered to be "just a game," something that Jim and Paul play and watch as a spectator sport "for fun." However, when Jim and Paul go to watch Manchester United, "their team," play at their home stadium at Old Trafford, soccer becomes very important to them. Standing at the "Stratford End" with thousands of other red-clad Manchester United supporters, Jim and Paul take soccer very seriously. The victims of violence in soccer stadiums testify to the fact that real intergroup conflicts can arise out of what may in other contexts appear to be rather trivial intergroup differences, that is, whether one supports soccer team red (X) or blue (Y).

Thus a wide array of evidence suggests that there are very few limitations on what could serve as the basis for social categorization in society. People can be grouped in many different ways, and what might seem in one cultural context to be trivial criteria for group formation can have important consequences in other cultural contexts. This process highlights the importance of culture in the ways in which individuals become integrated into society. For example, in some cultures social class serves as an important basis for social categorization and individuals perceive social class as relevant to all social life,

while in other cultures social class is far less salient and individuals do not view
the world through a lens of social-class distinctions.

American Exceptionalism as a Carrier

Social Class, the Flexible Category

Unlike gender, ethnicity, and other category memberships that one is unable to
change, social class can be changed (fortunately, though, most people would
never do what the "talented" Mr. Ripley did just to join the ruling class). Even
in the apparently rigid Hindu caste system, individuals sometimes manage to
move up to a higher caste; for example, by relocating to another geographic region and presenting themselves as a member of a higher caste than the one
into which they were born. In part because one can acquire the "markers" of a
higher or lower social class, and in part because the markers themselves are
constantly changing, it is often debatable as to what exactly constitutes social
class and how society is divided into social classes. Statistics on the numbers of
men and women in a society, and even the numbers belonging to various ethnic groups, can be agreed upon much more readily than the numbers of people in each social class.

Part of the difficulty with the concept of social class is that it has proved
very difficult to define on the basis of objective criteria. Although Karl Marx
discussed social class extensively, he did not get around to defining it precisely.
Nor did he foresee the rise in power of the "managerial class" and captains of
industry, who, despite not being important owners of the means of production,
enjoy immense power. The Marxist tradition places considerable emphasis on
the development of subjective elements relating to class, particularly *class
consciousness*, the perception that people are members of distinct classes with
competing material interests. According to Marx, subjective perceptions will
gradually come to accurately reflect objective reality, so that people will eventually come to see the social world as divided into two opposing and con-
tradictory classes, with class warfare as the inevitable outcome.

The Marxist tradition has fundamentally influenced the questions that
scholars, both those opposed to and those supportive of Marx's ideas, have addressed in relation to social class. Very broadly, these questions revolve around
the issues of (1) social-class characteristics as measured by objective criteria
(such as income, ownership of capital, and so on) and (2) social class as subjectively perceived by people. In practice, this distinction proves to be too simplistic, however, because subjectivity also influences the so-called objective

measures of social class. For example, in some instances the political ideology of researchers leads them to conduct particular types of "objective" studies to try to find support for their ideologies. An example of how subjective perceptions can color the entire debate on social class in a society is the influence of so-called American exceptionalism in the United States.

American Exceptionalism and Continuity in Class Relations

A discussion of social class must necessarily consider the idea of American exceptionalism. This assumption is explicit in Alexis de Tocqueville's *Democracy in America* (1835) and probably goes back even farther. If by American exceptionalism it is meant that there are fewer economic inequalities in the United States than in other industrialized societies, this is clearly not true. The actual state of affairs is suggested by the title of an influential book depicting the United States as a *Winner Takes All Society*, a place where the gap between the superrich and the rest keeps getting bigger at just as fast a rate, and arguably faster, than in other industrialized societies. If by American exceptionalism it is meant that the United States allows greater social mobility, then, again, the objective evidence suggests otherwise. For example, while upward mobility is slightly more prevalent in the United States than in England, it is slightly less prevalent than in Sweden, so that, for instance, a working-class person has a slightly better chance of joining the professional middle class in the United States than in England but a slightly lower chance in the United States than in Sweden. However, these differences are actually very small.

Another meaning of American exceptionalism could be that subjectively people perceive the United States as a classless society. On the surface this seems plausible, because according to some surveys about 90 percent of Americans see themselves as middle class. However, studies by Reeve Vanneman and Lynn Cannon are among many that have challenged this received wisdom, and in a definitive comparative study Fiona Devine showed that class consciousness is very similar in the United States and England. It appears that Americans are not blind to either their own social-class membership or to social-class divisions in their country. Detailed studies of the everyday lives of working-class Americans have revealed that class does matter and that lower-class individuals suffer from the stigmatization and negative stereotypes associated with their low-status jobs and life conditions. Life is not easier, or healthier, for working-class people in the "post–health care reform" era. The loss of stable manufacturing jobs, replaced by service jobs with less stability and fewer benefits, has created worse life conditions for them.

Given that the United States does not seem to be exceptional on objective criteria, and does not seem to have been so over the last few centuries, then how can we explain the persistence of the idea of American exceptionalism? One possibility is that the ruling class, the main owners of capital, are particularly strong in the United States and able to propagate the idea of American exceptionalism to serve their own interests. According to this view, North American academics have contributed to the success of this conspiracy by focusing attention on race and gender, rather than on social class by itself, and by insisting that social class always be considered in relation to race and gender, as reflected by the books of readings on "Race, Gender, and Class" typically used in North American colleges. By strengthening beliefs in a classless America, the ruling class could diminish the possibility of class warfare and thus safeguard its dominant position. This idea has been discussed extensively and possibly has some merit, but it is only part, perhaps a minor part, of the explanation. I want to put forward an alternative, less conspiratorial explanation, one that gives particular attention to the geographic and demographic features of the United States.

The United States is the largest immigrant-receiving country in the world, and the immigrant experience continues to be central to American identity. Each year about half a million people immigrate to the United States legally, and hundreds of thousands of others enter through other means and eventually become legal citizens. Perhaps as many as a million people a year are added to the U.S. population—around 285 million in 2001—through legal or illegal immigration. From the viewpoint of newcomers as well as the hundreds of millions of would-be immigrants around the world, America is the land of opportunity. Irrespective of the shortcomings, injustices, and inequalities that actual and would-be immigrants perceive in the United States, this country still presents them with better opportunities than any other country in the world—otherwise, they would not aspire to live in the United States. A first part of my alternative explanation, then, is the influence of the perceptions of actual and would-be immigrants, who continue to see the United States as the land of opportunty.

Second, my analysis implies that the United States is exceptional in that it has a class system that is open to individuals from *outside* the country. The social-class systems of the United States and Britain are actually similar, as Fiona Devine and others have shown, if they are compared as closed systems—that is, on the assumption that few people either leave or enter U.S. and British societies. However, in practice the United States functions as *an open system in the specific sense that vast numbers of people from around the world, and increasingly from Asian and Eastern European countries, join U.S. society each year.* The source of American exceptionalism, then, is the immigrant experience.

But the United States is not the only immigrant-receiving country, so why is it the only one that seems to benefit from a reputation of exceptionalism? Two factors seem to me to explain this situation. The first is that immigrant-receiving countries such as Canada, Australia, and New Zealand gained their independence much later and continued to be influenced by colonial ties for much longer. At least the trappings of the traditional British social-class system persisted in these countries until very recently. Second, and perhaps even more important, other immigrant-receiving countries do not compare to the United States in terms of the sheer size of their economies, and so the opportunties they offer immigrants are fewer. Having been an immigrant to both Canada and the United States, my own experience is that the vast size of the U.S. economy, the largest in the world, gives immigrants at least an impression of openness and vastness in terms of opportunities. This is at the heart of American exceptionalism.

Concluding Comment

From a Marxist perspective, which critics claim is overly conspiratorial, American exceptionalism is part of false consciousness, functioning to mislead Americans as to what are their true social-class memberships and interests. On the other hand, for supporters of the American system of capitalism, American exceptionalism is part of what makes America *the* superpower and the richest economy, because it gives individuals the hope and belief that anyone can make it in the American system, irrespective of their social-class background. In turn, supporters argue, this belief in American exceptionalism leads to exceptional entrepreneurial drive.

The traditional debate about social class has focused on the question of whether or not historical, social, economic, and other trends inevitably point to class warfare and revolution. I have not addressed this question, which seems untestable anyhow, but have looked at micro-level limitations, particularly the cognitive organizing principles that lead us to perceive the world in particular ways. I began this discussion by noting that information is limitless and that, in order to cope with the vast amount of stimuli around us, we tend to group things. We group on different bases, such as similarity and proximity. After phenomena have been placed into groups, certain consequences follow: Differences between groups are exaggerated, while differences within groups are minimized. The same processes are associated with the grouping of things and of people.

Although social categorization and some of its consequences seem universal, a perception of the world based on social class is not inevitable from this "ground-up" analysis. In other words, Marx's prediction of class warfare is not validated when we review basic cognitive micro-level processes. Indeed, such a review brings us back to the cultural level and the central role of carriers such as American exceptionalism in shaping the importance given to different criteria for social categorization in society. We can counter Marx's prediction with one that is at least as testable as his about class warfare and the inevitable historical march toward a classless society: As long as American exceptionalism survives, so will American capitalism.

Finally, and very importantly, I have given particular attention to the role of immigration in strengthening American exceptionalism. When considered as closed systems, there is very little objective difference between the social-class situation in the United States and that in other industrialized nations, even so-called class-based England. However, when looked at as an open system, the United States is very different from other industrialized countries. The American system is open to the rest of the world through immigration. Immigrants continually rejuvenate American exceptionalism. The continuation of widespread slavery and extremely hostile life conditions for the working classes in many third world countries means that the working-class conditions in North America still appear relatively luxurious for the masses looking at the situation from abroad.

While in this chapter I have referred to potential or predicted class conflict, and argued that carriers such as American exceptionalism prevent such trends, in the next chapter the focus is on actual conflict. However, instead of asking the traditional question "Why war?" I turn this question on its head and ask "Why peace?" This alternative question leads to new insights about conflict.

Suggested Readings

Anderson, M. L. (Ed.). (2000). *Race, class, gender: An anthology.* (4th ed.). Belmont, CA: Wadsworth.

Argyle, M. (1994). *The social psychology of social class.* New York: Routledge.

Bales, K. (1999). *Disposable people: New slavery in the global economy.* Berkeley: University of California Press.

Beeghley, L. (1996). *The structure of social stratificatioin in the United States* (2nd ed.). Boston: Allyn & Bacon.

Daniels, N., Kennedy, B., & Kawachi, I. (2000). *Is inequality bad for our health?* Boston: Beacon.

Devine, F. (1997). *Social class in America and Britain.* Edinburgh: University of Edinburgh Press.

Ehrenreich, B. (2001). *Nickel and dimed: On (not) getting by in America.* New York: Metropolitan Books, Henry Hold & Co.

Frank, R. & Cook, P. (1995). *The winner-takes-all society.* New York: Simon & Schuster.

Giddens, A., & Held, D. (Eds.). (1982). *Classes, power, and conflict: Classical and contemporary debates*. Berkeley: University of California Press.

Hall, J. R. (Ed.). (1997). *Reworking class*. Ithaca, NY: Cornell University Press.

Handler, J. F., & White, L. (Eds.). (1999). *Hard labor: Women and work in the post-welfare era*. Armonk, NY: Sharpe.

Highsmith, P. (1992). *The talented Mr. Ripley*. New York: Vintage (Original work published 1955).

Hooks, B. (2000). *Where we stand: Class matters*. New York: Routledge.

Joyce, P. (Ed.). (1995). *Class*. Oxford: Oxford University Press.

Lipset, S. M. (1996). *American exceptionalism: A double-edged sword*. New York: Norton.

Marx, K., & Engels, F. (1971). *The communist manifesto*. New York: International. (Original work published 1847.)

McGarty, C. (1999). *Categorization in social psychology*. Thousand Oaks, CA: Sage.

McMurrer, D. P., & Sawhill, I. V. (1998). *Getting ahead: Economic and social mobility in America*. Washinton, DC: Urban Institute Press.

Pessen, E. (Ed.). (1974). *Three centuries of social mobility in America*. Lexington, MA: Heath.

Putnam, R. D. (2000). *Bowling alone: The collapse and revival of American community*. New York: Simon & Schuster.

Rothenberg, P. S., Schafauser, N., & Schneider, C. (Eds.). (2000). *Race, class, and gender in the United States: An integrated study*. (5th ed.). New York: Worth.

Sennett, R., & Cobb, J. (1993). *The hidden injuries of class*. New York: Norton.

Taylor, D. M., & Moghaddam, F. M. (1994). *Theories of intergroup relations: International social psychological perspectives*. (2nd ed). Westport, CT: Praeger.

Turner, J. H. (1998). *The structure of sociological theory*. (6th ed.). Belmont, CA: Wadsworth.

Zandy, J. (Ed.). (2001). *What we hold in common: An introduction to working-class studies*. New York: Feminist Press at the City University of New York.

5 Why Peace?

The first time I personally experienced a major conflict was during the devastating 1980–1988 war between Iran and Iraq. I visited the Iranian war front several times as part of a United Nations mission. All the country was affected by the war in some ways, but nothing like the annihilation that took place in a number of large cities near the northwestern front. One scene of destruction remains particularly vivid in my mind. Traveling with a UN team, I arrived at what had once been a major urban center inhabited by several hundred thousand people but was now completely flattened and utterly empty of civilians. The only things standing upright were cars, hundreds of cars with their fronts dug into the ground and their backs sticking up into the air. The scene was suitable for a Salvador Dali painting. Apparently, the cars were supposed to defend against paratroopers, who might smash into them if they tried to surprise the defense forces by launching a night attack. As I looked around, I could not help but be overwhelmed by the massively destructive force that had killed or displaced so many people, flattened so many buildings, and created such a bizarre landscape covered with up-ended automobiles.

Through this devastating scene, there moved countless ghostly figures, soldiers of the "Army of Islam" sweeping forward, wave after wave, continually pressing toward the front. Here was yet another case of impressionable young men being directed to war by the cold calculations of old men, in this case Khomeini and his band of fanatical clergy.

As I write these words at the start of the third millennium, something like 30 major wars are going on around the globe. Millions of people are being killed, injured, made homeless, turned out to roam the world as refugees. The last century is estimated to have been the bloodiest in human existence, with about 110 million people killed in major wars, almost 50 million killed during World War II alone. This is one area of human behavior that sees little or no

70

improvement at all. Although the major religions and creeds espouse peace and universal love, in practice they continue to be used to justify large-scale killing and torture. Human ideals whisper peace; human practices shout war. Throughout recorded history, the theme of war and destruction is so strong that it seems to overwhelm every other theme. So pervasive and "normal" is this theme that I believe it is justifiable to invert the usual question of "Why war?" and instead ask "Why peace?" After all, peace has proven to be much more difficult to achieve than war. Why are we not able to change this situation? What accounts for our continuation of aggression and war?

After briefly reviewing a number of major causal explanations of war, I shall discuss a neglected but potentially very valuable alternative approach to understanding conflict, one that highlights culture and carriers that sustain traditions associated with militarism.

Received Wisdom on War

The pervasive nature of human aggressiveness and the persistence of war throughout human history seem to justify the idea that war is based on performance capacities and that something in our biological makeup leads us to be aggressive. One group of researchers, mostly adherents to a sociobiological perspective, has argued that there are certain genetic characteristics that cause humans to be aggressive toward particular others. These researchers propose that even large-scale warfare can be explained by reference to genetic makeup.

A basic sociobiological claim is that humans are moved by inherited characteristics, a "whispering within," to be aggressive toward others who are genetically dissimilar to them. We are, it is claimed, convenient vehicles, "gene machines," for the transportation of genes over time and place. The "whispering within" leads us to adopt behaviors that will maximize the probability of our genes being perpetuated. Given that in order to pass on genes, humans must have offspring, males behave aggressively toward rival males because they want access to females as well as to the resources that attract females. Thus researchers such as Napoleon Chagnon, who has studied the Yanomamo in northern Brazil for more than 30 years, have tried to document how aggressive males are more successful at attracting women and having offspring, and how the victims of aggression are more likely to be genetically dissimilar others. Chagnon chose to study the Yanomamo in part because of their reputation as one of the most aggressive people in the world, with apparently about 40 percent of the males having taken part in deadly violence (although Chagnon's research methods and results have proved to be controversial).

The sociobiological account of human behavior generally, and aggression specifically, has been severely criticized by a number of leading researchers, including biologists, as being too simplistic. In the words of the biologist Paul Ehrlich, "The idea that aggression, especially male aggression, is innate is too simple an explanation of the roots of war to do justice to the complexities of human behavior." In a recent book, Ehrlich targets the now-fashionable tendency to explain human violence and warfare as having genetic causes. One of the powerful arguments raised by Ehrlich is the following:

> People don't have enough genes to program all the behaviors some evolutionary psychologists, for example, believe that genes control. Human beings have something in the order of 100,000 genes, and human brains have more than 1 *trillion* nerve cells, with about 100–1,000 trillion connections (synapses) between them. That's at least 1 *billion* synapses per gene, even if each and every gene did nothing but control the production of synapses (and it doesn't). Given that ratio, it would be quite a trick for genes typically to control more than the most general aspects of human behavior. (p. 4)
>
> —*Human Natures*, p. 4

This estimate was made by Ehrlich in the late 1990s, but it was already out of date by 2001, when results from the Human Genome Project confirmed that there are probably around 30,000 protein-coding genes in the human genome (less that one-third of Ehrlich's estimate). This means that humans probably have only a few hundred more genes than a mouse! The clear expectation is that when the map of the chimpanzee genome is completed, our uniqueness in terms of genes will be shown to be even smaller.

The findings from the Human Genome Project provide further support for the view that the uniqueness of humans is to be found less in our biological makeup and more in our wider environment, particularly our collectively constructed human culture. The most important factor influencing human infants and ensuring that they become persons is the human culture into which they are born, rather than the few hundred genes they have that mice do not or the very few genes they have that chimpanzees do not. Of course, proponents of biological determinism have not allowed the findings of the Human Genome Project to thwart their efforts; they are now arguing that the genetic source of human behavior must be complex biological interactions yet to be discovered, rather than the number of genes unique to humans. Typical of this approach is a 2001 *Science* article by Peter McGuffin and others pointing the way "Toward Behavioral Genomes" but giving few hints as to the location of the genes that are supposed to be the source of behavior. This kind of maneuvering should be expected, because like all humans, scientists are influenced by personal ambitions, ideology, faith, pride, and so on, and those scientists who have invested their lives in explaining human behavior through biological models cannot be expected to change their views simply on the basis of objective criteria.

One of the challenges taken up by Ehrlich and a number of other sophisticated biologists is to stem the tide of naive thinking on "genetic determinism," as exemplified by scores of books appearing at the turn of the millennium, all proposing in one way or another that our genes determine our intelligence, our personality, our emotions—and our level of aggression. If we are to believe some evolutionary psychologists, everything is causally explained by our genes, including the murder rate and the twentieth century's two world wars.

The sociobiological account unravels when we consider the complexities of human behavior, such as found in alliances in war and peace. For example, consider even the most simple group relationships during World War II, when Germany fought against Britain, with Japan allied to Germany and India allied to Britain. Are we to believe that genetic similarity is the best explanation for such intergroup relationships? What type of genetic similarity led the Germans to ally with the Japanese against the British? And why should Britain have been allied with India? Clearly, ideology, colonial ties, and other such factors are better explanations of such alliances than genetic similarity. This is not to deny that genetic similarity can have some influence on social relationships, particularly at the intimate level of friendships and family. For example, genetic similarity may well be one factor, along with others, that helps explain why parents make sacrifices for their offspring and why they typically make more sacrifices for their biological children, "their own flesh and blood," than for adopted children.

Similarly, attempts to explain human aggression by reference to chromosomal abnormalities or brain malfunction or other physiological aspects of human functioning can be appropriate for explaining some cases of aggression manifested by some individuals but inappropriate for explaining collective aggression and conflict. For example, Charles Whitman had not been abnormally aggressive before he went on a rampage, shooting people randomly from the tower of the university administration building at the University of Texas at Austin, eventually killing 17 people before a police marksman ended his life. An autopsy suggested that a cause of his violent rampage may have been a malignant tumor that caused extensive brain damage. But such an explanation, which may be valid for this individual in this instance, is inadequate to explain wars or bloody revolutions involving millions of people. The German army was not comprised of millions of soldiers with brain tumors when they invaded neighboring countries from 1938 to 1940.

Materialist Explanations of Conflict

But biological determinism does not have a monopoly on causal accounts of aggression. While those seeking to find the causes of aggression and war in genes adopt a strictly reductionistic, bottom-up approach, another set of thinkers has attempted to find causes by adopting a strictly top-down approach. Aggression and war, they argue, is caused by economic conditions—more specifically, by competition for a bigger piece of the material pie. When John and Mike fight, or when nations go to war against one another, so the argument goes, the root cause of the fighting is a conflict of interests over scarce material resources.

There are a variety of materialist theories of aggression and war, from orthodox Marxist theory to more recent models such as realistic conflict theory, but they all share the basic assumption that psychological characteristics are primarily shaped by economic conditions. How we feel and act, they argue, is shaped by our economic situation. Modern social scientists have been particularly influenced by realistic conflict theory, in part because it was developed in the United States and has associated with it a number of peaceful solutions to intergroup conflict. Unlike Marx's model, which sees class warfare as inevitable, realistic conflict theory proposes that although the root cause of conflict is competition over material resources, intergroup harmony is possible.

Most importantly, realistic conflict theory proposes that it is possible to achieve intergroup harmony in a stratified society, one in which not all groups are equal. This is very different from a Marxist vision, which predicts conflict after conflict until the day when a classless society is achieved and equality is established.

Realistic conflict theory was launched in association with a series of field studies by the Turkish-American psychologist Muzafer Sherif. These studies involved 11- and 12-year old boys attending summer camp; unbeknownst to the boys, the camp staff included Sherif and his research associates. The studies involved four stages. In stage 1, the boys arrived at summer camp and got to know one another. Researchers observed the boys to identify friendship patterns among them. In stage 2, researchers divided the boys into two groups, making sure that those identified as "best friends" were separated and ended up in different groups. During stage 3, the boys participated in competitive intergroup games. A winning team not only won a prize but also gained in status. In-group cohesion developed, and more aggressive boys emerged as leaders in each group. "War" was declared, intergroup fighting intensified, and attitudes toward the out-group became more and more negative.

Having created a situation in which intergroup conflict took place, the challenge now was to create conditions in which the two groups would develop peaceful relations. In stage 4, Sherif introduced superordinate goals, that is, goals that were desired by both groups but only obtainable through the cooperation of the groups. For example, a truck bringing food to the camp "broke down," and the boys had to cooperate to pull it into the camp; in another instance, the water supply to the camp "broke down," and the boys had to cooperate to regain access to water. As a consequence of the boys' collaboration to achieve superordinate goals, attitudes and behavior across groups became favorable and, in effect, all the boys merged into one group.

The key theme of Sherif's research is that conflict between groups over material resources shapes intergroup attitudes and behavior: When material interests collide, the groups come to hate one another and they fight; but when their material interests coincide, the groups cooperate and come to like one another. The role of superordinate goals is to create compatibility between the material interests of the different groups. The model assumes that humans are rational and self-serving: They know what they are doing and why, and they make decisions that maximize their own profits. But even in Sherif's own studies there is evidence that in certain contexts, humans are not rational and they fail to behave in ways that would maximize their own profits. The groups of boys in Sherif's studies took part in raids and sabotaged and damaged rival camps and projects. Even these white, middle-class boys with healthy psychological profiles engaged in destructive acts that are difficult to justify on a rational basis.

Are Humans Rational?

Rational accounts of aggression and war assume that humans know what they are doing and why. Humans make assessments of the likely costs and benefits of conflict, so we are told, and then act in ways that minimize costs and maximize benefits to themselves. But are humans really rational? One group of thinkers does not believe so, arguing that humans are often unaware of the real reasons for their own behavior.

Freud, among others, has illuminated the irrational and destructive tendency of humans. He presents a picture of human experience as composed of (1) conscious experience, what a person is aware of at any moment in time; (2) the preconscious, what is not being attended to but can be brought to mind; and (3) the unconscious, what has been repressed and can only be brought to mind in extraordinary circumstances, such as a therapeutic intervention. Conscious and preconscious experience can be likened to the tip of an iceberg, with the vast bulk of the iceberg, the unconscious, hidden beneath the surface of the water.

Revenge, jealousy, envy, rage—all kinds of unconscious emotional motives can give rise to aggression and war, and the result may be destruction and worse material conditions for all the parties, even the "victors." From a rational materialist perspective, humans would do a lot better if they cooperated rather than fought. Intergroup cooperation and peaceful relationships would lead to better material conditions, because resources would not have to be diverted to destructive causes. A rational profit-making motive should mean that intergroup conflicts rarely occur. Unfortunately, intergroup conflict is common rather than rare.

Freud points out that humans are very good at rationalizing after the fact and providing "logical" explanations for past actions. After fighting and destroying another country, leaders will rationalize that their side fought for the sake of "freedom," "God," "democracy," and the like. However, this kind of rationalization should not be allowed to sidetrack us from the real motives, which lie deeper in our psyche and are generally unrecognized by those engaged in the fighting.

To understand the real factors leading to aggression and war, according to Freud, we should begin by unraveling the nature of libidinal ties between group members and their leaders. All such ties have positive and negative, love and hate, aspects to them. Positive aspects help to bind the group together, but negative aspects could potentially destroy the group. The group leader helps to displace negative sentiments onto out-groups, particularly dissimilar out-groups. Consequently, ethnic minorities become victims of aggression and discrimination on the part of the majority group, because they serve as scapegoat targets of displaced aggression. We can always bind people together in love, Freud claims, as long as there are some people left over to hate.

Like sociobiological and materialist accounts, then, Freud also sees aggression and war as causally determined. Although Freud is brilliant in his descriptive insights on the course of conflict, his explanations for why things happen the way they do is not necessarily convincing. For example, since the early 1990s research on animals, and more recently on humans, has demonstrated that stressful life experiences can lead to neuronal damage in the brain. This suggests that, at least in some cases, the explanation for people's "forgetting" negative early experiences may not be repression of memories into the unconscious, as Freud proposes, but memory loss due to physical damage to the hippocampus and other brain regions. Jet lag and other stressful experiences seem to cause structural changes in the brain, leading to memory impairment. This being the case, memory loss for "what happened during World War II" and other such experiences may be associated with neuronal damage rather than active repression of memories into an unconscious. This is not to deny the monumental contributions of Freud to our understanding of human conflicts but to suggest limitations to his interpretation of the role of the unconscious in such behavior.

The sociobiological, materialist, and irrationalist accounts each make interesting contributions to our understanding of aggression and war. The sociobiological account seems to explain some of the sacrifices people make for others related to them "by blood," such as the sacrifices parents make for their children. The materialist account, strongly influenced by Marx, highlights how conflicts of material interests can influence our feelings and actions, so that who comes to be seen as "friend" and "foe" depends on whether their activities lead to profits or losses for us personally. The irrationalist account, influenced particularly by Freud, casts the spotlight on our destructive tendencies as well as on the mistreatment of dissimilar others. More attention needs to be given to the cultural elements that perpetuate aggression and war, and it is with this need in mind that we turn to the role of carriers and their support of enormous facilities for the continuation of particular styles of behavior.

Carriers and War

Toward a Cultural Explanation of Human Conflict

The materialist, sociobiological, and irrational explanations of aggression and war are compelling in their different ways but inadequate for explaining the complexities of human behavior. For example, one aspect of this complexity is the enormous range of human societies, from those with few experiences with collective aggression, such as the Tiwi of northern Australia, to those with an almost continuous history of such experiences, such as the Yanomamo of northern Brazil. To use examples from modern nation-states, consider Switzerland's low level of involvement in war during the twentieth century compared to the Germany's high level of involvement. This variation suggests that conflict is not causally determined by fixed and unvarying mechanisms within individuals; it also suggests that more attention needs to be given to carriers, the cultural characteristics that sustain and strengthen collective aggression.

I will give particular attention to carriers that help sustain and strengthen aggressiveness, that is, behavior intended to harm others. A close examination of such carriers reveals that in many societies the facilities and avenues for waging war are much more readily available, and are ascribed greater importance and priority, than those for waging peace. Facilities for waging war include the vast military sector in modern societies, a sector that has enormous resources devoted to it. Contrast to this the typically meager resources available for waging peace. While the budget for the military is enormous in many kinds of societies, ranging from superpower to tiny, from technologically advanced to industrially underdeveloped, the budget devoted to peace is typically minuscule.

An examination of carriers that support aggressiveness and war reveals them to be fantastically varied and enormous in number. Such carriers sustain and expand ways in which violence is produced and absorbed in everyday life, such that it is intricately woven into the details of what we do and think. I will focus on just four categories of these carriers, pointing out some of their basic features.

A first type of carrier supporting war, which is both symbolic and behavioral, involves actions. An example is the national holidays observed in remembrance of war, such as Memorial Day in the United States, when communities celebrate with festivities, marching bands, and fireworks. On Memorial Day, people in the United States participate in various organized activities that are symbolic of the honor and glory given to members of the military, past and present. A second example is battlefield reenactments, such as those involving tens of thousands of people reenacting American Civil War battles. The actors use true-to-life reproductions of period clothes, food, weapons, and equipment. Large numbers of people are employed in numerous business enterprises to service this demand. A more everyday example is yellow ribbons, displayed as a show of support for troops and an indication of remembrance.

A second type of carrier supportive of militarism involves artistic symbols and depictions of military struggles and heroism. Examples are paintings, such as *Washington Crossing the Delaware*, painted by Emmanuel Leutze in 1850; prints commemorating special military events, such as those by Nathaniel Currier in the mid-nineteenth century featuring scenes from the war with Mexico; posters, such as James Montgomery Flag's World War I "I Want You" recruiting poster; photographs and postage stamps, such as the stamp adaptation of Joe Rosenthal's February 23, 1945, photograph of U.S. Marines raising a flag on the heights of Iwo Jima's Mount Surinachi; memorials, such as the Vietnam Veterans' Memorial in Washington, D.C., designed by Maya Lin and dedicated on Veterans Day weekend in 1982; songs, such as "The Ballad of the Green Berets," which was very popular in 1966; and films, such as *The Purple Heart* (released by 20th Century-Fox in 1944), which tells the heroic story of the crew of a B-25 bomber who are captured, tortured, and killed, without giving up their secrets. Among these carriers, film has probably had most resources devoted to it in recent years.

A third category of carrier involves individuals who embody heroism and dedication to the military life and cause. Historically these have tended to be "fighting men," the Davy Crocketts who really did fight and sometimes even die on the battlefield. In more recent years, these individuals have often been screen actors who play the part of fighting men—such as John Wayne, who played the role of Davy Crockett in the film *The Alamo* (1960)—and who have come to symbolize the "honorable fighting man," at least in the United States. But militarism has also been supported by entertainers who do not portray war heroes but help boost morale, an example being Bob Hope, who entertained U.S. troops for about half a century onwards from 1941.

Among the most powerful and insidious carriers are toys that support militarism, and these are so varied and pervasive that they represent a fourth category. Toy soldiers, toy weapons, toy uniforms, and the like were available well before modern warfare and the modern media and consumer culture. However, several things are new about the role of toys in support of modern militarism. First, from about the mid-twentieth century onwards, toys have been packaged as part of a larger sales program involving a multitude of related products. For example, when the toy soldier G.I. Joe was marketed in the 1960s, it was accompanied by G.I. Joe shirts, lunch boxes, books, posters, and so on. This kind of "holistic" marketing has become the norm in the twenty-first century.

A second fundamentally new feature of some toys is their use by both civilians and military personnel. In particular, some virtual-reality war games available on the mass market and popular among the civilian population are very similar to virtual-reality games used in professional military training. The teenager shooting at a virtual enemy in a fun game at the local mall could 1 or 2 years later be undergoing military training on a similar machine to learn to shoot at live enemy targets. The virtual-reality machinery serves to distance the shooter from the live target, so that the vital differences between virtual and real wars are more likely to become blurred.

A vast variety of carriers, then, serve to sustain and strengthen militarism in modern Western societies. A consequence of this process is a legitimization of the military, as well as a normalization and rationalization of it. That is, people come to view a vast military as part of the natural order of things, as normal rather than questionable. At the start of the twenty-first century, both major political parties in the United States are committed to increasing military spending.

Carriers, Militarism, and Non-Western Cultures

The role of carriers in support of militarism is not exclusive to modern Western societies. Rather, such carriers are found in all societies where militarism is prominent. In such societies, carriers function to sustain a normative system that gives extraordinarily high value to acts of physical bravery as well as to aggression and dominance over others. The history of such groups is characterized by bloody battles and death with honor according to the normative system of the group. Among the many possible groups we could use as illustrative examples, perhaps the Sikh community of India is among the most well known. Over the last three centuries or so, and more recently during the First and Second World Wars, Sikhs have come to be known for their amazing bravery and disregard for personal comfort and safety in the field of battle. It did not seem to matter who they were fighting, or why, or where—they fought with the same enthusiasm and valor. The contribution of the Sikhs to the British effort in World War I, particularly regarding the number of men in the army, was estimated at 10 times that of other Indian communities. Describing one of the many World War I battles in which Sikhs demonstrated their fighting spirit, a British general wrote:

> In spite of the tremendous losses, there was not a sign of wavering all day. Not an inch of ground was given up and not a single straggler came back. . . . The ends of the enemy's trenches leading into the ravine were found to be blocked with the bodies of Sikhs and of the enemy who died fighting at close quarters, and the glacis slope is thickly dotted with the bodies of these fine soldiers all lying on their faces as they fell in their steady advance on the enemy.
> —General Sir Ian Hamilton, writing about the contributions of Sikh soldiers in the third Battle of Krithis in 1915. Quoted in Madra & Singh, 1999, p. 109.

When World War II began in 1939, a large section of the Indian population was opposed to joining the British Indian Army to fight against the Germans and their allies, who had invaded and occupied several European countries, because the Indians considered themselves to be occupied by the British. But Sikhs proved more willing than other Indians to join in the fighting, and throughout the war Sikh combatants once again demonstrated outstanding military prowess. The high standard of military capabilities among Sikhs continued after World War II; after India achieved independence, Sikhs were disproportionately represented in the Indian armed forces.

How are we to explain the continued tradition of militarism among Sikhs? What has allowed the Sikhs to maintain this style of behavior? I believe the explanation lies in cultural carriers that have evolved as a central part of Sikh culture. Among such carriers are poetry, chants, and prayers that laud "the sword," bravery and honor in battle, and self-sacrifice in struggles against the enemy; these carriers are pivotal in Sikh spiritual life and are passed on from generation to generation. Becoming integrated into Sikh society involves taking on military values and behaviors. But this is not always an explicit and obvious process; in many ways it is subtle and implicit. For example, it involves a particular orientation toward the larger practical world.

An essential theme of Sikh spiritual life is engagement with the practical world and fighting to bring about change. A tradition of being engaged in the practical world was established by the very first Sikh guru, Guru Nanak

(1469–1539). By the time of the fifth Sikh guru, Guru Arjun Dev (1563–1606), a tradition of martial arts was being also established. This tradition was sustained by the spiritual teachings and poetry of important gurus, which were studied closely and passed on from generation to generation. Guru Arjun Dev, who was tortured and killed by enemies who were also Sikhs, taught that "a hero obtains for himself bliss both here and hereafter by the might of his arms."

The creation of the first Sikh standing army at the time of the sixth guru, Guru Har Gobind (1595–1644), was associated with the evolution of a number of symbolic carriers that served to sustain militarism. Two swords, and later the double-edged sword, representing the worldly and the spiritual, came to symbolize a delicate balance to be achieved in the lives of Sikhs, the "warrior-saints."

The sword is used in Sikh poetry as a metaphor for the Creator, as both mother of earth and all-powerful being. The tenth and final guru of the Sikhs, Guru Gobind Singh (1666–1708), wrote: "After the primal manifestation of the sword the universe was created." He also wrote: "I bow to You, who are the wielder of the sword./I bow to You, who are the possessor of arms."

The military tradition of Sikhs was sustained by a value system that gave highest importance to bravery in battle, to being devoted to defending personal honor and the honor of the Sikhs. Headgear was particularly used as a military marker, with peaked turbans being decorated with metal crescents, double-edged swords, tridents, knives, and tiger claws.

Factors such as material conditions, genetic characteristics, irrational motives, and the like may have played a role in creating the strong military traditions of the Sikhs. Be that as it may, the continuation and expansion of militarism among Sikhs has been strongly influenced by carriers, as is the case with most other groups who have such traditions (such as the Zulus of South Africa or the Gurkhas of Nepal).

Carriers and Children

They told us that we must not be afraid of violence or death and tested us to see if we could follow their command. Three different times people who tried to escape the base were brought back. The bandits brought all the children, including me, to witness their punishment. The bandits told us that we must not cry out or we would be beaten. Then a bandit struck the man on top of the head with an ax.
—12-year-old boy abducted and trained by Renamo, the Mozambique National Resistance, quoted in Neil Boothby & Christine Knudsen, "The Gun," p. 62

I have argued that major sources of continuity in human aggressiveness are the carriers that glorify militarism and the military hero. Among such carriers are stereotypes of the chivalrous male, who exudes physical strength and is willing to act violently in defense of honorable causes. Of course, just what constitutes an "honorable cause" is culturally defined, so that in some cultural contexts edicts such as "the only good Indian is a dead Indian" are put into practice, with John Wayne–type heroes holding both the blazing girl and the blazing gun in the final scene.

Powerful carriers are necessary to sustain continuity in aggression partly because killing fellow humans is not an easy thing for the vast majority of people to do. Detailed studies of children abducted into rebel or government armies—and there are currently about 300,000 children active in about 36 ongoing conflicts in Asia, Europe, Africa, Central and South America, and the former Soviet Union—reveal that it is actually a difficult task to train children to kill. David Grossman and other military experts have pointed out that despite thousands of years of refinement, military training still does not do a very effective job of molding killers. Accounts of actual combat conditions suggest that most soldiers feel sick rather than elated when they have to kill. The experiences of Vietnam veterans suggests that soldiers pay a very high price, particularly in terms of psychological problems, when they are forced to participate in actions that give rise to heavy human casualties.

Modern carriers sustaining aggressiveness include a new type of military hero, one who engages in "smart war." The new military heroes use highly sophisticated technology that allows killing to take place from a distance, sometimes from hundreds or even thousands of miles away. Rather than see and smell and touch the enemy at close quarters, the new military hero gives commands via a computer and only experiences the enemy as images or dots on a computer screen. This "virtual-reality war" is neat, clean, surgical, and impersonal to the extreme, at least for those who have the technology to wage "smart war."

Concluding Comment

My argument, then, is that to understand aggression and war, one must look to carriers that sustain this type of behavior. As an example, the readiness of the United States to use its armed forces to act as a so-called police force on the world stage and the readiness shown by U.S. citizens to use force in their everyday lives (as indicated by violent crime statistics) have their roots in, and are upheld by, carriers with long histories. One such carrier is the Second Amendment to the U.S. Constitution: "A well regulated Militia, being necessary to the security of a free State, the right of the people to keep and bear

Arms shall not be infringed." The right to bear arms is related to a strong tradition of citizen-soldiers in the United States, rooted in the militia system of colonial times and represented today by huge armies of military reserves. Cementing this together is a value system that lauds military action and honors the graduates of armed forces institutions, such as the U.S. Military Academy at West Point (established in 1802), the U.S. Naval Academy (established in 1845), the Naval War College (established in 1884), the Army War College (established in 1903), and the Air Force Academy and Air War College (both established in 1947).

Just how deeply ingrained and normalized militarism is in the United States is indicated by advertising for military academies for youth. Looking through almost any major newspaper in the United States, one can find advertisements for military academies for youth, institutions where "boys become men" and "character," "confidence," and "discipline" become part of the young man. The photographs in the advertisements show smart young men in military uniform, snapping to attention and following orders. These schools and their traditions are part of vast networks of carriers that sustain aggression and war. It is to such carriers we must look in order to explain the persistence of conflict and the fragility of peace.

Suggested Readings

Archer, J. (Ed.). (1993). *Male violence.* London: Routledge, Chapman & Hall.

Boothby, N. G., & Knudsen, C. M. (2000, June). The gun. *Scientific American*, pp. 59–65.

Chagnon, N. (1992). *Yanomamo* (4th ed.). New York: Harcourt Brace Jovanovich.

Das, V., Kleinman, A., Ramphele, M., & Reynolds, P. (Eds.). (2000). *Violence and subectivity.* Berkeley: University of California Press.

Ehrlich, P. R. (2000). *Human natures: Genes, cultures, and the human prospect.* Washington DC: Shearwater.

Freud, S. (1933). *Why war?* In J. Strachey (Ed. and trans.), *The standard edition of the complete psychological words of Sigmund Freud* (Vol. 22, pp. 199–215). London: Hogarth Press (Translation published 1964).

Goldstein, J. H. (Ed.). (1998). *Why we watch: The attraction of violent entertainment.* New York: Oxford University Press.

Gregor, T (Ed.). (1996). *A natural history of peace.* Nashville, TN: Vanderbilt University Press.

Grossman, D. (1995). *On killing: The psychological cost of learning to kill in war and society.* New York: Little, Brown.

Haas, J. (Ed.). (1990). *The anthropology of war.* Cambridge, UK: Cambridge University Press.

Holsinger, P. M. (Ed.). (1999). *War and American popular culture: A historical encyclopedia.* Westport, CT.: Greenwood.

Kaeuper, R. W. (1999). *Chivalry and violence.* Oxford: Clarendon.

Madra, A. S., & Singh, P. (1999). *Warrior saints: Three centuries of Sikh military tradition.* London: I. B. Tauris Publishers in association with the Sikh Foundation.

McGuffin, P., Riley, B., & Plomin, R. (2001). Toward behavioral genomes. *Science, 291,* 1232–1249.

Schubert, K., & Siegel, A. (1994). What animal studies have taught us about the neurobiology of violence. *International Journal of Group Tensions, 24,* 237–265.

Singh, G. (1979). *A history of the Sikh people.* New Delhi: World Sikh University Press.

Sponsel, L., & Gregor, T. (Eds.). (1994). *The anthropology of peace and non-violence.* Boulder, CO: Lynne Rienner.

Stein-Brehrens, B., Mattson, M. P., Chang, I., Yeh, M., & Sapolsky, R. (1994). Stress exacerbates neuron loss and cytoskeletal pathology in the hippocampus. *Journal of Neuroscience, 14,* 5373–5380.

Venter, J. C., et al. (2001). The sequence of the human genome. *Science, 291,* 1304–1351.

Weart, S. (1998). *Never at war: Why democracies won't fight one another.* New Haven, CT: Yale University Press.

Worchel, S. (2000). *Written in blood.* New York: Worth

6 Gender Relations

"Citizenship, sir?"

I looked blankly at the flight attendant.

"Your citizenship, sir?" she asked again.

For the first time I was traveling with a U.S. passport, and it felt strange to publicly declare myself to be "American." As I completed the arrival card, the flight attendant had given me, I felt somewhat apprehensive about what awaited me after landing.

I was flying to London to attend a research meeting, but I would also have an opportunity to spend time with an old friend and her family. But was this really a good idea, to suddenly drop in and stay at the home of someone I had not seen for such a long time?

When we finally escaped from customs at Heathrow, I saw that Maureen had come to meet me. I recognized her at once, even though 20 years had elapsed since our student days in England. She had the same shining round face surrounded by wavy brown hair, and the same exuberant energy and impatient style revealed itself as she slipped through the barriers in order to greet me earlier as I came out of the customs. My apprehension ended. If I needed further confirmation that she had not changed, it arrived as soon as we reached her car, the back of which was covered with stickers advocating feminist causes.

"I see you are still trying to level the playing field," I commented.

"That's right. We've come a long way, but we still have a long way to go."

As she launched into a passionate account of persistent discrimination against women and told me about the support groups, political activities, and marches she was involved with, it was as if time had stood still. She had always been involved in reform movements, always talking about changing the world, overturning the power structure, getting to a more just society. I was not surprised to learn that her home serves as the headquarters for several local women's groups.

But some things had changed. She was now the mother of two children, a girl and a boy, and she lived with her lawyer husband in a large, comfortable house in the suburbs of London. After we got back to her house, Maureen got busy feeding the two kids, getting them started on their homework, and preparing dinner for her husband.

"When does Dave get back?" I asked, referring to her husband, whom I also knew well.

"Usually not until 8:00, and sometimes much later."

"And how is your work?"

"I was born to be a pediatrician. I love it."

Over the next week as a guest in her home, I learned that Maureen had a thriving medical practice and thoroughly enjoyed her work, and I also learned the patterns of her home life, where she put in a "second shift" seven days a week. Her routine on weekdays was to get up at 5:30 A.M., prepare breakfast for the family, then get her children ready for school, leave the house for work before 8:00, return home around 6:00 P.M., prepare dinner for the family, check that the kids were doing their homework, get them bathed and ready for bed, clean up around the house, prepare materials for women's groups, socialize or relax in front of the television for an hour or so, and go to bed around 11 P.M. Two or three nights a week, her house helper would stay late to look after the children and cook so that Maureen could go out, usually to attend women's group meetings.

It was in the details of how Maureen and her husband behaved in the kitchen, and how they behaved with their children, that I found the greatest surprises. Although it was never explicitly stated, everyone acted as if the kitchen and everything to do with the kids was primarily Maureen's territory. In essence, "kitchen" and "kids" acted as powerful carriers, sustaining specific types of behavior in relation to the roles of husband and wife. These carriers were embedded in supporting social networks, such as family and church, that reinforced the relation of husband and wife to kitchen and kids.

Of course, some change had taken place. Like many twenty-first-century married men, her husband did attend to the children and he did help in the kitchen. But even on those occasions when Dave was doing the cooking, it was Maureen who continued to be the main person responsible for the kitchen and everything related to it. When Dave treated us to his special barbeque, it was Maureen who did the shopping, set up the utensils, and located the sauces and dishes. She supervised the weekly shopping and household routine. When Dave came back from a shopping trip without milk, his immediate response to her was, "You should have told me we need milk." It did not occur to him that he should look to see if milk was needed. When Dave did tasks in the kitchen or took the kids to a park, it was remarked on by guests and family members as if these were "extras"; but when Maureen did the same, they were treated as part of her routine responsibilities. In short, although Maureen and Dave had what everyone saw as a liberated relationship, the bottom line remained that Maureen was expected to do a second shift in relation to kids and kitchen but her husband was not.

Maureen's speeches constantly reminded me that at one level a great deal had changed. In the political and legal domains, on paper and in terms of how things are supposed to be in theory, women now enjoy full equality. They can vote and hold political office, and legislation has been enacted banning discrimination against women in just about every major domain, including employment. But the details of everyday life, sustained by subtle carriers, reveal a different picture, even for many highly educated and apparently liberated women such as Maureen. The minute-by-minute activities of the family in the kitchen show a pattern reflecting traditional gender relations. In some respects, then, Maureen and women like her have slipped back into behavior patterns of their mothers' generation.

Continuity in the Everyday Details of Gender Relations

The situation of women and ethnic minorities in the United States and other Western societies is puzzling in many ways. On the one hand, tremendous advances have been made by minority groups (referring here to any group that has less power, even though it may be a numerical majority), as represented by legal changes banning discrimination on the basis of sex, race, and sexual orientation. On the other hand, women and other minorities continue to report discrimination.

Perceived discrimination is not straightforward. How can we be sure that reports of discrimination on the part of minorities actually reflect objective reality? A solid body of research shows that when we ask individuals about their personal experiences as compared to what they assume their group has experienced, we discover that personal experiences of being discriminated against are typically lower. When we ask women, for example, "Have you personally been discriminated against because of your gender?" they give a lower rating than when we ask them, "Have women in general been discriminated against because of their gender?" One interpretation of this consistent finding is that women and minorities are exaggerating the level of discrimination experienced by their group, perhaps influenced by media reports of extreme cases of discrimination. The true level of discrimination experienced by minorities, the argument goes, is the lower level reported by individuals concerning their personal experiences. However, another possibility is that they are denying discrimination that they themselves have personally experienced. This "denial" explanation seems to be bolstered by objective indicators, such as the disproportionately small numbers of women who reach high political office, which suggests that equality is actually still a long way away, at least in some important domains.

The discrepancy between progress made in the formal sphere of law and the informal sphere of everyday social life highlights a fundamental paradox: Although cultures change, in some essential ways they remain the same. The impact of changes that occur at the macro level, such as changes in laws and even in political and economic systems, can be severely limited by stability at the micro level of common social practices. Examples of such practices are found in the details of everyday life, the many small actions involved in cooking, washing dishes, keeping track of food and kitchen supplies, taking responsibility for clothing, food, health, and other aspects of children's lives.

My argument, then, is that in order to better understand processes associated with continuity and stability in the integration of individuals into society, we must attend to the role that carriers and everyday social practices play in change. In some cases changes (such as those in the domain of sexual practices) take place at the micro level of everyday social practices but are resisted at the macro level by authorities, through censorship, religious rulings, and the like. For instance, the sexual liberation and the gay rights movements of the 1960s have been opposed by religious and governmental authorities, who continue to try to strengthen traditional lifestyles and to advocate conservative sexual morality. However, there are many other instances in which change is initiated from the top or macro level—by government, religious, and legal authorities—only to meet resistance at the micro level. For example, government legislation banning discrimination on the basis of gender and race has been resisted, sometime consciously, at the level of everyday interactions, at least in some communities.

We are reminded again of the different speeds at which change takes place at macro and micro levels, and of the insight that the maximum speed at which change can take place at the macro level, including the political and economic sectors, is faster than the maximum speed at which change is possible at the micro, social-psychological level. Laws and economic policies can change overnight, but informed social rules and norms regulating behavior relating to such laws and economic policies often take years—even decades and generations—to change. This means that while government policy, such as that on gender equality, can change relatively rapidly, and even overnight, the actual behavior of people in their everyday lives is generally influenced by carriers to change more slowly. The mundane practices of everyday social life, traditionally dismissed as unimportant, actually turn out to be pivotal in change processes. They lead us to ask "Why are things stable?" rather than "Why do things change?"

A concern to provide an explanation for continuity leads to a focus on the stabilizing, or anchoring, function of carriers that sustain particular everyday social practices rather than on the characteristics of isolated men and women, as in traditional research on "sex differences." The traditional approach has been to focus on performance capacity and to ask, "How do men and women differ?"—as if any differences found between men and women tested in isolation would explain the social behavior of men and women in the larger society. The traditional question of sex differences has led Alice Eagly, Eleanor Maccoby, and others to conduct grand surveys of sex differences. Some differences have been found consistently, such as that men are more aggressive. Other differences are found less consistently, such as that women score higher on tests of verbal performance. But the vast majority of the studies in the sex-differences arena have completely missed the point: *Most of the important differences between men and women manifest themselves only through social interactions, in the collaboratively constructed social relationships between men and women.* The differences arise in and through their relationships. In using traditional "exam-testing" methods—that is testing men and women in isolation and focusing only on performance capacity—researchers have actually washed away what they were most interested in measuring.

To better understand how women and minorities in the West have been influenced by these processes, it is useful to look to other cultures to their carriers, to use them as mirrors to reflect back on ourselves. Consider, for instance, the experiences of women in Iran and Japan, societies that contrast dramatically both with each other and with the West. Iran is an Islamic society with an ethnically diverse population, while Japan is a secular society that is ethnically more homogeneous. On the surface, the situation of women has changed dramatically in both Iran and Japan, but at a deeper level we see important stability. A close look at such stability reveals important similarities in the way change takes place in societies that are viewed as being very different.

Carriers and Gender Relations in Iran and Japan

Women in Iran

On the surface, the 1978 revolution against the Shah dramatically changed the situation of women in Iran. However, there is continuity in that both before and after the revolution the fate of women has been decided by competing groups of elite men. This is reflected by government policy toward the veil, traditionally worn by women in Iran and a fundamentally important carrier in that context. It is also reflected in the continuing tradition of so-called temporary marriage.

Supporters of the veil in Iran argue that it "frees" women by allowing them to escape being viewed as sex objects, thus protecting their "honor." Critics, on the other hand, point out that the veil prevents women from achieving a modern, egalitarian gender role because it stigmatizes them and severely restricts their activities outside the home. The veil has acted as a weather vane, signaling the direction of prevailing political winds in Iran. This direction changed dramatically several times during the twentieth century, and with these changes came the banning and legalization of the veil by different regimes. Each change has meant that women have had to march to a different tune. Thus the veil serves as a carrier that is symbolic of a larger ideal of womanhood and the role for women envisioned by ruling males.

The modernization of Iran speeded up soon after the first major oil find in the Middle East—in northeastern Iran in 1908. Internal corruption and the intervention of foreign powers enabled Reza Khan to seize power and establish his own Pahlavi dynasty (which lasted from 1926 to 1978). During the latter part of Reza Shah's reign, as part of his modernization plans, Iranian women were forcibly unveiled. However, as soon as the shah lost power in 1941, many women went back to wearing the veil, either voluntarily or because they were forced to do so by their husbands, fathers, or other family members.

In 1941 Reza Shah was replaced by his son, Mohammed Reza Shah (reigned 1941–1979), who was initially unable to dominate the larger national scene. During the early years of his reign, the veil once again became normal for many women in public places, although some of the more educated women did appear in public without the veil. After the collapse of a prodemocracy nationalist movement, led by Mohammed Mossadeq, who become prime minister in 1951, the shah was pushed back into full power by a CIA-directed coup after a brief exile in 1953.

Back in full control, the shah used Iran's growing oil revenues to push ahead with his version of modernization, which involved forcing women to abandon the veil. By the mid-1970s, women in Iran had to appear without the veil in the larger urban centers. A woman who insisted on wearing the veil could not take full advantage of opportunities in higher education or work in the modern sector of the economy. But although political and economic pressures pushed women to abandon the veil, in the family domain, fathers, husbands, brothers, and others often tried to enforce wearing of the veil. It became customary to see traditionally dressed women take off the veil at the entrance to universities, government ministries, and modern offices, and then put it back on when they left such places to go back to their homes, because back in the family domain men would often insist on their wearing the veil. Thus, during this period in Iran's history, women were forced by one group of men to take off the veil in official, government-controlled spaces but forced by another group of men to put on the veil in informal spaces not directly controlled by the government.

The situation changed again after the 1978 revolution. The veil now became symbolic of the ideal "Islamic sister" being propagated by the state, and within a few years after the revolution women had to adhere strictly to Islamic dress codes and wear the veil in all public places. As in the shah's Iran, in the new "revolutionary" Iran "correct" behavior for women has been established by an elite group of all-powerful men. But both before and after the 1978 revolution, some women tried to resist the established dress codes. Before 1978, some women showed disobedience by wearing the veil, and after 1978 some women show disobedience by refusing to adhere to the details of the Islamic dress code. Both before and after 1978, disobedience has been punished by rules set up by elite men.

Another important carrier sustaining continuity in the treatment of women in Iran is the tradition of multiple wives and so-called temporary marriage. Marriage arrangements reflect traditional assumptions about gender differences and sexuality. In the traditional Iranian value system, it is considered "correct" behavior for men to be driven by sexual urges but for women to be ambivalent about sex. This attitude endorses the view of women as objects of enjoyment for men. A manifestation of this in practice is the temporary marriage, which is a contract, often verbal, between a married or unmarried man and an unmarried woman. A Shiite Muslim man is legally allowed to contract simultaneously with as many temporary wives as he desires, in addition to the four wives legally permitted to all Muslim men. A woman can have only one husband of any kind at a time.

Marriage customs in Iran are based on everyday social practices that span centuries and have been only slightly altered by recent political events. These seemingly trivial everyday practices are powerful because they operate at an implicit and micro level. Although temporary marriage is legal in Iran, it is very seldom publicly acknowledged. Perhaps because women are often forced to enter temporary marriages out of financial need, a temporary marriage is regarded as something shameful. Many consider temporary marriage as a form of legalized prostitution, a topic to be avoided in polite company. But through collaborative avoidance of critical discussions of temporary marriage, Iranian communities tacitly endorse the practice and its continuation.

Perhaps in large part because it is seldom publicly acknowledged, the practice of temporary marriage has continued as an integral part of everyday social life across different political epochs. It is one of a number of means by which informal, implicit, and rarely acknowledged social practices prevail over the formal, explicit, and publicly acknowledged ones to support continuity in gender relations in Iran across revolutions and other macro politicoeconomic changes.

The same continuity in everyday practices and disparity between the formal and the informal are pervasive in many other non-Western societies. Detailed investigations of the lives of Moroccan women, for example, reveal that while the role of women has changed in the public, formal domain, change in private life has been much slower. Many Moroccan women still have little control over money, time, contraceptives, and other important matters that shape their *daily* lives. The case of Japan, which I consider in more detail below, is particularly interesting because Japanese society, although technologically modern, is still culturally traditional in important respects.

Women in Japan

During several periods in Japan's early history, some Japanese women enjoyed high status as goddesses, queens, and empresses. But after the introduction of Buddhism and the gradual absorption of Confucian ideas from China, the norms and rules regulating gender relations in Japan began to change, beginning around the middle of the sixth century. The establishment of a national system of administration in the seventh century made it easier to systematically exclude women from posts in major institutions. Buddhism and Confucianism, which served as carriers that sustained blatantly negative and deprecating views of women, had become entrenched among the Japanese populace by the end of the Tokugawa period (1600–1868). Important carriers emerged during the Tokugawa period, as women lost their rights to own land or to file for divorce. Adultery by women became punishable by death. Gender relations were regulated by the belief that women's chief value lay in bearing children and perpetuating the family line; as helpmates, women were enjoined to be subservient, uncritical of and loyal to men.

The defeat of Japan in World War II and the establishment of Western-style democracy through the influence of the United States and other Western powers paved the way for macro-level political, economic, and legal changes in the status of women in Japan. Japan's Equal Employment Opportunity Law (EEOL) went into effect in 1986, giving women equal rights in key areas of employment. The EEOL supported gender equality by prohibiting employers from discriminating against women in terms of on-the-job training and supplementary education, dismissal, retirement, and fringe benefits. It also forbade the establishment of specific hiring requirements that applied only to women, such as having to be unmarried, to be below a certain age, or to commute to work from one's parents' house. The law also encouraged, but did not force, employers to give men and women equal consideration in hiring, assignments, and promotions.

Industrialization, the expansion of the economy, and the EEOL did change the situation for women in some ways. Women now enjoy greater employment opportunities in Japan. However, in some subtle ways the EEOL seems to have had little effect on people's attitudes regarding women and work. It is still generally expected that Japanese women will quit their jobs when they get married, pregnant, or reach a certain age. A majority of companies still seek to place women in jobs in which their "feminine characteristics" can best be utilized, as opposed to the smaller number of companies that are willing to place women in all kinds of jobs. Most of the heads of large corporations still believe that women should not rise above the position of section manager. The practical consequence of this attitude has been the growth of a Japanese equivalent of the "mommy track" for educated women who want to pursue a career. They are given very limited opportunities for career advancement, because top management believes that women would be distracted from their primary duties to their children and husband if their job responsibilities become too heavy. In practice, then, a very effective and rather low glass ceiling has come into being.

In the political domain, too, the post–World War II era brought important legal reforms for women. The 1945 revision of the election law gave Japanese women equal rights to vote and to run for elected office. This equality has not resulted in women's achieving high political office. The one exception occurred in 1986, when Takako Doi was chosen to be chairperson of the Social Democratic Party of Japan (SDPJ). Doi's style became very popular on the campaign trail, especially with women voters, resulting in unexpected success for the SDPJ in the 1989 elections. The elections that year saw a record number of women voted into the House of Councilors and elected as assembly members of the Tokyo city government. Doi's triumph briefly introduced the possibility that a woman might become prime minister. However, her success was short-lived, and Japanese women failed to get more than even 5 percent of the seats in important representative assemblies.

How are we to account for this lack of improvement in the situation of women in Japan, despite the formal, macro-level changes in political, economic, and legal aspects of Japanese society? My explanation is to point to enduring carriers that sustain patterns of micro-level behavior, to what happens in the details of everyday life. Gender relations in contemporary Japan go back to the Tokugawa era. The rigid hierarchy characteristic of Tokugawa society was based on Confucian teachings that linked harmony in the state to harmony and order in the family. Consequently, the structure of the Tokugawa government resembled that of the traditional Japanese family or household, known as the *ie*.

The Japanese *ie* consisted of a main house, headed by the father, and a number of subordinate branch houses, in which lived the sons of the father and their families. Within each house, relations between members were hierarchically organized along lines based on age, sex, and expectation of permanence in the house. Younger members were seen as indebted to older members for their upbringing. Males, especially the father and the eldest son, were given power over females. The two main principles governing life in the *ie* were (1) that the good of the *ie* took precedence over the good of an individual and (2) that the continuation of the *ie* was the chief goal of all its members.

It is not just in gender relations that the *ie* system has infiltrated into the daily life of contemporary Japan. The same influence is apparent in modern Japanese companies. Just as the head of the *ie*, the father, expected loyalty and self-sacrifice from his children, so a company superior expects loyalty and self-sacrifice from his subordinates. The primary loyalty of the Japanese *sarariman* is to the company, the "main house," while the worker's own family, the "branch house," comes second. Just as loyalty to the *ie* was rewarded with paternalistic protection and support, so in exchange for the *sarariman's* loyalty and devotion to the company, the superior promises to take care of him and his family, even to the extent of arranging a marriage for him. Just as in the *ie*, authority relations in the company are arranged on the basis of age, permanence in the house (company seniority), and sex (males occupy most of the authority positions in Japanese companies).

Thus continuity in gender relations, spanning political epochs and even economic transformation, has been achieved in Japan through carriers that sustain rules, norms, and values, and in this way regulate behavior at the micro level of everyday social life. The same idea proves useful when applied to gender relations in the West.

Reflecting Back on Women in the West

The cases of Iran and Japan act as a mirror, reflecting back to illuminate the role of carriers in sustaining the political, economic, and legal status of women in the West, particularly in the United States, which acts as a weather vane for future trends. The formal macro system has changed dramatically for American women over the last century, and they now have the legal right to compete as equals in all major domains. However, critics of the status quo have argued that despite recent gains by women in the formal domain, inequalities persist. Women are still concentrated in lower-status occupations and receive lower pay even when they are in the same occupations as men. Women who work outside the home, even when they are highly educated, are still expected to take more responsibility than husbands for family life, as the case of my friend Maureen illustrates.

Additionally, women continue to be excluded from political power. The so-called year-of-the-woman U.S. elections in 1992 brought the number of women in the Senate to a grand total of six. Even young students do not see women as equally viable political candidates for top political positions.

In Chapter 2 I pointed out that in both developed and developing societies, women have tended to reach positions of power through a "widow's mandate" or by being closely related to male leaders. Research on ancient Egypt suggests that the "family ties" route to political power was used by women 5,000 years ago—and probably before. Hatshepsut, the best-documented female ruler of ancient Egypt, gained prominence through her lineage and was often represented as a man in sculpture and painting. Perhaps this was a way of making herself a more acceptable ruler, just as Margaret Thatcher presented herself as even tougher than the men in her cabinet.

In explaining this paradox between the formal and the informal, we once again point to the resilience and subtlety of carriers that sustain micro-level social practices. A similar idea is expressed by researchers concerned with aspects of the "new sexism." A study of the brightest women scientists, recipients of postdoctoral fellowships from the National Science Foundation and other prestigious sources, found subtle barriers working against them. For example, women do not receive the same quality of informal support and information, which is often provided through chats in corridors or by introductions to visiting scientists. In sum, much like their Iranian and Japanese counterparts, American women's advancement toward economic and political parity with men has to a considerable extent been stymied by subtle and unchanging everyday social practices.

Performance Capacity and "Causes" or Performance Style and "Norms"?

In the last few decades, as discrimination against women has become illegal in most industrialized societies, some writers, such as those who work under the banner of sociobiology, have argued that gender differences in behavior persist because they arise from biological factors. From this perspective, gender differences in behavior are caused by performance capacity, such as the childbearing abilities of women, the greater physical size and strength of men, and other similar biological differences. Two strategies for gathering evidence are particularly popular among supporters of this view.

First, gender differences in Western societies are identified and comparisons are made to show consistency across time. For instance, in the cognitive domain, men on average still score higher than women on mathematical and spacial tasks, while at least until the 1990s women scored higher on verbal ones. In the social arena, men tend to be more aggressive, while women tend to be more empathic.

Second, cross-cultural studies are conducted to demonstrate that key gender differences are universal, or nearly so. For example, in most societies brides are younger than grooms. In some societies the age gap is a year or even less, in other societies the gap can be 10 or more years, but the direction of the differences is consistently the same. Women are prized for health and youth, indicators of childbearing potential, and men are valued for experience and resources, indicators of a superior ability to take care of offspring.

Underlying these two strategies is the assumption that, since cultures change across time and across societies, then if the same gender differences are found across time and across different societies, the "cause" of consistency in gender differences must be biological. But this neglects two facts. First, there are important universals in the norms, rules, values, and other aspects of culture that regulate gender relations at the micro level of everyday behavior. Second, as in the cases of Iran, Japan, and the United States, the informal, implicit, and seldom-acknowledged aspects of everyday life prove to be enduring and effective in shaping gender relations. They also happen to be very similar in essential respects.

Biological factors were undoubtedly very influential in the ways in which gender relations evolved over the last 100,000 years or so. But this influence does not show itself in a mechanistic, causal manner. Rather, it shows itself indirectly, through the influence that biological factors have had on norms, rules, values, and other aspects of culture that pattern everyday social life. The persistence of certain types of gender relations is regulated through carriers that sustain certain types of performance style, everyday practices such as those pertaining to the kitchen and to children. The reason it is so difficult to change traditional gender relations is not because they are "caused" by biological factors but because of the deeply ingrained carriers sustaining cultural systems, particularly at the micro level.

Concluding Comment

"Becoming a woman" and "becoming a man," taking on gender roles in one's culture, is one of the central features of individual–society integration. The outcome of this integration is that men and women play roles that are in some ways fundamentally different, from what happens in the kitchen and around kids to what happens in the Senate and the highest levels of government. These differences are sustained through subtle but pervasive everyday social practices and are best understood by examining the details of how things are done by men and women in their collaboratively constructed and mutually sustained social relationships. I have pointed to kitchen and kids as important carriers in this domain, and arguing that in practice women rather than men are associated with, and responsible for, activities related to kitchen and kids. Changes in this arena are coming about very slowly, as men and women collaboratively renegotiate their social relationships. This renegotiation is influenced less by formal legislation or abstract discussions and more by practical requirements leading to changes in skilled performance of "how to be a man" and "how to be a woman."

Suggested Readings

Brettell, C. B., & Sargent, C. F. (Eds.). (1997). *Gender in cross-cultural perspective*. (2nd ed.). Upper Saddle River, NJ.: Prentice-Hall.

Capel, A. K., & Markoe, G. E. (Eds.). (1996). *Mistress of the house, mistress of the heaven: Women in ancient Egypt*. New York: Hudson Hills Press.

Cook, E. A., Thomas, S., & Wilcox, C. (Eds.). (1994). *The year of the women: Myths and realities*. Boulder, CO: Westview.

Eagly, A. H. (1995). The science and politics of comparing men and women. *American Psychologist, 38*, 971–981.

Fujimura-Fenselow, K., & A. Kameda. (Eds.). (1995). *Japanese women: New feminist perspectives on the past, present, and future*. New York: Feminist Press.

Haeri, S. (1989). *Law of desire: Temporary marriage in Shi'i Iran*. Syracuse, NY: Syracuse University Press.

Kimmel, M. S. (Ed.). (2000). *The gendered society reader*. New York: Oxford University Press.

Kumagai, F. (1996). *Unmasking Japan today: The impact of traditional values on modern Japanese society*. Westport, CT: Praeger.

Lambton, A. K. S. (1988). *Continuity and change in medieval Persia*. Albany, NY: Bibliotheca Persica.

Maccoby, E. E. (1990). Gender and relationships: A developmental account. *American Psychologist, 45*, 513–520.

Mackay, S. (1993). *The Iranians: Persia, Islam, and the soul of the nation*. New York: Plenum.

Matteo, S. (Ed.). (1993). *American women in the nineties*. Boston: Northeastern University Press.

Mernissi, F. (1989). *Doing daily battle: Interviews with Morrocan women* (M. J. Lakeland, Trans.). New Brunswick, NJ: Rutgers University Press.

Moghaddam, F. M. (1998). *Social psychology: Exploring universals across cultures*. New York: Freeman.

Ogletree, S. M., Coffee, M. C., & May, S. A. (1992). Perceptions of female/male presidential candidates. *Psychology of Women Quarterly, 16*, 201–208.

Sonnert, G., & Holton, G. (1995). *Gender differences in science careers: The Project Access study*. New Brunswick, NJ: Rutgers University Press.

7 Romantic Love

Belle laughed. For years, she had thought fairy tales could only be read
about in books. But as she looked into the adoring eyes of her Prince, she
knew what had happened was real. And she knew exactly what the ending of her real-life fairy tale would be. She and her prince would live happily ever after.

— A. L. SINGER, *Beauty and the Beast*

One of the most fundamental yet subtle themes in the integration of individuals into modern societies is romantic love, the view that happiness is achieved
when a person falls in love and marries for love. Individuals learn that in order
to be happy and fulfilled, they must be in love and live for love. Money, power,
fame, all the riches of the world will not be enough to make a person happy if
romantic love is missing.

This conviction directs the attentions of both women and men toward an
individualistic view of the world, so that fulfillment is seen as being achieved
only through interpersonal relationships. Love conquers all; it stands apart from
economic conditions, political ideology, and all the other aspects of the larger
society. As the popular Beatles song puts it, "Love is all you need." The pursuit
of romantic love leads to efforts to fulfill one's life through personal rather than
collective change, individual rather than societal transformation. Romantic
love is the most powerful reductionistic carrier in the twenty-first century, di-
recting attention to micro-level processes and dismissing everything else.

The process of teaching individuals about romantic love begins almost immediately after birth and involves countless powerful carriers, such as fairy
tales. By about 3 years of age, children have appropriated the basic ingredients
of the love story. Throughout childhood, an endless array of carriers, such as
the Walt Disney film–book–audiotape multimedia spectacular quoted at the

opening of the chapter, helps spread the ideal of falling in love, marrying the person one loves, and living happily ever after. Through fairy tales, children learn that romantic love is about real life and that in real life ultimate happiness is achieved by falling in love and marrying for love. In recent years, the message has become even more focused, such that falling in love and becoming paired with the loved one are seen as the *only* way to achieve true happiness.

By the time children have become teenagers, the ideal of romantic love is deeply ingrained in their behavior. They practice and improve their skills in presenting themselves as more attractive to potential love partners, and they learn more and more about different variations of the love story through songs, films, novels, dramas, and more fairy tales. In their relationships with others, they try out different ways of interpreting their role in the love story, and they learn to interpret feelings of love, their own as well as those of others. They exchange love stories with friends and collaborate in the crafting of love stories that are personal to their own lives. After learning the story of "Beauty and the Beast" as a 3-year-old, the teenage girl now tries out different ways to realize her ideals in practice, exploring different ways to improve her skills in romantic relationships, toward the ultimate goal that "she and her prince would live happily ever after."

In our new century, romantic love has been further transformed through a process of "democratization," in the sense that romantic love is now seen as the right of every individual, not just a privilege for a select few. For example, in the popular movie *Shrek,* (DreamWorks, 2001) just about every major character—all drawn from fairy tales—is integrated into a love story starring not a prince but an ogre and a princess who is not only physically unattractive but in just about every way opposite to the stereotype of the fairy princesses of traditional stories. Such mass market products are influential in creating a reshaped view of romantic love, one that is more inclusive and less elitist.

By the time a teenager has reached college, romantic love is a natural part of both present preoccupations and future plans. Ask groups of students, as I have done many times, about their ideal lives in the future, and romantic love will appear at the heart of the stories they tell. Young people today reach physical maturity earlier than did previous generations, and they have more sexual experience earlier. However, the impact of romantic love on their imaginations and actions is even greater, in large part because of the powerful influence of the mass media. More sexual experience has not lessened the belief of the younger generation in the fairy tale of romantic love.

But perhaps even more characteristic of modern times is the persistence of a belief among older people about the relevance of romantic love to their own personal lives. Middle-aged persons and senior citizens are also more prone today to see romantic love as central to their own lives. The idea is becoming more pervasive that age is no impediment to falling in love and that being in love is essential to happiness at all ages.

Universal and Local Features of Romantic Love

The pervasiveness of romantic love in modern Western societies might lead us to assume that all humans share this experience. After all, isn't falling in love a human thing? An exploration of human behavior across time and across cultures reveals that the twenty-first-century Western experience with romantic love is not universal, even though at its root are biological processes. These involve physiological changes that take place when a person experiences falling in and out of love. Of fundamental importance is the meaning given to these physiological changes, and this links directly to the role of romantic love as a powerful carrier in Western societies.

Biological Processes and Romantic Love

People in love talk about "being on a high," and they are not just imagining this. There are biochemical changes taking place in their bodies, and these changes can be interpreted by them as a high. The first "spark," or "head-over-heals" feeling of falling in love, is associated with a rush of chemicals—neurotransmitters such as dopamine, norepinephrine, and phenylethylamine that arouse people and lead them to feel energized and full of vitality.

Research has shown that individuals who are high in sensation seeking, a tendency to look for thrills and adventure, tend to be underaroused in those brain systems that control the level of norepinephrine. It would be simplistic to assume that the level of norepinephrine in particular brain systems causes a person to search for thrills, such as those associated with romantic love. However, the physiological characteristics of individuals may set certain limits to the arousal experienced. From this perspective, limitations are imposed on arousal by how much particular neurotransmitters are produced by the body at a given time, such as during a romantic date, and how the body reacts to the increased chemical output—for example, whether or not the body habituates to the increased chemical levels.

Of course, how arousal is interpreted—the meaning given to it—depends on cultural context.

Romantic Love and Social Context

Research shows that context plays a fundamentally important role in how physiological changes are interpreted as a romantic love experience. Several intriguing studies have taken advantage of situations in which males are physiologically aroused because of a threatening experience. In one of my favorite studies, female researchers interviewed male tourists either when they were halfway across a narrow, 450-foot suspension bridge over a white-water river or when they were back on solid land. Those who were interviewed while on the bridge found the interviewers more attractive. A compelling interpretation of this finding is that the male tourists thought back to their experience on the bridge, remembered how aroused they were, and misattributed their arousal to the female interviewer. Such studies suggest that even when the cause of physiological arousal is *not* another person, if it seems appropriate in the context this person will mistakenly be seen as the cause and may well come to have romantic appeal.

In the modern Western context, it has become normative to interpret certain physiological changes as falling in or out of love. Our language reveals the centrality of romantic love in our personal experiences. We describe romantic love, as we do great art, as a "moving" experience. Our beloved "moves" us to experience agony and ecstasy, despair and elation, swinging through moods of elation and back to the ground again. Love transports us, and often it seems we are powerless to resist. We uncontrollably "fall" in love and then can fall out of love again with just as little control, with each change leaving us in a new situation. Most importantly, although the normative system encourages us to look for love, to want to fall in love, the assumption is that love is out of our control—it is something that happens *to* us. In order to better appreciate the distinctive power and pervasiveness of romantic love as a carrier in modern Western societies, it is useful to explore the concept across time and cultures.

The Cultural Roots of Western Romantic Love

At a superficial level, it appears that romantic love is universal. Examinations of songs and folklore in hundreds of societies have shown that what we recognize as romantic love is found in about 86 percent of them. The experience of falling in love is recognized by almost all major cultures. For example, romantic love is a theme in Arabic and Persian literature, the main languages of the Islamic world. But a closer examination of *traditional* practices in Islamic societies such as Saudi Arabia and Iran reveals that there has not been a pervasive belief in the right of every individual to fall in love and marry for love. To the contrary, the actual marriage choices of individuals, particularly women, have been determined through family and community norms and expectations, resulting in unions that are closer to arranged marriages than to Hollywood-style romantic love (I am referring here to traditional practices, not to the behavior of the Westernized elite in these societies). Of course, through the internationalization of communications, trade, and travel, the idea of Hollywood-style romantic love is reaching Islamic societies, but it is still a small minority of people in such societies who are moved in their thoughts and actions by romantic love.

Similarly, when we look across time, we find that in earlier historical eras romantic love was recognized in Western societies, but it was not democratized; the vast majority of individuals did not feel they had a right to make marriage choices on the basis of romantic love. From Homer, to Shakespeare, to Hemingway, romantic love is a major theme in Western literature, but it was only in the twentieth century that romantic love became democratized. This came about through an enormously important shift that began with industrialization and the emergence of mass markets in the late eighteenth century.

Modern romantic love is distinct in that it involves two individuals *free to fall in love and to make their own choices as to who will be their partner.* The conditions for such choices came into existence very slowly, through political reforms and, in the latter part of the twentieth century, the economic independence of women. A careful reading of pre-twentieth-century literature reveals that, because of economic and political conditions, the possibility of romantic love as we know it did not exist for the vast majority of people. The medieval troubadours who sang of courtly love are often described as a major influence on the development of romantic love in the West, but the main focus of the troubadours' songs was a very small elite of knights and ladies, not the commoners.

Even the pre-twentieth-century literature that is popularly regarded as romantic proves, on closer inspection, to place romantic love within very strict economic limits. This is particularly true of works by women authors. In Charlotte Brontë's (1816–1855) *Jane Eyre*, the heroine wins the freedom and gains the courage to make a choice and follow her love after she has inherited a fortune and her beloved has lost his. In George Eliot's (1819–1880) *Middlemarch*, the heroine herself chooses her first and second husbands, but she happens to be financially independent, and the freedom of choice she exercises comes at the cost of losing the bulk of her fortune. Even in the more personal novels of Jane Austen, romantic relationships are located firmly within economic relationships, and breaking out of the economic mold proves very difficult. In *Emma*, the heroine fails in her matchmaking endeavors in large part because she tries to match her friend Harriet with men who are economically unsuitable for her. In *Pride and Prejudice*, the main male character, Mr. Darcy, even makes it clear in his first proposal to Elizabeth that he considers her to be beneath his station. It is not until he overcomes this repulsion that he succeeds in gaining the hand of the woman he loves.

Perhaps the clearest example of limits set on romantic love by economic conditions is found in *Sense and Sensibility,* in which Jane Austen contrasts the behaviors of two sisters, Elinor and Marianne, who in important ways have different approaches to life generally and to romantic love specifically. Elinor has common sense and is self-controlled. She is concerned to maintain societal proprieties, is composed and less inclined to give public display to her private whims and passions. Marianne, in contrast, makes few concessions to social conventions and proprieties. She expresses her inner feelings, even if it is at the expense of transgressing local norms and hurting the feelings of others.

Marianne finds it oppressive to be surrounded by individuals who are restrained and unexpressive, as she sees Elinor and some others surrounding her to be. When Marianne learns that her sister might be attracted to Edward, she is disappointed because Edward seems to her to lack spirit and "fire." When Edward reads to them, Marianne objects: ". . . how spiritless, how tame was Edward's manner in reading to us last night! . . . To hear those beautiful lines which have frequently almost driven me wild, pronounced with such impenetrable calmness, such dreadful indifference!" (1997, p. 33).

In appearance, too, Elinor and Marianne are contrasts, the former is described by Austen as having a correct and the latter a striking figure. This difference becomes greater as each sister experiences difficulties in love. Elinor remains composed and struggles to maintain social decorum even when it seems the man she loves has married another. Marianne, on the other hand, experiences severe psychosomatic illness when her lover abandons her. She completely disregards her own appearance as well as societal conventions. Her initial striking and later chaotic physical appearance is symbolic of her passionate and emotional way of dealing with love.

Marianne, then, is a person who tries to live out the ideal of romantic love. She declares that each person falls in love once in a lifetime and should sacrifice everything for that one true love. But Marianne has little money, and her lover abandons her to marry a woman with a large inheritance. Marianne suffers a breakdown and emerges from her illness with changed views. She eventually marries a man who is twice her age but economically secure. In the language of Leon Festinger, she experienced cognitive dissonance, because her attitude (each person has only one true love in a lifetime) was incongruent with her own behavior (the person she imagined to be her one true love married another woman, and she was forced by circumstances to marry a suitor she had previously declared to be unacceptable). She changed her attitude to resolve the dissonance. In the language of Daryl Bem, Marianne observed her own behavior (she married the alternative suitor) and concluded that she must actually be happier with the alternative choice (Do I prefer him? I must—I married him).

It was only in the final decades of the twentieth century that romantic love became democratized and pervasively sought by both women and men. This transformation came about on the one hand through women's entering higher education and the labor market, thus gaining economic independence, and on the other hand through the mass marketing and consumerization of romantic love. With more than 50 percent of college students being female in 2001, and with women making enormous progress in the marketplace, the economic independence of women gives them the power to make choices, including the choice of romantic partners. At the same time, romantic love has been adopted as a powerful means through which sales of consumer products can be increased. The mass media in tandem with popular culture, particularly films and pop music, continually add countless images and phrases to the already-rich collectively constructed and shared view of romantic love.

Through consumer products and the images conveyed by the mass media, individuals come to appropriate collaboratively constructed and shared ideals of romantic love. As Western products are exported to non-Western societies and Hollywood films reach even the most remote corners of the globe, the democratization of romantic love spreads to non-Western societies. Of course, this does not mean that even in Western societies everyone has exactly the same idea of what love is. In Western societies, there is some variation in what people mean when they say they have fallen in love. Some love relationships are based more on friendship ("We are each other's best friend"), some on passion ("It was love at first sight"), some on pragmatic issues ("I made a list of the qualities my future lover should have, and then found a person to fit the picture") or even game playing ("I like to tease my lover and maintain an air of uncertainty"). Common to a number of these types of love is the idea of a basic "spark" at the initial stage.

Romantic Love in Western Social Life Today

"Tell me about your divorce. Why is it you are breaking up?"

"Well, there is really not much to say," began the man sitting opposite me, "I just felt—my wife and I both sensed—that the fire has gone."

I was interviewing Jim, a 46-year-old man, as part of my research to find out more about romantic love. He had been married for 19 years and had two children, 18 and 16 years old. He was an engineer, and his wife was a business manager. They both looked fit and attractive, they were doing well in their careers, and their home seemed to be a happy one, from the outside at least.

"Can you tell me more about that?" I prodded. "What do you mean when you say the fire has gone?"

He took a deep breath and leaned back. He did not find it easy to talk about his ongoing divorce. "The first few years were great. There was passion in our lives, real passion. The chemistry was right. Being with her was a natural high. Better than anything else I had known, and I am not boasting when I say that when it came to women I was quite successful, and I experienced relationships with a lot of different woman during my college years. I met my wife in my senior year at college, and we made sparks fly." He paused again and just sat back and sighed several times as he remembered past experiences. "Things have changed; we've lost the magic," he added pensively.

Interestingly, his wife gave a very similar explanation for their breakup when I later interviewed her on her own.

A strong sense of déjà vu came over me as Bill and his wife talked about "having lost the magic." It was like being in the middle of the same conversation again and again. In almost every case during the course of my research on the experience of romantic love, individuals having marital problems talked about losing the magic, missing the spark and excitement.

"I need the passion back in my life; I need the excitement," Bill repeated.

"How did the change take place?"

"How? I really don't know," he began thoughtfully. "I mean, I really hadn't thought about it. It's not that I wasn't interested, but the opportunity just didn't arise. We've been so busy, just running around and getting on, trying to make it. You know, thinking back, maybe we only had real passion for a year or two. But who had time to think? The kids were born and we had to go through diapers and sleepless nights. Then we got to the stage of starting them in kindergarten and school and soccer and music and a million birthday parties and God knows what. It was endless. For the last 20 years I feel I have been a glorified nanny and cook and cleaner and chauffeur for the kids."

"And now?"

"Well, now they can drive themselves around, and all they want from us is money and an occasional bit of advice. My kids are very independent. At this stage I feel as if there's nothing holding Jean and me together. Some respect and lots of good times in the past, but no excitement left. It's like flat warm beer."

"What will you do next?"

"You mean after the divorce? Well, I've met somebody, somebody special who makes me feel alive again. Don't get me wrong. I'm not trying to relive my youth. She's not a lot younger than my wife, but the important thing is that when I'm with her I feel excitement. I'm on a high again."

After hesitating he added, "Even if it doesn't work out with her, even if it only lasts six months, it will still be worth it. I feel I have to make the break and find a way to live again."

Like most people who talk about romantic love, Jim focused a lot on finding the romantic spark again. Of course, in an ideal world, love would be constant and unchanging, lasting "to the edge of doom" as Shakespeare puts it. But this ideal is an end result. It is the fulfillment of love, when the process of "falling in love" is over. The process itself involves a great deal more, because much of the excitement arises from the journey there and back again, the act of falling in love and falling out of love.

In Bill's case, the key point was that he felt a change in his relationship with his wife. He no longer sensed excitement and passion when he was with her, but he did experience these feelings when he was with his newly found lover. As he put it, romance was back in his life, she made sparks fly and gave him that magic high feeling again.

The fundamental shift in behavior in the twenty-first century is that the pursuit of romantic love has become a lifelong goal. Increasingly, middle-aged people and older people now try to keep romance in their lives; they are willing to go through the traumas of divorce and family breakup when they feel that their marriage lacks magic, that they are no longer in love with their spouse. What begins as a fairy tale about the prince and princess living happily ever after in a far-away castle, takes such a strong grip and becomes so powerful in personal lives that its influence shapes lifelong development.

Romantic Love as a Carrier

Romantic love has become the most important destination in the lives of many people, particularly in Western societies. When asked if they would marry a person who had everything they desired in a spouse but with whom they had not fallen in love, over 80 percent of both men and women now say they would not. This has changed from the 1960s, when about 70 percent of men and less than 40 percent of women replied "no." Clearly, on this question the difference between male and female students has disappeared.

Interestingly, cross-cultural research suggests that as non-Western societies become Westernized and influenced through trade and communications by Western values, there is a greater tendency for young people to say "no" in response to the question "If a man (woman) had all the other qualities you desired, would you marry this person if you were not in love with him (her)?" Even in collectivistic societies such as India and Pakistan, about half of the young people interviewed said "no" to this question, and indications are that this percentage is rising with increasing Westernization. In Iran after the 1979 revolution, I found that about 70 percent of more Westernized young Iranians said "no," whereas only about 35 percent of the more traditional young Iranians said "no."

These changes are important, because they reflect how romantic love has become integral to ideas about freedom and happiness. In modern Western societies the freedom to pursue happiness is seen as a right of all individuals, with romantic love being the most important way in which personal happiness can be guaranteed. When I ask young people to describe what would make them happy, reciprocated romantic love is at the top of their lists. To fall in love with a person who also loves you: That is the ultimate picture of happiness.

This view of happiness is glorified by the entertainment industry, with all its many arms in films, music, magazines, novels, theater, and so on. Again and again, the message we get from Hollywood movies and popular music is that falling in love and being with the one you love is the most important ingredient to happiness. If you have any doubt of this, try the following exercise—one that has never failed for me. Turn on a radio and tune in to a popular music station that is playing a song (rather than broadcasting a commercial, or a talk show, or anything other than a song). When that song ends, immediately switch to another station that is playing a song. Do the same again when that song ends, so that you are continually changing to different stations playing songs. Now see how long you have to keep doing this before you find a station playing a song that is *not* about a romantic love relationship. I have found that it can take many hours, or even days, before this happens. Love is in the airwaves 24 hours a day.

It is now seen as an essential *right* for everyone to fall in love and marry the person they love. More people want to participate in this feature of modern democracy than in any other. Even in the most important political elections in the United States, only about 40 to 50 percent of the eligible voters actually cast ballots. In most state and local elections, only about 20 to 40 percent of eligible voters bother to vote. Electoral participation among the young is particularly low and unstable, depending on factors such as the weather. Inclement weather means that most young people will not show up to vote. However, the same young people who do not see it as necessary to exercise their right to vote see it as imperative to exercise the right to fall in love and to marry the one they love.

Romantic Love and Personal Stability

So far I have highlighted the association of romantic love with change, such as couples falling in love or breaking up, but there are at least two fundamental ways in which love is associated with stability. The first, and more mundane, is the stability love brings into the personal lives of individuals. As countless popular songs remind us every day, love is supposed to be forever. In the ideal, love transcends time, remaining fixed despite the passing of time and a changing physical world; love, as Shakespeare wrote, "bears it out even to the edge of doom" (Sonnet 116).

Thus, in the ideal at least, love forms the bedrock of lifelong partnership and ensures the stability of the family. Although divorce rates have risen over the last half-century, to about 50 percent for first marriages and about 60 percent for second marriages, the ideal is still lifelong marriage and fidelity. Although the odds of divorce are well known, young people getting married believe they will stay together "to the edge of doom."

The role of romantic love in maintaining stability in relationships is obviously fundamental, in part because of the central place of family in modern human societies. Despite the continued decline of the percentage of Americans who live in traditional families, the role of the traditional family in raising the next generation remains pivotal. The traditional family remains the most effective institution for inspiring individuals to make enormous altruistic sacrifices for the sake of the next generation.

Romantic Love and the Social Status Quo

In addition to sustaining stable interpersonal relationships at the micro level, romantic love supports stability—that is, the status quo—at the macro level of societal and collective relationships in at least three main ways.

First, romantic love reduces goals and desires to the level of interpersonal relations. The passion and joy of love, the agony and ecstasy, all hinge on relationships with the loved one. But more than this, if the lover succeeds in winning over the beloved, then fulfilment is assured. The world starts and ends in this relationship, and so everything is reduced to the interpersonal level. Romeo is only concerned with the injustices of the larger society insofar as they impact on his relationship with Juliet. Romantic love thus directs all attention to the micro level of interpersonal relations rather than the macro level of social and political causes and ideologies.

Romantic love further supports stability and the status quo by endorsing the picture of society as merit-based. Love knows no boundaries, so the popular image implies. In fairy tales, princes often fall in love with poor girls—or at least girls who appear to be penniless. For example, Snow White is wandering in the forest alone when she meets the prince, who immediately falls in love with her despite the fact that she seems to be a commoner. This theme of rich boy/girl meets and falls in love with poor girl/boy is repeated in countless Hollywood movies. The implication is that romantic love is a path to social mobility and that the outcome of the story is completely dependent on personal characteristics. If you have the right qualities, a millionaire may fall in love with you and lead you up to enjoy life among the rich.

But rich lovers are equally likely to abandon all their wealth and titles for the sake of their true loves, so the fairy tales relate. Love is so important that, in comparison, nothing else matters. Edward VIII abandoned the British crown for Mrs. Wallace Simpson, an American divorcée who had won his heart. Such examples seem to endorse the popular view that love conquers all and that, for rich and poor alike, love is the most important thing in the world. To be rich but not be with the one you love is to be miserable, whereas to be with the one you love is to be happy even if you are materially poor (of course, the former monarch continued to live an opulent life as the Duke of Windsor).

And this leads us to yet another way in which the idea of romantic love endorses the status quo: It allows the poor to imagine ways in which they can be better off than the rich. Life seems fair after all. The poor may not have material comforts, but they can fall in love and become happy. The rich have money, but the poor can do even better by experiencing love. Romantic love endorses the message that money does not matter; ironically, this message is loudest in the United States, where the gap between rich and poor is larger than in other industrialized societies. If Karl Marx were alive today, he would probably proclaim romantic love rather than religion to be the opium of the masses.

Concluding Comment

A major function of carriers is to sustain ways of life and, ultimately, to bolster the continuation of societies. Romantic love functions extremely effectively in this respect, because it implies the achievement of bliss through personal rather than societal transformation. It is the fulfillment of the American Dream through "falling in love . . . again" and being carried along by personal relationships, unconcerned with the larger society. Lovers do not need the rest of society; they have each other.

Romantic love is at one level about personal fulfillment through change. Individuals fall in love, become different in some important ways, and (ideally) find happiness through a relationship with another. But romantic love is at another and more fundamental level about stability, both personal and societal. It is an experience that cements marriages and families, and it also endorses the idea that happiness is within the reach of both poor and rich. There is no need to be concerned about the increasing gap between rich and poor around the world, because who needs money when you have love?

Suggested Readings

Austen, J. (1997). *Sense and sensibility.* Originally published 1811. New York: Signet Classics.

Bloch, R. H. (1991). *Medieval misogyny and the invention of Western romantic love.* Chicago: University of Chicago Press.

De Munck, V. C. (Ed.). (1998). *Romantic love and sexual behavior.* Westport, CT: Praeger.

Hatfield, E., & Rapson, R. L. (1993). *Love, sex, and intimacy: Their psychology, biology, and history.* New York: HarperCollins.

Hendrick, C., & Hendrick, S. S. (1993). *Romantic love.* Newbury Park, CA: Sage.

Illouz, E. (1997). *Consuming the romantic utopia: Love and the cultural contradictions of capitalism.* Berkeley: University of California Press.

Jankowiak, W. R. (Ed.). (1995). *Romantic passion: A universal experience.* New York: Columbia University Press.

Janov, A. (2000). *The biology of love.* Amherst, New York: Prometheus.

Johnson, R. A. (1985). *We: Understanding the psycyhology of romantic love.* San Francisco: Harper.

LeVine, R., Sato, S., Hashimoto, T., & Verma, J. (1995). Love and marriage in eleven cultures. *Journal of Cross-Cultural Psychology, 26,* 544–571.

Person, E. P. (1989). *Dreams of love and fateful encounters: The power of romantic persuasion.* Harmondsworth, UK: Penguin.

Singer, A. L. (1992). *Beauty and the beast.* New York: Disney Press.

Sternberg, R. J., & Barnes, M. L. (Eds.). (1988). *The psychology of love.* New Haven, CT: Yale University Press.

Walsh, A. (1991). *The science of love: Understanding love and its effects on mind and body.* Amherst, NY: Prometheus.

Zuckerman, M. (Ed). (1984). *Biological bases of sensation seeking, impulsivity, and anxiety.* Hillsdale, NJ: Erlbaum.

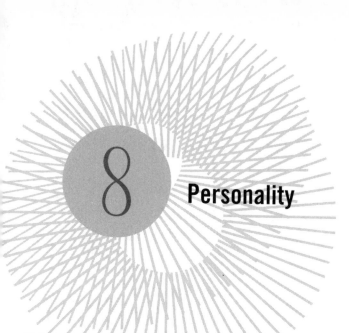

8

Personality

"Well, my son is back from the Marines, and it's as if he never left," said the middle-aged cashier. We were having our usual weekly chat as I bought a few things from the neighborhood grocery store.

"How long was he in the Marines?"

"Five years, from the time he was 18. And you know he went all over the world, and he really seemed a different person. When I went to see him with his friends in the Marines, he was so different."

"And now?"

"Now he's back home, it's as if he never left. His personality has stayed the same."

"Interesting. Why do you think that is?"

"I don't know. I read once that people are born with their personalities. He was always like that, as long as I can remember."

"But how about when he was with his Marine friends?"

"Well, he seemed different, and now he is back home and his old self again. You know, his personality hasn't really changed since he was little."

"Oh?"

"It's the same with his younger brother—same personality since he was a toddler."

The idea of personality as a stable set of characteristics, as something inside each person that leads them to think and act the same way across contexts, is pervasive in everyday life. Personality functions as a carrier, leading us to look to assumed characteristics within individuals for explaining behavior. Thus in the above episode the mother explained the behavior of her older son according to an intriguing assumption: that his personality has been the same since he was a little boy, and that is why he behaved as he always did when he returned home from the Marines. Notice that she dismissed her own observation that her son seemed very different when he was with his friends in the Marines. Also, very interestingly, she mentioned that she had read somewhere that people are born with certain personalities. This is one of many ideas that has been exported from academic psychology to the mass media and popularized in countless magazines and television talk shows.

A very different interpretation of her son's behavior, one she did not attend to, is that how he behaves is largely dependent on the social context he is in at any given time. When he was in the Marines and interacting with his Marines friends, he was actually behaving differently from when he was at home with his family. The stability of his behavior in the context of his family could be explained by the influence of his family on him, rather than by stable characteristics within him. As the family context changes over time, with some individuals leaving and others joining, with the family moving to another house in a different neighborhood, and so on, the influence it has on its members changes, and thus we should expect her son to change to some degree over time even if he remains with her at home.

For others to perceive changes in me, there must also be some stable features in how I present myself. Something must stay the same, or at least change at a noticeably slower rate, for others to recognize the things that *do* change. But other people see me only from the outside; they do not have direct access to my private thoughts and feelings. The challenge of getting to dispositions from what we see as outsiders is implied by the term *persona*, the mask worn by Greek actors telling audiences the characters they were playing and the origin of the term *personality*.

Personality functions as a carrier through *commonsense personality*, the assumptions people hold and apply about personality in everyday life. I discuss this in the first major part of the chapter. In the second major part, I argue that the power of personality as a carrier has been dramatically increased through the cultural biases inherent in modern psychology.

Commonsense Personality and Culture

So Cinderella was brought from the kitchen. Blushing, she put on the dainty slipper, just as the Prince himself entered the house to see how the search was proceeding. "It was you!" he cried, looking down at Cinderella's lovely face. "Please be my bride and we shall never be parted again.

—THE STORY OF CINDERELLA AS RELATED BY
NICOLA BAXTER IN "CINDERELLA"

What kind of investor reads *Forbes*? Larry Light thought long and hard
about that question before editing the Investment Guide. . . . He divides
the world into three personality types. . . . Type I is the passive
investor. . . . Type II is the hyperactive investor. . . . That leaves a middle
ground of rationality (Type III).

      —WILLIAM BALDWIN, "SIDE LINES"

The story of Cinderella, in one form or another, continues to be one of
the most popular fairy tales for children around the world. We all recognize
Cinderella as a good, kind, and patient person, while her stepmother and two
stepsisters are just as clearly recognized as selfish and mean-spirited. The story
ends with Cinderella marrying the prince, rising from her lowly position as
nothing more than a servant to her ugly stepmother and stepsisters, to live
alongside her prince, rich and happy. In Cinderella and countless other fairy
tales, the behavior and destinies of individuals are explained, sometimes explicitly, as determined by their personalities. Individuals with good personalities
enjoy happy and *successful* endings, such as Cinderella's rising to the top to
become a princess. In such stories, the prince marries the girl despite the
huge social-class gulf between them. She is his "type," and nothing else
matters.

Commonsense personality has been particularly influenced by the idea of
personality types. A browse through any popular magazine will turn up examples of how individuals are supposed to fit into "types," such as the three types
of investors discussed in the *Forbes* editorial at the opening of this section. No
doubt the popularity of typologies is in part a result of the proliferation of
personality typologies in the discipline of psychology, something I will discuss
further in the second part of this chapter. For now, let us focus on *why* personality should be such an important carrier in everyday life.

A fairly extensive body of cross-cultural research has a bearing on the role
of personality as a carrier. For example, researchers have addressed questions
such as whether Americans are more likely than Indians to see the cause of an
event, such as a traffic accident, as lying within individuals rather than in the
environment. Joan Miller and others have shown that people in collectivistic
cultures, such as India, typically attribute causes more to external factors, while
people in the United States and other Western societies tend to attribute them
more to factors internal to individuals. Also, in collectivistic cultures there is a
greater tendency to describe individuals as connected to their context, whereas
in individualistic cultures the independence and personal responsibility of each
individual are emphasized. This type of research, then, suggests that there are

some cross-cultural differences in the extent to which focus is placed on the characteristics internal to individuals.

But such cross-cultural research does not negate the proposition that personality is an important carrier in most human cultures. That is, to a greater or lesser degree, people tend to believe that there is something we refer to as personality and that characteristics within individuals lead them to behave consistently across contexts. Commonsense personality is a human thing, albeit with some variations across cultures. The universality of commonsense personality is intriguing and requires attention.

One obvious explanation is that the person is a physically independent entity and thus a convenient explanatory unit. A person is perceptually identifiable, an entity that moves around separate from others. Even when individuals conform and act the same as others around them, they are still physically separate entities. This makes it convenient for individuals to be perceived, evaluated, and made sense of as independent units.

This independent unit, the individual, has physical continuity. When we see Sam on Monday and again on Friday, he has changed little physically. He might be wearing different clothes or have noticeably shorter hair, but we still recognize him because he is physically very nearly the same on the two occasions.

These two factors—the physical independence and continuity of individuals—constitute the platform leading to a strong expectation of consistency in behavior. Individuals are treated as if their behavior should be consistent across contexts. No doubt this expectation induces greater behavioral consistency than might exist if individuals were expected to *differ* in their behavior across contexts. In addition, the expectation of constancy also influences others to perceive consistency, even when there is little or none. Thus the mother ignores her son's different behavior when he is with his Marine friends and focuses on his (assumed) consistent behavior before and after he went away to the Marines.

Associated with this focus on the individual is a reductionism, whereby the influences of context and larger societal processes are given less attention. This arises in part because "context" and large categories such as "social class" seem abstract and intangible relative to "a person," who is a clearly demarcated and easily identifiable physical entity. Those large-scale features of the social world that are more clearly visible, such as ethnicity and gender, are more often incorporated as a basis for making judgments about personality and behavior.

No discussion of commonsense personality could be complete without an exploration of the role played by modern psychology in how people think about personality in everyday life.

Modern Psychology, Culture, and Personality as a Carrier

Personality is probably the most central and expansive topic in all of psychology. The term *personality* has been used by psychologists to refer both to how an individual acts and to the private and internal thoughts, motives, and feelings that are assumed to underlie such action. The most influential psychologists in the history of the field, including Sigmund Freud, Carl Jung, B. F. Skinner, Abraham Maslow, Hans Eysenck, and Carl Rogers, have provided their own somewhat differing explanations of how personality takes shape. Terms such as *ego, self, reinforcement, extroversion, introversion,* and *unconscious* are part of our everyday vocabulary, indicating that psychological explanations and theories of personality have spread into popular culture. In a sense we are all psychologists now, particularly Freudians, because we very often use ideas such as Freudian slips and repression to explain what makes people tick.

The powerful influence of personality research is also evident in applied domains. Clinical psychologists and counselors use various theories of personality, sometimes made explicit, to guide them in their everyday work in the treatment of psychologically disturbed patients. In order to provide therapy and guidance, all clinicians begin with assumptions about how personality "works" and what healthy personalities have in common. Psychologists in educational and industrial contexts use theories of personality to advise individuals in making career choices, as well as in helping managers to make hiring and promotion decisions. On the basis of personality assessments, psychologists guide individuals onto some career paths rather than others and select some employees for promotion rather than others. Marriage counselors provide particular types of advice depending on what they see to be the personalities of members of different couples. Thus the topic of personality is central to both the theoretical and applied work of psychologists.

Of fundamental importance is the fact that psychologists have conceptualized personality as performance capacity rather than performance style. That is, they have tried to measure what they assume to be basically stable and quantifiable characteristics within persons, characteristics that people have more or less of, just as they have more or less height, for example, or faster or slower reaction time. These personality characteristics are assumed to allow people to do certain things to greater or lesser degrees, such as withstand stress or express emotions outwardly.

The focus on performance capacity is perhaps understandable, given that psychology has, over the last one-hundred and fifty years striven to be accepted as a science, and it is assumed that a focus on performance capacity rather than performance style is more compatible with scientific criteria. The search for valid and reliable tests of personality is a clear reflection of these trends.

Personality Tests and Performance Capacity

Despite their variety, all major personality tests have one thing in common: They try to measure personality as performance capacity. Based on traditional criteria, these tests are broadly of two types: structured and projective. Structured tests have specific questions and require specific responses: "Do you have trouble sleeping at night?" Yes or No? "Do you hear voices?" Yes or No? "Do you sometimes think people are following you?" Yes or No? Structured tests typically allow for the computation of scores on various subtests, each presumed to measure a particular personality trait, such as extroversion or introversion, by what are taken to be characteristic responses to the questions. These various traits are assumed to be stable features of personality, and together they make up the personality profile of the individual.

Trait theorists attempt to describe human personality in terms of underlying dispositions. These dispositions are assumed to be not only stable but also universal. There is some disagreement among trait theorists about which particular underlying dispositions are universal, but the so-called Big Five traits are seen as best fitting this bill. These five are *extroversion/introversion* (the extent to which a person is sociable/reclusive, outspoken/silent, and so on), *neuroticism* (the extent to which a person is calm/anxious, composed/excitable, and so on), *agreeableness* (the degree to which a person is good-natured/irritable, gentle/rough, and so on), *conscientiousness* (the extent to which a person is responsible/irresponsible, careful/careless, and so on), and *openness to experience* (the extent to which a person is intellectual/unreflective, imaginative/simple, and so on). The trait theory approach is closely associated with structured tests, which are seen as identifying traits underlying behavior.

The main function of structured tests is to help categorize people, to determine the extent to which they are one type or another (neurotic, extroverted and so on). Thus questions on structured tests result in scores on traits and lead to the identification of "types" of personalities, such as Type A (people who are competitive, hard-driving, hostile, impatient) and Type B (easygoing, less hurried, less competitive, and more friendly than Type A). Toward this purpose, the questions, or "items," on structured tests are designed independent of content. If a question about stamp collecting, or doodling with a pencil, or eating habits, or anything else for that matter, differentiates between neurotics and non-neurotics, this question can be included with no regard for how its content relates to the topic of neuroticism. Thus, while the questions used in structured tests are specific, there is no limit to what they could be specific about.

Among the hundreds of structured tests available, the most widely used and well established are the Minnesota Multiphasic Personality Inventory (MMPI), developed particularly for use with abnormal populations, and the California Personality Inventory (CPI), used more often for assessing individuals whose personality falls in the normal range. These both have multiple subtests, and clinicians use the profiles of test-takers on the subtests to identify possible personality disorders. Profiles of test-takers are compared to the profiles of people who fall into different personality categories, such as depressive, extroverted, neurotic, and so on, so as to "place" the test-takers. If the profile of a test-taker maps onto the profile of typical depressives, for example, then the test-taker is labeled a depressive.

Projective tests are different from structured tests in several important ways. First, they use ambiguous questions or stimuli, and they require the test-taker to answer open-ended questions. For example, a picture of two ambiguous figures apparently arguing may be shown, with the test-taker asked to explain, "What led to this scene? What is happening now? What is going to happen next?" Test-takers are free to respond to such questions in any way they see fit. They could, for example, construct a story that includes the two figures shown but also involves numerous other persons in various roles in a plot. Second, projective tests get at meaning and focus on subjective interpretations.

Among projective tests, the most widely used are the Rorschach and the Thematic Apperception Test (TAT). The Rorschach involves presenting test-takers with inkblots and asking them to describe what they see. The idea that individuals have different interpretations of inkblots goes back at least to the nineteenth century, but the Rorschach attempts to use these interpretations as a means of revealing the inner characteristics of test-takers. Similarly, the TAT uses a series of picture cards showing characters in ambiguous situations to assess how test-takers project their inner selves when describing the scenes on the cards. Other projective tests, such as word-association tests (psychologist says a word, test-taker responds with first word that comes to mind) and sentence-completion tests (test-taker is asked to complete sentences with beginnings such as, "What I fear most is . . .""I wish my life was . . ."), also aim to reveal the hidden dispositions of the test-taker.

Thus both structured tests and projective tests attempt to identify key dispositions underlying personality. Trait theorists using structured tests propose that they have uncovered universal traits, the Big Five, and that these are inborn. The implication is that central features of personality are fairly fixed from birth. However, while I accept that *the disposition to have dispositions is universal,* the particular dispositions one develops are to a large degree a result of interactions with the social and physical environment. The so-called Big Five have emerged through research with respondents from either Western societies or Westernized sections of other societies, typically students in modern universities modeled on Western universities.

University students in Turkey or India or other non-Western countries are in many ways more similar to students in Western countries than they are to the vast majority of the population in the traditional sector of their own societies. Modern universities throughout most of the world teach students basically the same things and train them to take standardized tests in the same way. To find these students answering in similar ways to standardized tests in the university context is not surprising. Indeed, this finding supports the idea that the same dispositions can be nurtured in people living in many different societies and that what is shared by all is a disposition to have dispositions.

The Exclusive Focus on Stability

An implication of treating personality as performance capacity is the focus on stability in behavior. A wide variety of different schools of thought assume that a large number of human characteristics are shaped early in life and remain stable throughout the life span. Thus, in both theoretical and applied research, a central feature of personality psychology is the almost exclusive focus on stability. Freud, perhaps the most influential psychologist of all time, must bear a major part of the responsibility for this biased focus.

The idea that early experience marks us for life and shapes our adult personalities is shared by various schools but was popularized most widely by Freud. The newborn infant behaves according to the pleasure principle, demanding instant gratification. "Feed me, clean me, hug me, NOW!" the baby seems to be demanding as it cries and cries (many new parents have covered their ears and said silent, desperate prayers at this stage). As infants grow, caretakers place more and more restrictions on them and try to teach them correct behavior, in areas such as potty training, table manners, conversation with elders, and so on. At first the child displays correct behavior because of the direct presence of caretakers. But after a while, the normative system of society has been thoroughly learned. In other words, a conscience develops, like a little police force inside each of us. The 5-year old will now say to herself, "I'd better not take the cookie; it would be wrong," and behave correctly a lot of the time even though nobody is there to enforce rules.

The internalization of norms, rules, and other aspects of the moral order comes at a cost. Most societal rules and norms go against basic instincts, particularly in the realm of sensuality and things related to the human body. I recently witnessed a bunch of toddlers arrive at a wading pool, led by three adult supervisors. One of the little girls impulsively took her swimming suit off and splashed into the water. The immediate reaction of the nearest adult supervisor was to say, "Shame on you! Girls don't swim with nothing on!" The little girl did not yet seem to have a clue as to what shame is, but within a few years she will learn which circumstances she is supposed to feel shame according to societal norms. Similarly, the little boy who is punished by his father for playing with his penis and told not to repeat this "dirty act" begins to internalize societal ideas about shame and guilt, although as a 5-year old he had not, until now, felt he was doing anything "dirty" when he touched his penis.

Becoming a human being, then, requires the subjugation of egocentric desires and wishes in order to participate as a citizen in a larger community. Freud was highlighting a theme already developed by Thomas Hobbes (1588–1679), among others, over the last 2,000 years. Hobbes lived through a particularly turbulent era in English history, when civil war raged and Roundheads and Cavaliers fought each other up and down the land. His rather negative view of human nature was no doubt influenced by the chaos and destruction he witnessed, which he saw as the result of the breakdown of central authority. He came to believe that the natural inclination of humans is to act selfishly, steal, cheat, rape, kill, subdue, and, in short, satisfy their own desires in every way if left unchecked by authority. Hobbes would interpret events in Bosnia and other parts of Eastern Europe—indeed, throughout much of the world—in the 1990s as evidence that his negative views on the natural inclinations of humans were justified.

For Hobbes, the conflict between the needs of individuals and communities had been resolved historically through a social contract, whereby individuals submitted to be ruled by a central authority and to accept limitations on their freedom in exchange for the protection of their lives and property. Modern social contract theorists, such as John Rawls and Robert Nozick, have worked out a variety of schemes by which different compromises are reached between the inclinations of individuals and the requirements of authorities. But for Freud the social contract is negotiated, often painfully and with much damage to individuals, by each person in the course of growing up. Every one of us experiences a tug-of-war, with our basic pleasure-seeking instincts pulling on one side and societal norms and rules on the other. This experience scars us for life. One should notice the negative emphasis in Freudian thought. The great Russian psychologist Lev Vygotsky would have said that this prepares us for life.

Thus, to find the roots of psychopathology, Freud looked back to the past, particularly to childhood experiences. Following the same Western tradition, modern researchers are positing a variety of factors as causal predictors of future personality. Prominent among these are thinkers who believe that genes shape personality development. Of course farmers have known for thousands of years that, through selective breeding, they could have some control over the characteristics of horses, cows, dogs, and other domesticated animals. The basics of genetic inheritance was worked out by Gregor Mendel (1822–1884), an Austrian monk. Whereas Mendel researched the peas in his monastery garden with the most elementary resources, modern genetic researchers have attracted enormous resources and are in the spotlight. Research in genetics is seen by some as a potentially effective way to tackle mental and physical illness in the long term. If we can identify the genes that make people more prone to heart disease, diabetes, alcoholism, aggression, and so on, then we have the option of dealing with these problems through genetic manipulation (which seems, by the way, to be a new and scientifically respectable synonym for the discredited eugenics movement, the deliberate planning of human breeding). If the sex, height, eye and hair color, and other characteristics of babies can be determined through genetic manipulation, why not shyness, adventurousness, and so on?

Temperament

> Steve was like that even as a little baby. He would get into everything. If there was trouble to be found, he would find it and get into it before you had time to turn around. But Mike was always different. He was always the more careful one. As a kid he never went where he was not supposed to, and as an adult he has always been cautious. Even when he was a student in college he never did anything risky, whereas "risk" is Steve's middle name.
>
> —AMERICAN MOTHER TALKING ABOUT
> HER TWO ADULT SONS

The treatment of personality as performance capacity fits well with assumptions about inherited characteristics. The idea that people are born with certain temperaments, characteristic and consistent ways of behaving, has been with us for at least the last 2,500 years. An early belief was that an individual's temperament would depend on the balance between the four humors—hot, cold, wet, and dry. An excess of one or several of these humors would tilt temperament in a particular direction.

In modern times, the notion that some personality characteristics may be inborn is interpreted by some through evolutionary theory. From the point of view of evolutionary theory, it makes sense that people would be born with a variety of personality characteristics, such as neuroticism and extroversion, because variation within populations is advantageous. Variation allows a population to achieve an evolutionary stable strategy, so that through a mix of personality characteristics best suited for environmental conditions, survival chances are maximized. Environmental conditions are continuously changing, and some personality characteristics are better suited than others for coping with particular environmental conditions. If environmental conditions call for risk-taking behavior, it is a handicap for a population to have fewer risk-takers. However, if environmental conditions favor cautious individuals, it is disadvantageous for a population to have fewer cautious people. These considerations have led to attempts to develop an evolutionary justification for a proposed genetic basis for temperament.

But there are also opponents of the view that temperament, transmitted via genes, shapes adult personality. The behaviorists, such as B. F. Skinner, argue that different people behave differently in the same situation because they have experienced different reinforcement histories. Steve was positively reinforced for taking risks in the past, but Mike was positively reinforced for cautious behavior. They are brothers and were brought up in the same home, but environmental conditions differed dramatically: Steve was the firstborn, Mike was the third and youngest child. Steve was shaped at the hands of parents and other family members, friends, teachers, and so on to become a risk taker; Mike was shaped to become cautious. They grew up in very different environmental niches.

Attempts to study hereditary and environmental influences on personality—and human behavior generally—and to identify the contributions of each one in isolation from the other are misguided and lead to misrepresentations of both. We need to reconceptualize hereditary and environmental factors in such a way that they become an integrated part of understanding behavior. One point of departure for this integration is the recognition that the activities of every individual are embedded in social networks. Another is that the individual's participation in these activities plays a central part in all aspects of development, including personality development.

"Personality" is not something fixed inside individuals, to be "triggered" by environmental factors at particular "stages" in individual growth. Personality is not a "potential" that the environment brings to realization. Rather, the participation of individuals in different activities is associated with particular styles of doing and thinking.

Activities themselves are sustained over time through various carriers. For example, war memorials, such as the Vietnam War Memorial in Washington, DC., serve as carriers, sustaining patriotism, promulgating respect for the military, giving honor to those who fought and died in wars, and so on. When individuals come to the Vietnam War Memorial, the kind of behavior they engage in is fairly standard: They tend to stand in silence or speak in hushed tones, pray, hold hands, touch names engraved on the wall, take off their hats, place flowers, and so on. Such behavior is not a "part of their personalities" that is triggered by the environment; rather, it is part of a web of activities in which they participate. In this sense, personalities are inherently cultural.

Participation in activities leads to the internalization and appropriation of ideas, values, and styles of thinking. Through participation and appropriation, individuals become integrated into societies. Thus it is the activities of the individual in the social world that give rise to what traditionally has been called "personality."

Dilemmas Arising out of Treating Personality as Performance Capacity

The treatment of personality as performance capacity has given rise to a focus on stability and heritability in behavior, particularly on the part of researchers who adhere to a traditional positivist view of science. Major dilemmas have arisen, however, and the entire field of personality studies is mired in what seem to be unresolvable questions.

Is Personality Stability Good or Bad, Illusory or Real?

A central dilemma concerns the topic of personality stability. On the one hand, humanistic psychologists, such as Carl Rogers and Abraham Maslow, have proposed that individuals should strive to achieve personality growth; that is, to develop their talents as fully as possible and to become better people in every way they can. Humanistic psychologists have highlighted potential change and movement toward what Maslow refers to as *self-actualization*, the realization of one's maximum potential. On the other hand, a wide variety of major personality theorists, from Freud and other psychodynamic thinkers to Eysenck and other trait theorists, have underlined stability in personality.

Personality stability is not only assumed to exist but is also thought to be a good thing. From one perspective, to describe people as "unstable," "changeable," or "shifting" in behavior is to insinuate negative characteristics about them; it is to suggest that they are unreliable and perhaps even unprincipled. Alternatively, to describe people as "stable," "consistent," and "remaining the same" is to suggest positive characteristics; it is to imply that they are reliable and can be counted on.

In the psychological literature, the tendency has been to view personality stability as normal and change as unusual. Indeed, psychologists with perspectives as different as those of Freud and Skinner have argued that personality is shaped early in development and tends to remain stable throughout life. This tradition is continued in modern research on temperament as well as on a variety of other topics central to personality and social psychology, such as attitudes, which are evaluations of the world, including oneself, with some degree of favor or disfavor.

Research on attitudes is a good example of how the consistency assumption has guided thinking among scholars. At least since the early field studies of Robert LaPiere in the 1930s, and the attempts by L. L. Thurstone to develop better scales for attitude measurement around the same period, researchers have tried to find ways of predicting future behavior from reported attitudes. It has been assumed that there is attitude–behavior consistency and that the main challenge for researchers is to develop accurate measures to capture this consistency. If Jane expresses negative attitudes toward ethnic minorities, then her behavior will be negative toward members of those groups when she interacts with them in the future. In other words, what people say will predict what people actually do.

This assumption is highly influenced by Western conceptions of what a human being should be like. One can almost see John Wayne or Clint Eastwood shaking hands and expressing a view, and then being honor-bound to keep his word. We know that bad guys don't keep their word and get called out on it. In non-Western societies, there are instances when the role of host demands that one be agreeable and not say "no" to a guest. But it is also understood that an "agreement" arising from such situations need not be kept when the guest leaves. Western negotiators, such as (the first) President Bush and his negotiating teams in the early 1990s, have often been surprised and pleased that their hosts in Japan, for example, agree to a lot of their terms. But they have become angry when they find the other side not sticking to its word after the host/guest relationship is ended and they are all back in their respective countries.

But some critics, such as Walter Mischel, have argued that even in the West consistency of behavior across situations is an illusion. The consistency that we see arises in part because the observer is the same person each time and elicits the same type of response from the other person. Also, when we see the same individuals in different contexts, we expect there to be continuity in their behavior (after all, physically they look the same) and therefore perceive their behavior as consistent. In other words, we find what we expect to find in their behavior.

In actuality, behavior is shaped by the contexts in which individuals live out their lives and the socially enmeshed activities in which they engage, not by attitudes or other processes assumed to take place inside individual minds. A prime example of this is the relationship between what politicians say when they are running for office and what they actually do when they get into office. Again and again, we find that expressed attitudes fail to predict behavior, and voters become cynical because of what looks like broken promises.

Since the 1960s, when this line of attack was opened up against the idea of personality consistency, defenders of the "stability" position have regrouped and counterattacked to try to show that there actually *is* consistency. Unfortunately, this debate has been reduced to methodological issues. In looking for the trees, we have lost sight of the forest. The search for cross-situational constancy in behavior has led people to use larger and larger numbers of narrow behavioral indexes, while keeping the indexes as specific as possible. The thinking has been: If a large enough number of the "right kinds" of behavioral measures are taken, then a higher level of cross-situational behavioral consistency can be shown. But the question becomes: "How many measures and of what kinds?"

What Is Normal—To Change or to Stay the Same?

Received wisdom tells us that structured tests are scientifically better than projective tests. A major reason for this is that structured tests have higher reliability, meaning that they are more likely to yield a similar result when a person is tested more than once. Projective tests are faulted because of low reliability; that is, the test-taker is more likely to be rated differently when tested repeatedly on a projective test. The assumption, of course, is that personality is stable and that people do think and behave consistently over time. But another possibility is that the normal state of affairs is for people to shift their attitudes and behavior—not only over years, but also over months, and weeks, and even days, hours, and minutes.

This suggests that the stability identified by structured tests such as the MMPI and the CPI may well be illusory, in that the very restrictive closed-ended questions posed by these tests are not sensitive enough to catch shifts in attitudes and behaviors. Structured tests call forth the same responses from people, responses that might not be forthcoming in different circumstances. They allow less room for the test-takers to show a range of responses; they simply leave room for yes/no–type responses to set questions. The open-ended questions posed by the projective tests allow the test-takers more room to creatively reveal their inner selves changing over time.

The issue of the range of attitudes measured by different personality tests is reminiscent of earlier debates in the history of psychology about restrictions placed by psychological tests on the behaviors of test-takers, both animal and human. For example, for much of the first half of the twentieth century behaviorism was the dominant school of academic psychology. In their typical learning experiments, behaviorists placed animals in cages (e.g., Thorndike's puzzle box, the Skinner box, and so on) in which they could either press or not press a lever in response to reinforcement. Such procedures were severely criticized by Gestalt psychologists, who placed animals in situations in which they could behave in many different ways and show insight in solving problems. In Gestalt research, chimpanzees climbed on furniture and put sticks together to reach bananas hanging out of their immediate reach, thus demonstrating novel problem-solving strategies. The greater range of behaviors allowed by Gestalt experiments meant that there was less likelihood of a particular behavior being exactly repeated, and thus on the surface it might appear that "reliability" in the strict sense was lower.

Although structured and projective personality tests are different in major ways, they do, however, share a fundamental similarity: They both treat personality as performance capacity and search for causes to explain performances. In both cases, the causes of behavior are measured as capacities, although they differ as to the nature of the causes. Structured tests assume traits to be causal determinants. Projective tests are more influenced by psychodynamic traditions and look for causes in the past life experiences of the respondent. It is assumed that often such past experiences can only be discovered through therapy that digs into the unconscious, where the real causes of behavior are assumed to be buried.

Concluding Comment

Personality has become an important carrier, particularly through the influence of the "science of personality" as it is traditionally taught and researched in universities. Received wisdom in academia and the mass media treats personality as performance capacity; behavior is seen to be explained by factors, typically traits, that are assumed to be fixed and in large part inherited. This fits in with and strengthens reductionism and also helps to maintain the status quo: If individual traits are responsible for behavior generally and for performances and outcomes particularly, then there is no need to seek large-scale changes or reforms. The fate of individuals is determined by factors within themselves. But dilemmas arise, because at the same time the meritocratic ideology, particularly as propagated in the United States, requires us to assume that individuals can change themselves—and thus their personalities.

Indeed, modern American heroes typically represent vivid demonstrations of the power of human agency, the ability of individuals to act on the world and change people, including themselves. Americans reserve special admiration for persons who take command and bring about changes, such that one could say their personality has changed. As I write these words, I am very conscious of a classic example of such "personality change" in the case of George W. Bush, the forty-third U.S. president. Bush's appeal is in part his "born-again" nature: Having been a "hell raiser" as a young man, he changed himself and now claims Jesus to be the most important figure in his life. Such wondrous transformations come about through individuals moving from one context to another, participating in different activities, and through this appropriating new personalities. They literally change themselves through transforming the social world in which they participate.

Suggested Readings

Anastasi, A., & Urbina, S. (1997). *Psychological testing* (7th ed.). Upper Saddle River, NJ: Prentice-Hall.

Baldwin, W. (2001, June 11). Side lines. *Forbes*, p. 22.

Baxter, N. (Ed.). (1994). *Cinderella*. In *My treasury of stories and rhymes* (pp. 74–77). New York: Barnes & Noble.

Benson, C. (2001). *The cultural psychology of self: Place, morality and art in human worlds.* London: Routledge.

Church, A. T., & Lonner, W. J. (Eds.). (1998). Personality and its measurment in cross-cultural perspective. *Jounal of Cross-Cultural Psychology, 29*, (1), 5–270.

Giddens, A. (1991). *Modernity and self-identity: Self and society in the late modern age.* Stanford, CA: Stanford University Press.

Heatherton, T. F., & Weinberger, J. L. (Eds.). (1994). *Can personality change?* Washington, DC: American Psychological Association.

Kagan, J., & Snidemand, N. (1991). Temperamental factors in human development. *American Psychologist, 46*, 856–862.

Lamiell, J. T., & Weigert, S. C. (1996). One step forward, two steps back. *Psychological Inquiry, 7*, 335–339.

Leontev, A. N. (1978). Activity, consciousness and personality. Englewood Cliffs, NJ: Prentice-Hall.

Lessnoff, M. (Ed.). (1990). *Social contract theory.* New York: New York University Press.

McAdams, D. P. (1996). Personality, modernity, and the storied self: A contemporary framework for studying persons. *Psychological Inquiry, 7*, 295–321.

McCrae, R. R., & Costa, P. T., Jr. (1997). Personality trait structure as a human universal. *American Psychologist, 52*, 509–516.

Mischel, W. (1990). Personality dispositions revisited and revised: A view after three decades. In L. Pervin (Ed.), *Handbook of personality: Theory and Research* (pp. 111–134). New York: Guilford.

Sloan, T. (1997). Theories of personality, ideology, and beyond. In D. Fox & I. Prilleltensky (Eds.), *Critical psychology: An introduction* (pp. 87–103). London: Sage.

Vygotsky, L. S. (1978). *Collected works of Vygotsky: Vol. 1. Problems of general psychology* (N. Minick, Trans.). New York: Plenum.

9 Intelligence and the Social Order

"And why did you come to America?" I asked the Irish mother of six children sitting in front of me. We were fellow passengers on a train from Washington, D.C., to Boston. Her children were not with us, but I felt I knew them all because she had told me dozens of very funny stories about the six of them, talking almost nonstop since we had left Washington five hours earlier.

"Why did I come to America? Oh, that was a long time ago, dear," she responded. "I came to America back in 1958."

"And was it to be with relatives?"

"Not exactly. It had more to do with Tommy, my firstborn." She sighed, then went on, "You see, in those days I was living in Kilburn, a neighborhood in London, and my Tommy failed the eleven-plus."

"A test?"

"A test the schools gave 11-year-old kids in England to decide what they were going to do," she stopped in midsentence and heaved out the next phrase very slowly, "for the rest of their lives. Can you imagine that? Tommy did not do well on the eleven-plus, and the teachers assumed he was stupid and not at all fit for university."

"I think I remember reading something about that test. Wasn't it based on the ideas of a psychologist named Sir Cyril Burt? He thought people get to their peak intelligence by the age of 11."

"Well, I don't know who he was or what exactly was on his mind when he came up with that idea, but I know he was dead wrong!" She declared, giving emphasis with a little stamp of her feet. "And that's why I came to America. At least over here they don't think life stops at 11. You know, Tommy got into university over here," she added triumphantly.

"Well done for him."

"Yes, and after he finished his engineering degree, he got a wonderful job and is now senior manager. But if we had stayed in London, Tommy would be cleaning office floors or maybe working in a bar, or something like that, all because he failed a test when he was 11. Why would anybody in their right mind think that intelligence stands still at 11, or 16, or 21, or even 70? I'll be 70 soon, and who says I may not be more intelligent tomorrow than I am today?"

"You have a good point there," I agreed.

I returned home with a strong curiosity to learn more about what the Irish mother had told me, so I researched the topic and discovered that there continues to be a fierce struggle between supporters and opponents of the eleven-plus examination in Great Britain (just look up "eleven plus, UK" on the Internet, and you can enter the debate). Opponents point out that success on the eleven-plus is highly correlated with income; for instance, relatively few children needing free lunches pass the exam and gain entrance to the better schools. In line with this trend, social class is also a fairly accurate predictor of entrance to elite universities in England. Of course, Americans are familiar with this controversy, because in the United States there is a strong correlation between income and the type of college students enter. For instance, community colleges are predominantly filled with students from lower-income families and Ivy League colleges are predominantly filled with students from higher-income families. To some, this suggests that tests such as the eleven-plus are measuring the quality of the environment in which children grow up. But supporters of the eleven-plus and similar tests claim that something else is being measured: intelligence independent of context.

Intelligence as a Carrier

Intelligence plays a very powerful role as a carrier, a role that is becoming more important globally as Western intelligence tests and related knowledge are exported to non-Western societies. Just as in the case of personality, this carrier role is closely tied to the treatment of intelligence as performance capacity and the assumption that behavior, specifically intelligence, is basically fixed and inherited.

Intelligence as a carrier helps to shape our understanding of ourselves, how we fit into society, and how fairly or unfairly we think we are being treated. If Jack is poor and holding down a job with very few opportunities for improving his situation, and if at the same time Jack believes that his situation is a result of low inherited intelligence, he is likely to accept that he "naturally" should have fewer resources and lower status. He "deserves" his lower position because he was born with lower intelligence. There is nothing he can do to change this situation. Senior managers in his company were born with higher intelligence, and they "naturally" enjoy greater resources and status. This is only fair. Thus a view of intelligence as inherently fixed and of society as being stratified on the basis of ability, so that those of lower intelligence remain at the lower levels and those of higher intelligence maintain their places at the top levels, is more likely to lead individuals to accept the status quo.

In contrast, a perception that scores on intelligence tests are fundamentally determined by educational and general environmental conditions is more likely to lead the economically disadvantaged to seek to change the status quo. Such a view leads to the children of the economically disadvantaged being seen as condemned by environmental conditions, from quality of formal education to informal networking opportunities, rather than by inherited characteristics. Environmental conditions are unstable and external to the individual, and they can be reformed through political commitment and the application of sufficient economic resources.

Societal Inequalities and "Fixed" Intelligence

The conceptualization of intelligence as fixed and inherited has helped to justify the status quo in society. Inequalities in power, status, and resources generally have been explained by referring to assumed differences in inherited intelligence: More intelligent people have more intelligent children, and because they are more intelligent, they rise to the top status levels in society.

Proponents of this view have often tried to tie such explanations to Charles Darwin's scientific elaboration of the theory of evolution. Darwin pointed out that all organisms reproduce in excess of the numbers that can actually survive. If all the eggs spawned by fish survived, oceanic waters would quickly be displaced by fish. In practice, only a few of the thousands of spawned eggs reach maturity, becoming fish that reproduce. To explain how some organisms survive and others do not, Darwin pointed to variation within species. The ways in which individuals vary from one another prove advantageous, or disadvantageous, or irrelevant to survival under given ecological conditions. Individuals who have the advantageous characteristics survive and pass on their characteristics to their offspring, and those offspring who are more advantaged will compete more successfully. Thus inherited characteristics lead some individuals to perform better than others.

In the nineteenth century, Herbert Spencer and other social Darwinists argued that societal inequalities are a reflection of natural selection. Those who inherit better characteristics rise to the top of society and have offspring who share their superior characteristics. Much more recently, basically the same assumption is made by Richard Herrnstein and Charles Murray in their much-publicized book *The Bell Curve*. They argue that as we become a meritocratic society, social class will be determined by intelligence quotient (IQ). Given that IQ is basically inherited, the result will be a stable stratification, with low-IQ individuals permanently staying at the lower-class positions. Add to this the claim that there are cross-race differences in intelligence, and we have a pessimistic picture: Some races will be overrepresented in the lower strata of society. Starting from the idea that IQ is fixed and inherited, these researchers reach the conclusion that a meritocratic society will inevitably result in a stratification with fixed membership: the poor begetting offspring who remain poor and the rich begetting offspring who maintain their elite position, with certain races disproportionately remaining poor.

An interesting consequence of this thesis is that class inequalities are now justified on the basis of IQ. It is not John's fault if he is a billionaire and the owner of the company in which Jack works for the minimum wage; it just so happens that John was born with a high IQ and Jack must have been born with low IQ.

A major shortcoming of the social Darwinist thesis is that society is not open and meritocratic, and it is far too simplistic to assume that where a person stands in the social hierarchy depends on IQ. Clearly, IQ is only one of many factors that determine the social class of a person; other, and far more important, factors include the social class of one's parents and the lifestyle that goes with it.

Promising New Views of Intelligence

Since the 1970s there have been serious efforts by Howard Gardner, Robert Sternberg, and others to broaden the conceptualization of intelligence. Traditional concepts of intelligence have been described by some critics as too narrow and too similar to the paper-and-pencil tests given in schools. We all know of people who were not particularly successful in school examinations, never managed to get high grades, yet did very well in meeting the practical challenges of the real world. We also know that being brilliant in school does not guarantee success in the outside world, in social relationships, in leadership, in teamwork, or in everyday practical matters.

To overcome some of the limitations of traditional measures of intelligence, researchers are focusing on contextual abilities, such as *emotional intelligence*, the ability to effectively express and regulate one's own emotions and interpret the emotions of others; *practical intelligence*, problem-solving commonsense strategies that are not formally taught but are based on tacit knowledge; and *Machiavellian intelligence*, strategies of manipulating others for personal gain, even at times against the other's self-interest. Rather than treat intelligence as unitary, researchers are also exploring typologies. For example, Howard Gardner's idea of *multiple intelligences* includes linguistic, logical-mathematical, spatial, musical, bodily-kinesthetic, and personal (both interpersonal and intrapersonal) intelligences. These developments could gradually pave a path away from a static conception of intelligence to one that is more contextual and characterized by change. In practice, however, we are a long way away from this realization.

The idea that intelligence is something fixed, something set either at or near birth, plays too central a role in the maintenance of the status quo to be abandoned so easily. Intelligence as a carrier helps to explain and justify the position of individuals in the social hierarchy and the unequal distribution of resources to individuals and groups.

Theories of Intelligence

Intelligence as Something "Fixed"

Since that meeting with the Irish mother of six children some years ago, I have had many occasions to ponder her questions and to critically think through the ways in which traditional psychology has tackled the issue of intelligence. The Irish mother clearly believed that intelligence can be different across contexts and can change over the life span. This idea does not correspond closely to traditional views.

Traditional psychology has distinguished between "fixed" and "changing" aspects of intelligence, and then focused on the assumed fixed aspects. This distinction is reflected in the terms *fluid intelligence*, referring to basic mental abilities concerned with the perceiving relationships, organizing and remembering information, drawing logical conclusions, and problem solving, and *crystallized intelligence*, intellectual performance heavily influenced by education, social experience, and cultural practices. Fluid intelligence is generally assumed to be causally determined by inborn characteristics, while crystallized intelligence is generally assumed to be constructed through environmental factors. Traditional psychology has tried to measure fluid intelligence in isolation, because this is seen to be the universal component that distinguishes between less intelligent and more intelligent people irrespective of their cultural experiences.

The Wechsler and the Stanford-Binet continue to be the most widely used tests of intelligence. These tests are *structured*, that is, they ask specific questions and require specific answers; *convergent*, that is, only one answer is accepted as correct, as opposed to a divergent test, which measures creative thinking and gives credits for different answers; and *static*, that is, they involve presentation of test items that are answered by the examinee without feedback. The Wechsler and the Stanford-Binet are supposed to measure general intelligence independent of educational and cultural experience. Interestingly, however, they are very similar in important ways to the most widely used college ability tests, the SAT and the American College Test (ACT), which are supposed to tap educational experiences.

Thus traditional psychology has tried to develop decontexualized measures of intelligence, on the assumption that performance on intelligence tests is independent of past experience and present circumstances. Traditional psychology has acted as if it were possible to measure the intelligence of people independent of their past education—such as whether they attended a well-funded private school or a dilapidated inner-city school or did not attend a school at all—and independent of whether they presently live in a ghetto where there are no suitable libraries and computer facilities or whether they live in a mansion that has in it superb libraries and computer facilities and hired instructors to give training on how to take intelligence tests. According to traditional psychology, intelligence can be measured independent of whether children are brought up in an emotionally and materially rich family environment with their own mother and father or simply survive in a string of inappropriate foster homes, never even knowing the identity of their father. Intelligence is assumed to be something that exists outside of all such experiences.

The notion of intelligence as fixed, as something specific that can be measured precisely and will remain the same, allowing it to be measured again and again, is associated with the idea that each person has one "true" intelligence score. Any deviation from the "true" score is seen as measurement error. If George is tested on his thirtieth birthday and gets an IQ score of 110, and is then tested again on his thirty-first birthday and gets a score of 125, it is assumed that the discrepancy arises from measurement error, not from a real change in George's intelligence. Each measure taken is expected to deviate from the true score by some margin of error. If the test is given enough times, then the average of test scores will aggregate toward the "true score."

Associated with the idea of intelligence being fixed is the notion that intelligence "peaks" at an early age and that the main challenge for researchers is to ascertain the age at which this occurs. Some have thought it peaks at age 7 or even earlier, some at age 11, and others in the teenage years. Once the peak is reached, it is assumed, intelligence becomes fixed and that is an end to that.

Searching for the "Hidden Hand"

Throughout the history of intelligence testing, traditional researchers have tried to find a "hidden hand" that they imagine exists above and beyond experience, is universal, and can be captured by a single number, a unitary indicator of intelligence, such as IQ or *g,* standing for "general intelligence." Since the cognitive revolution that began in the 1950s, the search for a hidden hand has tended to lead to investigation of so-called cognitive mechanisms or mental processes.

Initially, those in the cognitive camp basically ignored cultural experiences and focused on developing decontextualized tests. Over the last few decades, supporters of decontextualized intelligence tests have developed more sophisticated arguments. They now accept that there is a role for culture and context, but only a peripheral one. They argue that "mental processes" are universal but that their instantiations in contexts are not. The same yardstick can be used to measure "cognitive mechanisms" used by everyone, although the practical problems tackled by people will differ depending on their cultures.

Imagine the cases of Sanchez and Harry, both with a "true" IQ of 135. The same universal cognitive processes will be behind their intelligent behavior, but the ways in which their intelligence is manifested will be different depending on local cultural conditions. Sanchez lives in a rough neighborhood in Los Angeles, and his intelligence will be shown in the ways in which he copes with living in a poverty-stricken, drug-infested neighborhood with high crime rates. Harry lives in an affluent suburb of Los Angeles and faces a different set of challenges, but the success he has in problem solving is assumed to depend on the same "mental processes" that determine success for Sanchez.

Thus terms such as *mental processes* and *cognitive mechanisms* are used to describe invisible universal "causes" assumed to lie behind the problem-solving activities of people. They are supposed to act like a hidden hand common to all human beings, never directly viewed but ever-present and discernible through the skills people show in solving problems. This hidden hand is the cause behind problem solving, the reason some people succeed and get high intelligence scores and others fail and get low scores.

Physiological Measures

For those determined to demonstrate the hereditary basis of intelligence, the most direct route would be to show that intelligence is linked to physical differences between people. Just as some people are taller or slimmer or faster than others, some are more intelligent. Francis Galton, a distant cousin of Charles Darwin, was one of the first to march down this path. Galton, like Darwin, was a prototypical English gentleman-scholar, meaning he did not have to work for a living and could pursue his scholarly interests. Galton is often described in texts as a child prodigy and a genius with an estimated IQ of close to 200, but he did not do well at university. His creative genius revealed itself only after he left formal schooling, when he had the opportunity to pursue his own diverse interests. One of these interests was the theory of evolution—and with it, the obsession to demonstrate that intelligence is inherited.

Galton's research on intelligence is a combination of silly and sublime ideas. Among his sublime ideas, one that still influences modern research, is that a very effective way to get at the relative contributions of heredity and environment is to study twins. But, alas, silly ideas also came to him. Starting with a Lockian notion that all knowledge comes to us through the senses, Galton concluded that individuals with sharper senses must be more intelligent. Following this logic, he proceeded to measure intelligence through tests of reaction time, auditory and visual perception, and the like. Fortunately, by the end of the nineteenth century the idea that sensory ability reflects intelligence had fallen from grace, for the excellent reason that it was contradicted by research evidence. However, the idea of finding a causal link between behavioral/physiological measures and intelligence is too appealing to be discarded by those adamant to prove that intelligence is heredity-based—just as criminologists, starting with Cesare Lombroso in the nineteenth century, have not been able to avoid the temptation of trying to prove that criminals are physiologically different from law-abiding citizens. Thus Arthur Jensen is among those who have taken up the challenge in recent times, trying once again to show that reaction time and the like correlate with intelligence. Although these modern hereditarians use more sophisticated techniques, such as ways of measuring the time an injection of glucose takes to reach and be absorbed by the brain and the electrical response of the cerebral cortex to visual and auditory stimuli, their basic assumption is the same as Galton's and just as naive.

These behavioral/physiological approaches often have popular appeal and get a lot of attention from the media. When a group of researchers reported that a "crucial" region of Albert Einstein's brain, in the parietal lobes, was different from that of a comparison group of people with normal intelligence, journalists jumped up and took notice. A *New York Times* headline declared: SO, IS THIS WHY EINSTEIN WAS SO BRILLIANT? Since the turn of the twentieth century, researchers have tried to find anatomical correlates of intelligence, and their efforts have often involved detailed case studies of geniuses. But there has been a fundamental flaw in this research strategy: What about the thousands of other individuals who are similar to Einstein in this "parietal lobe abnormality," and similar to other geniuses in their anatomical abnormalities, yet have failed to produce the equivalent of the theory of relativity? A more complete research design would also compare geniuses with normal people who share their anatomical abnormalities, and then try to find out why the geniuses proved exceptionally creative and the normal group did not.

What the article on Einstein's brain and others like it reveal is a confusion about causation: Just because Einstein had a brain that was physiologically different from many other people's does not show this difference to be the cause of his creativity. The tendency for both professionals and laypersons to want to find causes for creativity and other behaviors leads to such incorrect assumptions being made.

"IQ Gene"—Another Modern Myth

Well, it was bound to happen! In this era of media hype about a "genetic revolution," it was only a matter of time before claims would be made about the discovery of an "IQ gene." For example, an experiment by Princeton University molecular biologist Joe Z. Tsien and his colleagues has fueled publicity about an "IQ gene" and brought to the surface many generally held assumptions about the causal role of genes in determining individual intelligence. It is useful to consider this study by Tsien and his colleagues, because it is probably the first of many of its kind that will be conducted in the next few decades.

Tsien and his colleagues experimented on mice by adding a gene during the zygote stage of development (these manipulated mice are referred to as *transgenic*). The outcome of this manipulation was an increase in the protein subunit NR2B, which is part of a complex of proteins that form the NMDA receptor. This receptor is situated on the surface of brain neurons and, when triggered, leads to a chain of biochemical changes associated with improved memory.

The transgenic mice, once adults, outperformed a normal comparison group of mice on a number of learning tasks, such as remembering the location of a previously encountered object, moving through a water maze, and working out that a negative feature of the environment was no longer present. The transgenic mice also had about twice as much of the NR2B protein in the cerebral cortex and hippocampus, brain regions crucial to learning. The NR2B protein is more plentiful in key brain regions of young mice but decreases after sexual maturity. This has led to some speculation that by increasing the amount of the NR2B protein in adults, mature animals will gain the kind of plasticity and learning ability enjoyed by youngsters.

Pharmaceutical companies are already attempting to build on this kind of research to develop effective "memory pills," designed to enhance memory performance in human adults. Given the central role of memory in all aspects of human behavior, including performance on academic tests, we seem to be on the verge of enormous breakthroughs toward using genetics to make people "more intelligent." There has already been considerable debate on the ethics of bringing about such changes: Will it mean that rich people will be able to pay for their children to become smarter through genetic engineering? Will this research doom children from poor families to fall behind "genetically enhanced" kids from rich families with the ability to pay for such treatments? Countless such questions have been raised, again highlighting misunderstandings about the nature of intelligence. I want to correct three common misconceptions.

It is simply wrong to conceive of a gene "for" intelligence. No feature of human behavior or anatomy is determined by a single gene alone; the influence of any particular gene is manifested through complex interactions with other genes and countless environmental factors. A gene that influences memory could also influence other aspects of behavior, including personality characteristics and emotionality. On the other hand, intelligence is also not a single entity, but a social construction, with multitudes of different manifestations that can and often do vary across groups and cultures. Thus intelligence may be influenced by numerous genes that at the same time influence many other aspects of behavior; there is no gene "for" intelligence.

A second misunderstanding is that genetic manipulation will make it possible for intelligence to be boosted independent of environmental changes. The picture is conjured up of a person going into an operating room and coming out after the operation with "more intelligence." But a close reading of the study by Tsien and his colleagues discredits this idea, since the genetic manipulation they introduced simply allowed adult mice to be more *open to learning*, as youngsters *can be*. Neural openness is only a starting point: There also has to be an environment rich in learning opportunities.

A third misunderstanding concerns the assumption that genetic engineering would make the educational system more unfair, through the advantage it would give the rich. Implicit in this assertion are the assumptions that education is at present more or less a level playing field and that genetic factors will prove to be far more important than environmental factors in determining intelligence. This viewpoint is misguided and unfair to the poor, because *the rich already enjoy the greatest advantage available: access to superior educational environments, both at home and at school.* Critics, particularly Americans with strong beliefs in self-help and individual responsibility, point out that academic success is not determined by economic wealth. I agree that the term *determined* is not appropriate here, because a small number of children from lower-class families do succeed against the odds and gain entrance to the top colleges, but these are the exception rather than the rule. Nor will the situation be changed by giving the poor access to genetic-engineering breakthroughs. Even if sometime in the future government subsidies were provided to give lower-class children free "memory pills," as they get free lunches today, for the most part the relative intellectual poverty of their environments would still place them at a disadvantage. Being open to learning would not be enough; there would also have to be dramatic changes in their environments.

Rather than focusing on anatomical or biochemical bases of intelligence and seeking solutions in "memory pills," let us move toward a more dynamic view of intelligence.

Intelligence and Context

As an alternative to viewing intelligence as performance capacity—something fixed, inherited, and independent of context—we should view it as performance style, a way of doing things (solving problems) that is intimately related to context. First, let us put aside the idea of "mental processes," because they do not serve a useful purpose in this discussion. Intelligence is simply the problem-solving skills people show; there really is no need to conjure up a universal invisible hand behind problem-solving skills. Second, rather than being fixed, intelligence varies across contexts, depending on how well trained a person is for solving particular types of problems in particular contexts. Once we have accepted the idea that intelligence varies across contexts, then there is no need to assume there to be a hypothetical "true" fixed score.

The idea of a peak in intelligence is based, once again, on the assumption that context does not matter and that behavior is causally determined by fixed factors internal to the individual. The inborn factors that inevitably lead intelligence to peak at age X are assumed to operate automatically, independently of context. Where people grow up and what they experience—whether it is in the Kalahari Desert, or the Amazon jungle, or Paris, or New York, or any other part of the world, for that matter—would not influence the peaking of intelligence, either *when* it happens or *what level* it reaches. Like the "mental processes" that act independently, and invisibly, and operate at some hypothetical universal decontextualized level, the peak of intelligence is also supposed to be in that untouched and unreachable sphere. The factors that causally determine the characteristics of the peak are not influenced by mortal hands.

As an alternative, I suggest that in practice there is no fixed "peak age" for intelligence and that a peak reached by a person in context A will be different from peaks the same person could reach in contexts B, C, D, and Z. The very subtle ways in which contexts can influence test scores is shown by an interesting set of studies by Claude Steele involving mathematically bright young men and women taking tests in math. In one context, researchers purposely made salient the traditional stereotype of women being bad at math compared to men. The female test-takers did worse in this context compared to when they took the test without the traditional stereotype being made salient.

An assessment of intelligence as performance style, rather than capacity, makes comprehensible certain puzzles that have bedeviled scholars in this area. One of these is the issue of a possible decline in population IQ.

How Can We Stop the Decline? The Problem of Population IQ

Modern intelligence testing started with the French psychologist Alfred Binet (1857–1911), who was the first to try to measure intelligence as reflected in comprehension, reasoning, imagination, and other aspects of "higher mental abilities," rather than reaction time and other such behavioral/physiological measures. Soon after the introduction of Binet's pioneering intelligence test (1905), the First World War provided psychologists opportunities to expand intelligence testing enormously. The Army Alpha and the Army Beta were intelligence tests administered, respectively, to literate and illiterate soldiers in the U.S. army, totaling about 1.7 million test-takers. This massive testing exercise generated a huge body of raw data, which in turn provided fodder for political debate. The two key alarmist issues raised at that time are still with us today and reflect the fundamental impact of the role of intelligence as a carrier: (1) the idea that some races are more intelligent than others and (2) the idea that IQ for the population as a whole is declining.

In the 1920s, a number of influential politicians were eager to make use of "scientific" evidence "proving" that some groups of people, particularly those from Southern and Eastern Europe had inherently lower intelligence than Western and Northern Europeans. Such evidence could be used to support the view that immigration to the United States from some parts of the world should be severely restricted, because people from those parts had lower intelligence and their immigration to the United States would cause intelligence levels in the U.S. population to decline. There were also a number of psychologists—including Robert Yerkes, a president of the American Psychological Association—eager to provide "scientific" evidence to support this viewpoint. The result of this political fervor and "scientific" evidence was that the 1924 immigration laws reduced immigration quotas from the "weaker gene pools" of Southern and Eastern Europe.

In the rush to make political use of the results of the Army Alpha and the Army Beta, supporters of this policy of restricted immigration neglected all explanations except the idea that IQ differences reflect fixed inherited characteristics. They neglected, for example, the fact that analyses of Army Alpha and Beta results revealed that the longer immigrants remained in the United States, the higher their IQ scores became, in large part because their English proficiency improved over the years. They also ignored the fact that socioeconomic status accounted for the lower performance of some groups. For example, better-off blacks in the North scored higher than both poor blacks and whites in the South.

These kinds of more complex environmental factors are typically over-looked as a result of a powerful fear created by the idea that national IQ could be falling, with its implications for a decline in national economic and military strength. It seems that we are still unable to overcome this fear, as reflected by a resurgence of interest in "falling IQ" since the 1980s. When Richard Herrn-stein wrote an article about "IQ and Falling Birth Rates" in the *Atlantic Monthly* in 1989, the specter of national decline loomed again. Herrnstein argued that more intelligent women of all races were having fewer children, and so their "intelligent genes" were not being passed on to the next genera-tion. The result is scary: a decline in national IQ (not a new idea).

While the idea that national IQ is declining is scary, some proposed solu-tions to the problem are even scarier. According to some supporters of the hereditarian hypothesis, Head Start and other environmental programs fail to boost IQ because they do not get at the root genetic cause. One possible solu-tion is eugenics, the selective breeding of humans in order to improve the human stock. Francis Galton is seen as the pioneer of modern eugenics, but despite serious efforts to give eugenics a scientifically "objective" face, the movement is primarily associated with the Nazis and other racist groups. Clearly, in the democratic atmosphere of the twenty-first century, overt eugen-ics is not acceptable. On the one hand, then, environmental efforts to boost IQ have been attacked as a failure, and on the other hand, genetic solutions are dis-missed as draconian and unacceptable in democratic societies.

But a solution to the problem arises from very unexpected sources: A nonpsychologist saw a positive trend that psychologists had missed.

Surprise! IQ Has Been Increasing, Not Decreasing

Throughout the twentieth century there were a succession of scary predictions about falling IQ, predictions associated with eminent psychologists such as Henry Goddard and Robert Yerkes at the beginning of the century and Richard Herrnstein and Arthur Jensen at the end. Essential to these predictions have been the ideas that intelligence is inherited and fixed and that the United States is being overrun with people of lower intelligence, because the wrong kinds of people are being allowed to emigrate or because more intelligent women are having fewer children, among other reasons. With the birth rate in many Western European countries falling well below the replacement rate, and with rising numbers of ethnic-minority immigrants and refugees in these countries, the same specter of a fall in population IQ has been raised in Eng-land, France, Germany, and other European countries. Thus, while the scare-mongers depict intelligence in individual persons as fixed, they claim that the average intelligence in a population is variable and falling.

Indeed, if the assumptions made by the hereditarians are correct, then average intelligence can only fall under recent conditions. If intelligence is inherited, then we must rely on more intelligent individuals and races to have more children. But since more intelligent women have been having fewer children and proportionally fewer members of more intelligent races have been emigrating to the United States, then the average intelligence of the U.S. population has only one place to go—down. The only problem with this analysis is that average intelligence scores have been *going up, not down*. We owe this groundbreaking discovery not to a psychologist but to James Flynn, a political scientist of American origin working in New Zealand.

Flynn is one of the genuine heroes of modern social science research, being equipped with both humanitarian zeal and extraordinary sharpness of mind. In researching the IQ debate as part of his efforts to fight racist ideology, he discovered that the Stanford-Binet and Wechsler tests of intelligence, among others, have both old and revised versions and that in some instances both versions had been administered to the same group of test-takers. Comparing the scores that the same people had gotten on the old and the revised versions, Flynn noticed an astounding trend: Test-takers performed much better on the old tests. After more thorough analysis, Flynn reported in 1984 that Americans had gained about 14 IQ points in 46 years.

A simple explanation for this could be that the Stanford-Binet and other standard intelligence tests have a higher educational content than had previously been supposed and that, as the U.S. population becomes more educated, there is a corresponding increase in IQ scores. To check this possibility, Flynn scrutinized scores achieved by different people around the globe on an intelligence test that is supposed to be as culture- and education-free as possible, the Ravens Progressive Matrices. The Ravens requires test-takers to make judgments using patterns, rather than numbers or words. Flynn has found that in more than 20 countries, IQ as measured by the Ravens has been *increasing* from anywhere between 5 and 25 points.

Indeed, international and U.S. data all show the same trend: The lower the educational content of an intelligence test, the *larger* is the increase in IQ points shown by the test across generations. While there is a gain of something like 18 IQ points every 30 years or so on the Ravens, there is almost no change on achievement tests that focus on the contents of school-taught subjects. This is exactly the opposite of what hereditarians such as Jensen predicted: They expected Ravens-type tests that focus on so-called fluid g—that is, problem solving not related to educational/cultural experiences—to remain more stable.

IQ gains over generations represent a real puzzle that as yet has no satisfactory explanation, at least not from the hereditarian viewpoint that IQ is basically inborn and fixed. What they do suggest strongly is that IQ tests do not actually measure intelligence in a way that is directly related to the quality of problem solving in the real world. In other words, the IQ gains shown by the tests are not real gains in intelligence; otherwise we would have generations that vastly outperform their predecessors. Instead of debating why there is a decline in educational standards we would be celebrating extraordinary rises in educational standards and a renaissance in human creativity. The continuing, and warranted, dialogue about how to stop the "dumbing down of America" suggests that such a renaissance is not at hand.

More importantly for our central theme, the continuing rise in population IQ puts the spotlight not on the role of inborn, fixed characteristics within individuals, but on the fluid features of human social life, which are very much related to context. Next, I point out that when we review IQ over the life span, we find that the treatment of intelligence as performance style rather than capacity is supported.

IQ over the Life Span

The first modern IQ tests, starting with Binet's, were designed for use in schools. Items were selected for inclusion in these tests to show a trend of more children getting the correct answer with increasing age. The general assumption was that at some age intelligence reaches a peak, and for this reason it becomes difficult at some point to find items that a greater proportion of people get correct with increasing age. Ideas about the age at which intelligence peaks have been based in large part on cross-sectional studies, which involve comparing samples of people belonging to different age groups, including children, teenagers, young adults, and seniors. However, a major problem with cross-sectional studies is that we have to assume that these samples are comparable in every way except age. This assumption is obviously wrong, because seniors who are 75 years old now were not like the teenagers of today when they were 16. Their nutritional, educational, and cultural conditions were very different, for a start. A much more effective approach is to conduct longitudinal studies, focusing on the same individuals over the course of their lives.

Longitudinal studies pose both practical and theoretical challenges. In practical terms, it is very difficult to keep track of the same group of people over a long time. Just think about what a challenge it is for each of us to keep in touch with even a few friends from our elementary school days. Now consider the challenge of keeping in touch with hundreds of individuals for decades. Theoretical difficulties also arise, in part because longitudinal studies involve the same group of respondents being repeatedly tested, and the more they are tested the more they might be influenced by practice effects. Despite such difficulties, a number of excellent longitudinal studies focusing on intelligence have been successfully conducted.

A consistent, if surprising, finding of longitudinal studies is that so-called "peak performance" on intelligence tests tends to be reached and sustained much later than had been expected. The Berkeley Growth Study, one of the most extensive efforts to examine changes in intelligence with age, found a peak in intelligence not in the teens but in the mid-20s, with declines in some areas starting in the mid-30s. The Seattle Longitudinal Studies, perhaps the most rigorous research ever conducted on age and intelligence, led to even more intriguing and promising conclusions. While perceptual speed and numerical ability were shown to peak in the 20s, verbal ability and inductive reasoning did not decline among healthy individuals until the 70s and 80s.

A number of smaller-scale longitudinal studies reveal the same trend: Intelligence peaks later than traditionally expected, and the peak lasts longer. William Owens conducted a follow-up study of a sample of soldiers who had taken the Army Alpha in 1919; he found no declines on average scores in any of the Alpha subtests about three decades later—and even a rise in scores on subtests involving verbal skills. A similar surprising rise in scores was demonstrated by David Campbell in a study of students who had first been tested in the mid-1930s. A quarter of a century later, they were found to score higher. This trend of people's maintaining or even exceeding peak performance in later years was confirmed by Lewis Terman's famous studies of gifted children, which identified 1,000 gifted children between 1911 and 1924 and subsequently tracked their individual development.

The general conclusion one reaches from studies of aging and intelligence is that as long as good health is maintained, significant declines in abilities do not take place until the 60s and 70s, and in the case of verbal abilities, not until the 80s. Medical research is adding details to this picture. For example, a study reported in the *Journal of the American Medical Association* confirmed that cognitive abilities do not decline with age for healthy individuals. This study, which tracked about 6,000 senior citizens over a decade, showed that for about 70 percent of individuals evaluated, there was no decline in cognitive abilities over the course of the study. However, individuals with diabetes or high levels of atherosclerosis or an apolipoprotein E4 gene (often associated with Alzheimer's disease) were eight times more likely to show a decline in cognitive functioning.

Concluding Comment

As in the case of personality, discussed in the last chapter, we have seen that intelligence performs as a powerful carrier in large part through the influence of traditional research, conducted in the positivist tradition. This research aspires to identify hypothetical "true" scores of intelligence, ones that are assumed to be fixed at or near birth and unchanging throughout life. A vast technology, centered on psychometric tests and having all the features of pseudo-science, has been manufactured and extensively used in Western, and increasingly non-Western, societies. The main objective of this technology is to identify intelligence independent of context.

Perspectives on intelligence are particularly powerful because they are presented to the lay public as being based on science. In the popular media, references are made to "IQ scores" in the same way that "height in inches" or "weight in pounds" is referenced. This objectification of intelligence helps to justify resource inequalities: Joan and her family do not have health care, did not do well in school, have poor career prospects, and so on, and this is all in line with their low scores on "scientifically developed" intelligence tests. North Americans may look across to Great Britain and wonder how those Brits could possibly justify using the eleven-plus examination to create so-called educational apartheid for children from such an early age, but the role of intelligence as a carrier is just as powerful on this side of the pond.

Ultimately, intelligence as a carrier endorses and upholds the existing social order. Intelligence depicts the fate of individuals as being determined by fixed abilities within themselves, abilities that are assumed to exist independent of context.

Suggested Readings

Cole, M. (1996). *Cultural psychology: A once and future science.* Cambridge, MA: Harvard University Press.

Fancher, R. E. (1987). *The intelligence men: Makers of the IQ controversy.* New York: Norton.

Flynn, J. R. (1999). Searching for justice: The discovery of IQ gains over time. *American Psychologist, 54,* 5–20.

Gardner, H. (1993). *Multiple intelligences: The theory in practice.* New York: Basic Books.

Goleman, D. (1995). *Emotional intelligence.* New York: Bantam.

Gould, S. J. (1996). *The mismeasure of man* (2nd ed.). New York: Norton.

Greenfield, P. M. (1997). You can't take it with you: Why ability tests don't cross cultures. *American Psychologist, 52,* 1115–1124.

Haan, M. N., Shemanski, L., Jagust, W. J., Manolio, T. A., & Kuller, L. (1999). The role of APOE e4 in modulating effects of other risk factors for cognitive decline in elderly persons. *Journal of the American Medical Association, 282,* 40–46.

Herrnstein, R. J. (1989, May). IQ and falling birth rates. *Atlantic Monthly,* pp. 73–79.

Herrnstein, R. J., & Murray, C. (1994). *The bell curve: Intelligence and class in American life.* New York: Free Press.

Jensen, A. R. (1998). *The g factor: The science of mental ability.* Westport, CT: Praeger.

Schaie, K. W. (1996). *Intellectual development in adulthood: The Seattle Longitudinal Study.* Cambridge, UK: Cambridge University Press.

Sternberg, R. J. (Ed.). (1999). *The handbook of intelligence.* Cambridge, UK: Cambridge University Press.

Tang, Y. P., Shimizu, E., Dube, G. R., Rampon, C., Kerchner, G. A., Zhue, M., Liu, G., & Tsien, J. Z. (1999). Genetic enhancement of learning and memory in mice. *Nature, 401,* 63–69.

Witelson, S. F., Kigar, D. L., & Harvey, T. (1999). The exceptional brain of Albert Einstein. *The Lancet, 353,* 2149–2153.

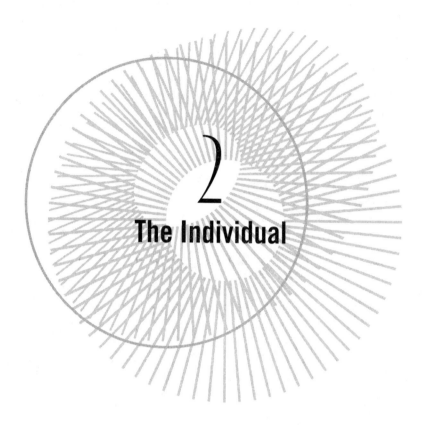

2

The Individual

10 Memory as Carrier

The faded photograph fell out of a book, and suddenly a multitude of faces from my past were staring at me: the shiny faces of the younger boys sitting at the front of the group, the uneasy glances of the young adolescents slinking in the back row, and the more confident stares of the oldest boys standing with the schoolmasters in the center. Then I found myself, a figure at once familiar and unfamiliar, squeezed in between two little chums. The passing of years had not dimmed the warmth of that comradeship, forged at that pivotal moment in our lives and captured in a school photograph.

A glance at the photograph brought back the excitement, the sounds, the smells, and even the comedy of my boarding school years in England. The most vividly remembered parts of that era are those I have re-created again and again. For many years afterward, I kept in touch with a few of the boys and schoolmasters. Through these contacts I have retold, adapted, negotiated, recreated, and reconstructed our adventures and the various parts played by each of us. While some adventures faded and eventually were dropped from my repertoire of favorite stories about my early life, others gained luster and acquired new details, becoming enlarged and playing more central parts in my recollected past. The more years pass by, the less it seems I rely on an ability to remember my school adventures as facts and the more on an ability to recount them as reconstructed stories.

We remember the past not as a frozen picture but as constantly changing scenery. We actively relive and remold the past, not just privately in our individual minds but as members of communities who collaboratively construct how the past is to be remembered. As a member of a family, a school, a neighborhood, a city, a nation, a religion, a race, among other groups, we participate in the collaborative reconstruction of the past.

Much of the past stretches back to a time before our own birth, but it can still influence our notions of who we are. The histories and traditions of our families, schools, nations, religions, and so on shape our personal identities. Just as these histories and traditions are reconstructed, so, too, our identities are transformed and our memory of who we are changes. For example, since the 1960s the Catholic Church has reconstructed its history and its relationships with other religions. As one indication of this, in 2000 the pope openly expressed regret for the policies of the church toward the Nazi regime in Germany and toward Jews. This reorientation touches on the identity of all members of the Catholic Church.

Through the evolving memories of their social groups, then, individuals come to appropriate particular identities for themselves and their societies and to participate in particular skilled activities. The Catholic child in Northern Ireland "remembers" through the collective stories of the Irish past, just as Jewish and Palestinian children "remember" through the collective stories of the Jewish and Palestinian past. Each child is embedded within constructed traditions of how he or she is to fit into the larger society, and although each child has personal and subjective memories, such memories are intricately enmeshed in the collective memory. No memory is an island.

Reconstructing Memory

Brave New Past

Although Susan Engel and others have convincingly articulated how in everyday life *Context is Everything* with respect to memory, traditional memory research has almost completely neglected context and social relations. Traditional research has treated memory as performance capacity, focusing almost exclusively on how *accurately* individuals remember the past. Such research on memory as "reproduction" has involved isolated individuals tested in laboratory settings, and only a small number of researchers have explored the social processes involved in remembering the past, memory as "reconstruction" in social context.

The two lines of research—memory as reproduction and memory as reconstruction—are in some ways complementary. Traditional research has gauged our memory capacity and addressed questions such as "How much do isolated individuals remember under controlled conditions over different time periods?" while more novel research has explored memory as addressing questions such as "How do people actually remember things in their everyday lives as members of communities?"

The dominant tradition, memory as reproduction, has conceptualized changes in memory as equivalent to defects: Memory changes come about because we are unable to reproduce past events accurately. This defect may arise because we did not take in the information accurately in the first place, or because we failed to store the information efficiently, or because we are unable to retrieve the information effectively, or because of some other type of "malfunction" in memory. In contrast, according to the more innovative tradition, memory as construction, change is an integral and indispensable feature of memory. Our remembrances of the past change as we interact with others and relive the past through exchanged accounts and as our changing personal lives give new meaning to what occurred before.

Thus, according to this alternative tradition, change in memory is not a defect but a development as natural and inevitable as aging itself. And, importantly, what the future will be is related to what we take the past to have been. Thus memories of the past are continually being transformed to form a changing basis for possible futures.

The Carrier Role

Memory has a complex and central role as a carrier. First, the ability to remember—memory as performance capacity—enables individuals to be influenced by carriers in the first place. The national flag can act as a carrier of national values, pride, loyalty, and so on only if individuals are able to recognize the flag when they see it and remember the values, norms, and other phenomena it sustains. Thus at a basic level memory is a prerequisite for carriers to function at all.

Second, memory as it has been conceptualized traditionally is reductionistic and directs attention to individual rather than collective remembrances. This reductionistic bias in memory research, which arises out of the self-contained individualism of Western societies, has so far ensured a neglect of collective memory—the type of memory that is inherently conflict-laden and threatening to the status quo. I elaborate on the history of this bias later, but for now I want to draw attention to another question: What happens when the contextual, social, and collective aspects of memory do become a focus? My argument is that such a focus almost inevitably leads to open intergroup conflict. A timely example is at hand to illustrate my point.

The city of London began the twenty-first century with a new mayor and a lot of controversy. Mayor Ken Livingstone (nicknamed "Red Ken" because he is seen by some as having extreme left-wing political views) has decided to try to find a new home for some of London's statues. Mayor Livingstone has argued that some of the statues around London represent individuals who should not be considered as heroes and who, if they were alive today, would be condemned for their actions. The statues represent aspects of a colonial past that some people, particularly the younger generation, find reprehensible. An example, situated on Parliament Square, is the statue of H. J. T. Palmerston, the prime minister who directed the invasion of China in 1856, forcing the Chinese government to open the country up to British opium traders.

Palmerston and the bombardment of Chinese ports in 1856 can be remembered in many different ways. For example, Palmerston can be remembered as a strong leader who expanded the British Empire, opened up new trading routes, and paved the way for Britannia to rule the waves for another half-century or so. But some people choose to remember all this very differently: Palmerston as a racist colonial leader, forcing the Chinese to import opium and opening the floodgates to social disintegration, corruption, and exploitation in Chinese society.

What should be remembered about Palmerston? How should the colonial history of Britain be remembered? The mayor of London has opened up this controversial debate by addressing collective memory, how the past is remembered collaboratively. By proposing to move the statue of Palmerston and other heroes/villains to a less prominent place, the mayor has attacked the status quo on the traditionally sanctioned view of the past. This reminds us of other conflicts that have arisen because of challenges to the traditional ways in which nations and other groups remember the past, such as conflicts over Columbus and the "discovery" of America, the Confederate emblem on the flags of a number of U.S. states, and the controversy over moving the capital of Germany back to Berlin.

Memory as it is traditionally treated in psychological research does not allow for attention to such debates, because traditional research focuses on performance capacity by isolated individuals. How well does Jane do on a test on Palmerston's foreign policy? Does she remember the facts correctly (how many ships took part in the bombardment of Chinese ports, the dates of the conflict, and so on)? Such questions concerning performance capacity do not bring to the forefront the very different issue of collective remembering: What is to be the national view of Palmerston and his foreign policy? Should the British government apologize to the Chinese? This kind of collective reconstruction of, and reorientation toward, the past is continually taking place, sometimes in explicit ways. Consider, for example, the reorientation of the American people and government toward the Japanese Americans interned during World War II or the reevaluation of the Vietnam War by Americans since the early 1990s.

Thus the dominant research tradition, memory as reproduction, has serious shortcomings, in that it neglects collective processes and the collaborative construction of memory. Nevertheless, this dominant tradition has led to in-depth information about the memory capacity of isolated individuals. It is instructive to review this tradition.

Measuring Memory Capacity

What is memory? Traditional research has treated the brain like a container. Some individuals have larger containers, some smaller, and so the number of bits of information the brain can hold varies across individuals. How do bits of information get put into the container, stored, and taken out again? Traditional research has addressed this question by attempting to test containers under controlled conditions.

Memory Capacity: Ebbinghaus

In the latter part of the nineteenth century, psychophysics was a new hybrid science, bringing together elements of physics and psychology to make revolutionary breakthroughs, just as biochemistry, biophysics, and other hybrid sciences continue to lead to breakthroughs in the twenty-first century. Gustav Fechner (1801–1888), the great pioneer in psychophysics, used rigorous experimental techniques to get precise measurements of human sensory capacities, such as how well people can see, hear, and sense through touch. Hermann Ebbinghaus (1850–1909) was glancing through the books in a Paris bookstall when he came across a copy of Fechner's *Elements of Psychophysics*, published in 1860. The book immediately captured Ebbinghaus's imagination. Just as Fechner had applied new experimental techniques to measure sensory capacities, Ebbinghaus would apply similar techniques to measure human memory capacities.

Ebbinghaus set about achieving this goal with Herculean resolve. He conducted hundreds of memory experiments, almost always using himself as the only subject and keeping the general conditions of the experiment as constant as possible. Whereas most previous research had focused on memory of past events already known to the subject, Ebbinghaus studied memory of completely new material. He tried to standardize the material to be learned by using about 2,300 nonsense syllables, each consisting of two consonants with a vowel in between that do not make up a word (for example, ZUN and KOL). By using nonsense syllables, Ebbinghaus intended to avoid the problem of words having different associations for different people, and thus being different in how difficult they are to learn for different individuals. (Later research showed that even nonsense syllables are not meaningless and actually have different associations for different people.) He standardized the rate of presentation of the material to be learned at two-fifths of a second per syllable.

One of Ebbinghaus's first important findings was that he could generally learn about seven nonsense syllables in one reading. But if he tried to increase the number to be learned to more than seven—to nine or ten, for example—he required considerably more time. This was an early report of a limited capacity in *short-term memory*, involving a duration of a few seconds, for which researchers in the mid-twentieth century formulated the famous "seven-plus-or-minus-two" rule. Most people can hold seven bits of information, plus or minus two, in their minds. After about 20 seconds, this information begins to fade. If new bits of information are introduced, they will displace the original seven bits. For example, if John tells Jane his telephone number, she will be able to remember it for a short while but will lose it if Dave immediately tells her his telephone number, because Dave's number will displace John's (assuming Jane is equally motivated to remember the two telephone numbers). Of course, through rehearsal a number could be transferred from short-term to long-term memory.

Ebbinghaus realized that learning is not a matter of all or none but a matter of degree. He learned lists of nonsense syllables under standard conditions and then tested how many repetitions it would take to relearn a list after a given interval. He found that by overlearning material—continuing to present the material to himself after he had already learned it—he could cut down on, or "save," the amount of effort needed to relearn the material after a given period. An advantage of this "saving method" was that the degree of forgetting could be quantified. The general shape of the forgetting curve for most material—an initial drop, but gradually getting less steep until it becomes almost flat—has been verified by modern research.

Ebbinghaus also made a contribution that should be particularly appreciated by students everywhere, because he showed how exam-takers can best use their time. If Anne is going to dedicate four hours to studying for her history exam, she would get a higher grade if she studied in four one-hour sessions rather than in one four-hour session. Later research showed that Anne would do better to read all the material she has to learn from start to finish rather than breaking up the material and learning bits at a time.

Continuing the Exam Tradition

Ebbinghaus had thus established what is aptly described as an "exam tradition" in memory research: the study of individual memory performance under controlled conditions through paper-and-pencil-type tests. It is not surprising that his findings provide useful hints for students taking exams. The exam tradition continues its dominance today, but now the focus of researchers has shifted to different systems of memory as well as to the biological basis of memory.

The traditional view was that memory involves a sequential process, starting with short-term memory and moving to long-term memory. Of course, only things that received attention and were rehearsed would become part of long-term memory. But this view has been superseded by the idea that short-term memory is actually part of working memory, the active part of memory. Working memory is believed to consist of several components, including a central organizing part, a verbal memory store, and a visual memory store. Evidence to support the distinction between verbal and visual memory comes in part from patients who, sometimes because of head injuries suffered in accidents, have either verbal or visual memory intact but not both.

Rather than consisting of one system, working memory functions as several systems and is able to sidestep the seven plus or minus two bottleneck traditionally ascribed to short-term memory. Despite this, however, verbal working memory remains rather simplistic, being influenced both by the sounds of words and the order in which they are presented, as well as by their meaning. Long-term verbal memory is more sophisticated in that it is more influenced by word meaning than sound. Thus words with more important meaning are given more attention and retained better in long-term memory.

Visual memory can last just a few seconds, in which case it is referred to as iconic memory, or it can last up to half a minute, in which case it becomes part of working memory. Rather like a negative that fades, visual memory in the iconic and the working memory forms will disappear quickly. However, the negative can be developed to become a more long-lasting photograph, and the "development" in this case requires rehearsal—that is, revisiting the visual scene so that it becomes more solid.

"Locating" Memory in the Individual

The insistence that memory must reside within the individual has perhaps inevitably led to attempts to locate memory inside the person and to identity exactly how memory is stored. Is it in images? Is it in the unconscious or the conscious? What physical part of the brain is it in?

Imagery and Memory

The role of visual imagery in memory, and in thinking generally, has been controversial for centuries. In the latter part of the nineteenth century, a heated debate ensued between those who argued that all thinking necessarily involves imagery and opponents who proposed that thought without imagery is possible. How was this debate to be resolved? A favored research method of the time was introspection: Individuals were trained to reflect on their own thought processes and report their experiences. But reports from introspection exercises in different laboratories contradicted one another, some claiming that thought without imagery is possible and others that it is not. Introspection came to be seen as an unsuitable method for resolving this dispute, because claims made by persons about their thought processes could not be independently verified. An important consequence of this impasse was the decline of nineteenth-century structuralism, paving the way for the rise of behaviorism early in the twentieth century and the rejection of thinking as an appropriate subject for psychological research. So one way in which this dispute was resolved was through the abandonment of research on thinking. However, by the 1950s behaviorism was in decline, and cognitive psychology, together with research on memory, was on the rise. Recently, advances in technology have allowed us to solve the ancient puzzle of images and thinking: Yes, it seems that visual imagery is an indispensable part of thinking.

This helps explain why at least since the time of the Greek orator Simonides 2,500 years ago, the method of *loci*, which involves encoding information by visualizing the placement of things in familiar locations, has been successfully used to improve memory. For example, Mike remembers a speech he is giving by walking around his house and associating each part of the speech with a different part of his house (as Winston Churchill used to do). Frances Yates has discussed how for centuries a number of "Memory Theaters" were used as standard "familiar places," with hundreds of locations in which to "place" things visually. Indeed, most mnemonic strategies for improving memory use visual imagery, which makes a lot of sense given that imagery is foundational for memory, both working and long-term.

In practice working memory overlaps with long-term memory because it functions more effectively through access to information in long-term memory. Consider, for example, why it is that in tests of working memory, meaningful words (e.g., *bug*) are better remembered than meaningless bits of information (e.g., *kug*). Presumably this is because the words are more easily linked back to information in long-term memory. The same overlap between working memory and long-term memory is apparent when individuals chunk information as an aid to remembering, such as when George chunks the things his wife asks him to buy in groups of "fruits," "vegetables," "dairy," and so on. By using labels for groups of foodstuffs, George is able to increase his working memory capacity from seven to thirty. But this is only possible because chunking uses information from long-term memory, information such as which items fall into the categories of fruits, vegetables, and dairy.

Consciousness and Memory

One can think of working memory as the tip of an iceberg protruding out of the water, with long-term memory being the vast submerged mass of the iceberg. This image immediately brings to mind Freud's distinction between the conscious and the unconscious, the idea being that the conscious is like the tip of an iceberg and the unconscious equivalent to the vast mass hidden beneath the water. Insofar as both working memory and the conscious are visible, like the tip of an iceberg, the analogy works. However, while Freud saw the unconscious as repressed material and difficult to access, cognitive psychologists have put far less stress on the role of repression and irrationality in long-term memory.

The distinction between explicit and implicit memory is probably the closest cognitive psychologists have come to considering the unconscious nature of memory. Explicit memory is what can be recalled consciously. It is related to declarative memory: the information that people explicitly remember about things and events. Charlie knows the names of all the basketball players on the visiting team and makes a point of shouting them out throughout the game, attaching colorful adjectives to each name as he does so. Implicit memory is memory that shows itself in behavior, without a person's expressing it or even being conscious of it. Implicit memory is related to procedural memory, which comes into play with skills and abilities. Sean is unable to explain to his son how to open the puzzle box, but when he holds the box in his own hands, he finds that the ability to open it automatically comes back to him. Somewhere in his long-term memory, he had the necessary knowledge but was not conscious of it. One's ability to speak and understand one's mother tongue is the most important kind of procedural memory.

Another way in which the unconscious has found a place in modern cognitive psychology is as an explanation for forgetting. The main explanations for forgetting attended to by researchers have been rational ones: decay, meaning that an *engram* or memory trace literally fades away, and interference, meaning that similar bits of information interfere with one another and get in the way when an attempt is made to remember. But explanations based on irrational behavior—a person's intentionally suppressing something in the past or unintentionally repressing it—have also found some favor among experimental researchers in recent decades. This is in part because of the controversies created by cases of supposed repressed memories of sexual abuse in childhood and the general topic of so-called false memory syndrome.

In an intriguing case of memory distortion, Donald Thompson, a psychologist researching this very topic, was falsely accused of rape as a result of false memory. Thompson did fit the profile of the rapist, but at the time of the crime he was on live television talking about ways in which people can improve their memories for faces. Apparently the victim remembered his face but confused this memory with her memory of the rapist's face. This kind of source amnesia, in which a person remembers something (such as a face) but forgets the source of the memory (where did I see the face?), accounts for numerous mistakes. No doubt his own frightening experience with source amnesia motivated Thompson to do more to show the nature of false memory syndrome.

There is no doubt that some victims of sexual abuse have repressed parts of their earlier experiences and are amnesic for certain traumatic incidents in their childhood, such as being raped. While there is some evidence for repressed memories, there is also evidence that people can sometimes be influenced to "remember" events from their past that never actually happened to them. Such influence has sometimes been exerted, it seems, by clinicians, lawyers, and others determined, sometimes even with good intentions, to discover abuse in the "victim's" past. This has led to some innocent people being blamed for crimes they never committed.

The issue of repressed memories of sexual abuse highlights a fundamental feature of memory in real life: People often remember the past in collaboration and through interactions with others. Any event will be remembered differently by different people, and the version of the past that is agreed upon as "the truth" will often be some sort of compromise between differing versions put forward by different people. But this social feature of memory still remains neglected, relative to the much greater attention now being given to the biological basis of memory.

"Locating" Memory in the Brain

Over the last few decades technological advances have enabled researchers to monitor brain activity with some degree of accuracy and in this way to explore the possible locations of particular types of memory in the brain. The new technology adds considerably to the information already gathered through the traditional method of conducting postmortem examinations of the brains of individuals with memory disorders. A great advantage of the new technologies is that they can allow us to gather evidence about brain–memory relationships while the patient is still alive.

A useful way to discuss the new neuroimaging techniques is to divide them into two groups: *structural* techniques, which show brain structure or anatomy, or a cross section of the brain, and *functional* techniques, which provide views of some particular aspect of brain activity. The structural techniques include cerebral angiography, computerized tomography (CT), and magnetic resonance imaging (MRI). One set of functional techniques, characterized by high spatial resolution, measures aspects of brain metabolism, such as cerebral blood flow, glucose metabolism, and oxygen consumption. These techniques include positron emission tomography (PET), single photon emission tomography (SPECT), and functional magnetic resonance imaging (fMRI). A second set of functional techniques, characterized by high temporal resolution, measures brain electrical activity (using an electroencephograph) or brain magnetic activity (using electrophysiological neuroimaging).

The best we can do at present is to combine information attained from all these techniques to better understand brain and memory relations. Reliance on just one technique typically leaves too many questions unanswered. For example, in two recent studies lists of words were presented to respondents with no mention made of needing to memorize the material. In a later task, the same words were classified as to whether they were forgotten, remembered weakly, or remembered well. Researchers used fMRI, which gives a measure of brain metabolism, to establish that brain activity associated with words that were remembered was higher in two brain areas, the prefrontal and the parahippocampal cortices, than brain activity associated with words that were weakly remembered or forgotten. But brain-lesion studies are needed to tell whether both these brain regions are essential for this kind of remembering, and techniques with better temporal resolution are needed to clarify whether the two identified brain regions are acting serially (one after the other) or at the same time. No doubt combinations of more advanced techniques will lead to a clearer picture of the relationship between brain and memory.

There are already available some fascinating case studies involving brain lesions that do indicate some localization of different types of memory. A famous case is that of H. M., a patient who had a part of his brain—the amygdala, hippocampus, and other parts of the medial temporal lobes—removed as a way of ending his uncontrollable epileptic seizures. After the operation, H. M. suffered from an inability to store new memories, but he had not lost the ability to learn new procedures. When given an opportunity to learn a new drawing task through repeated trials, H. M. actually improved with practice, but each time he started he had no memory of ever having done the task before. This suggests that the parts of the brain removed in the case of H. M. are essential for explicit memory but not so for implicit memory.

But it is too simplistic to assume that there is a one-to-one relationship between different parts of the brain, or engrams or "memory traces" in parts of the brain, and our past experiences. Memory is much more likely to depend on the integrated and coordinated working of multiple parts of the brain. This is indicated by cases of patients who lost aspects of their memory after suffering damage to parts of the brain not assumed to be directly involved in remembering. For example, a British patient referred to as P. S. suffered a stroke that affected his thalamus, which is not generally thought of as being involved in memory storage, yet he lost all memory for his past life except for a brief period when he was on leave from the navy during World War II. P. S. believed that his leave would end and he would have to report back for active duty. Even if this dislocation and highlighting of a particular slice of his life 50 years ago could be localized to a particular part of the brain, which is not the case, what exactly would it signify?

Let us imagine, for argument's sake, that over the next 50 years more sophisticated technology allows us to pinpoint the location of just about all the different types of memory in the brain. What exactly would this localization of memory allow us to say?

Well, it might allow us to make causal statements, and it would add to our understanding of the psychology of capacities. This research would allow us to make statements such as, "If location X in the brain is injured, it will cause impairment to type Y memory." This would be very important in the long term, because it might eventually lead to the ability to repair damaged brain parts.

However, we need to take care not to jump to false conclusions at this point: While it is true that higher mental capacities, such as those involving memory, can be incapacitated through damage or disruption to a single factor, it is *not* true that by influencing the same single factor we can improve performance. Just because memory is disrupted when X is damaged, it does not mean that we can improve memory performance by manipulating X (genetically or otherwise). To give an analogous example: By treating my damaged toe, my doctor can enable me to play tennis again, but no amount of improvement of my toe will get me to the U.S Open next year (unfortunately!).

Most important, information about the localization of memory in the brain tells us nothing about the meaning of what is remembered, either for the individual remembering it or socially for the context in which the remembering is taking place. For example, person A and person B may both recall the number 100, and the same part of their brains may be particularly active when they are remembering 100. For person A, 100 may be his grandmother's age, while for person B this number may represent his score on an exam. For person A, 100 might have a particular meaning because his culture honors older people like his grandmother, while for person B, the number 100 might have a very different meaning because the exam he took had a possible total score of 200. Thus, the "location" of memory in the brain does not tell us about the meaning of a thing remembered or, indeed, about the techniques historically used to improve memory.

Moreover, research on the biological basis of memory does not have any implications for the psychology of constructions: It will not tell us, for example, anything about how people evaluate and give meaning to memories in social context or interact with one another to reconstruct memories. In order to better understand these aspects of memory, we must move to the social sphere and consider memory as part of a psychology of constructions rather than as part of a psychology of capacities.

Memory as Performance Style

Traditional research on memory informs us about the capacity of isolated individuals to remember and forget under certain controlled conditions. Recent brain-imaging techniques also inform us about biological changes in specific parts of the brain as remembering is going on. But unless we take the examination situation, where an isolated individual tries to remember and to problem-solve, to be the norm, traditional research tells us little about memory in everyday life—that is, social, collaboratively constructed memory.

Memory in everyday life tends to be negotiated and continually changed through interactions with others; in other words, it is a social phenomenon. Another feature of memory in everyday life is its intimate connection with socially shared carriers, which sustain meanings, values, and styles of thought across time. Because memory relies in large part on the social, external world of meaning systems and the carriers that sustain them, how people remember is highly dependent on experience, as indicated by research on memory and aging—the point to which we now turn.

Memory as Construction

The way I had remembered it, the substitute Latin master we had for a week in the 4th form (U.S. 9th grade) collapsed in class because we treated him very badly. We played tricks on him constantly, even putting a firecracker under his desk. He fainted and had to be taken to the hospital by ambulance. That was my recollection. About five years after I left that school, I met up with some of the other boys who had been in the same Latin class, and in reliving our past adventures we talked about the substitute Latin master and his collapse. Somebody said he remembered him having a heart attack, another person said the teacher had hit his head on a desk as he fell, while still another remembered the teacher being hit by the paper plane fired from the back of the class, no doubt by one of the usual rowdies who occupied the back corners. But someone else said he had heard that the Latin teacher had been feeling unwell in his earlier classes that day. We finally decided that maybe the Latin teacher had been feeling unwell but that it was our antics that had caused him to collapse. This helped to support our view of ourselves as mischievous and rowdy schoolboys.

Several years later, at another reunion, one of the former classmates told us he had by chance bumped into the our former substitute Latin master. He said he felt bad about what had happened, so he had apologized to the teacher. However, the teacher had told him that he had really enjoyed teaching us and that his collapse had had nothing to do with any jokes we might have played, which he could not remember anyway. He remembered us as well behaved. So over the years my remembrances of that day in class, and the emotions associated with it, have changed quite a lot, mainly through recollecting the event with others and reconstructing what happened. The question of whose version is the truth becomes irrelevant to what is remembered.

While traditional research has told us much about memory as capacity—how well isolated individuals can remember under controlled conditions using standard "meaningless" material—and also about which parts of the brain are involved in different types of memory, more novel research is also available on memory as construction: how people actually remember in everyday life. I have already pointed out that everyday memory is special in that it is highly influenced by interactions with others, but it needs to be added that everyday memory is also guided by intentions and is part and parcel of emotional experience.

Imagine that you visit a house for the first time and wander around for half an hour. What will you remember from this visit? Well, that depends a lot on why you visited. If your purpose was to look over the house as a prospective buyer, you will remember one set of things, such as the general architectural plan, the number of bedrooms and bathrooms, the possibility of fitting a table and some chairs into the kitchen, and so on. But if you have been hired to paint the house, you will be motivated to remember a whole set of other things, such as the square footage of the walls, the present color of the walls, the general condition of the surfaces you will have to paint, and so on.

What we remember is also typically associated with emotions, with a whole array of feelings and moods. When Bob recalls the day he arrived late for his own wedding ceremony, he feels embarrassed. But the feelings associated with that recollection, and what they lead to, are not so simple as to be put in one box labeled "embarrassment." In *Remembrance of Things Past*, Marcel Proust wrote, "An image presented to us by life brings with it, in a single moment, sensations which are in fact multiple and heterogeneous" (p. 146), adding "an hour is not merely an hour, it is a vase full of scents and sounds and projects and climates, and what we call reality is a certain connection between these immediate sensations and the memories which envelope us simultaneously with them" (p. 147).

Adding to this complexity is the fact that in everyday life we often want to remember things in a way that supports our values and views, irrespective of accuracy. Thus different groups have different remembrances of major events, such as government-sponsored activities against communists in the United States during the 1950s, and major personalities, such as Senator Joseph McCarthy. When left-wing and right-wing political activists discuss the McCarthy era, differences in the pictures they paint of that era arise not so much because of differences in the "accuracy" with which they recall events but because of the interpretation and meaning they give to what they recall. Some of these differences arise because left-wingers and right-wingers have constructed their own versions of the past.

Different versions of the past are supported by carriers, and part of the competition between groups is the struggle to give greater prominence to carriers that support their particular memories of how things happened. "McCarthyism" has become a left-wing carrier in the United States, signifying a conspiratorial view of threats from right-wing groups against democracy and basic freedoms. Meanwhile, right-wing interpretations of events in the 1950s focus on real threats from communism and real communist collaborators in the United States, people who were ready to "sell us out" to the Soviets.

Aging and Memory

An assessment of memory as performance style and as integral to social processes, rather than as performance capacity and as confined to intrapersonal cognitive processes, helps to better explain the surprising memory abilities of older people. Despite doing less well when tested in isolation, older people do well in social situations.

■ **What Older People Do Less Well** Research on the capacity of individuals has shown that older people do less well at more complex working memory tasks, such as dividing their attention and recalling things while attending to a second task (only 20-year-olds seem to be able to watch television, make coffee, talk on the telephone, and do their research assignments all at the same time!). Younger people also need less time to learn new material. It is not just that they are more open to taking in new information; they are also quicker at doing so.

With respect to information already stored in memory, older people have more difficulty retrieving information. Older people do better at recognizing words (when presented with a list of words and asked to select the ones they encountered earlier) than they do at recalling words (when asked to remember a list presented earlier).

The poorer performance of seniors in these situations is not just a matter of "worn-out hardware," such as damaged brain cells; it also seems to stem in part from differences in "software." Older people seem to make less use of memory-enhancing thinking strategies, such as chunking (grouping bits of information together), as a means of increasing the number of bits of information remembered.

■ **What Older People Do Better** Thus research in the exam tradition—testing the memory capacity of isolated individuals—shows that older people do less well in recalling some types of information and in learning new material. But a rosier picture emerges for seniors when we look at memory in everyday life, where people remember through interactions with others. When older people hear a story, they will not be able to remember the details as well as younger people, but they will be more likely to identify the real meaning of the story. They are less likely to "miss the point."

Studies of married couples suggest that older couples remembering together can be just as accurate as younger couples. One reason may be that older couples know each other better, enabling them to become more focused on the task of remembering. Greater experience allows older people to compensate for some of the "capacity" (hardware) losses they suffer, with the result that their productivity does not decline as much as might be expected solely on the basis of physical deterioration. A similar compensation strategy seems to be used at work, where older employees have been found to maintain productivity.

One of the reasons for the better collaborative performance of older people has to do with the greater availability of carriers to them, which they use as hooks on which to hang things to be remembered. Seniors have greater experience with and knowledge of carriers, including those that serve as cultural symbols and guides to "how things were done and should be done" in different contexts. This allows them to effectively use their past experiences as support for things to be remembered today.

Concluding Comment

William Butler Yeats begins his poem about a visit to an art gallery with the line, "Around me the images of thirty years." He proceeds to describe the images in the gallery, most of which are associated with special memories for him, in terms of both his personal identity and the collective identity of the Irish people. Images of an ambush, a revolutionary soldier kneeling to be blessed, a beautiful woman he met in an art gallery, a famous painter, an abbot or archbishop, and on and on—the images revive in him memories of who he is and who his people are.

Without memory we would have neither personal identity nor collective identity. We would still know "that we are," since our existence would not be in doubt, but we would know "who we are," since all traces of our past experiences would be lost. "Who we are" both individually and collectively is supported by carriers, such as the poems of Yeats and the paintings he writes about. Works of art are powerful carriers of collective memory, and although they remain the same, their interpretations continuously change. The *Mona Lisa* and *Hamlet* are both part of Western memories, but what they mean changes for each generation.

Rock music illustrates this point vividly. Elvis, the Beatles, Nine Inch Nails—just about all the popular musicians were at one time regarded as radical, unacceptable, and even evil. What was once considered to be "just noise" is later remembered as "revolutionary music." But this remembering does not occur in isolated minds; rather, it occurs through social processes. Although each of us inherits a past, it is a new past with a new interpretation. In this change, memory is never an island, nor is it ever static.

Suggested Readings

Adams, C. (1991). Qualitative age differences in memory for text: A life-span development perspective. *Psychology and Aging, 6,* 323–336.

Baddeley, A. (1990). *Human memory: Theory and practice.* Hillsdale, NJ: Erlbaum.

Brewer, J. B., Zhao, Z., Desmond, J. E., Glover, G. H., & Gabrieli, J. D. E. (1998). Making memories: Brain activity that predicts how well visual experience will be remembered. *Science, 281,* 1185–1187.

Craik, F. I. M., Anderson, N. D., Kerr, S. A., & Li, K. Z. H. (1995). Memory changes in normal ageing. In A. D. Baddeley, B. A. Wilson, & F. N. Watts (Eds.), *Handbook of memory disorders* (pp. 211–241). New York: Wiley.

Dixon, R. A. (1996). *Compensating for psychological deficit and decline.* Mahwah, NJ: Erlbaum.

Engel, S. (2000). *Context is everything: The nature of memory.* New York: Freeman.

Kosslyn, S. M., Pascual-Leone, A., Felician, O., Camposano, S., Keenan, J. P., Thompson, W. L., Ganis, G., Sukel, K. E., & Alpert, N. M. (1999). The role of area 17 in visual imagery: Convergent evidence from PET and rTMS. *Science, 284,* 167–170.

McEvoy, G. M., & Cascio, W. F. (1989). Cumulative evidence of the relationship between employee age and job performance. *Journal of Applied Psychology, 74,* 11–17.

Middlebrook, D., & Edwards, D. (Eds.). (1990). *Collective remembering.* London: Sage.

Proust, M. (1970). *Remembrance of things past: Vol. 7. The past recaptured* (A. Mayor, Trans.). New York: Vintage. (Original work published 1927)

Schacter, D. L. (1996). *Searching for memory.* New York: Basic Books.

Wagner, A. D., Schacter, D. L., Rotte, M., Koutstaal, W., Maril, A., Dale, A. M., Rosen, B. R., & Buckner, R. L. (1998). Building memories: Remembering and forgetting of verbal experiences as predicted by brain activity. *Science, 281,* 1188–1191.

Yates, F. A. (1966). *The art of memory.* Chicago: The University of Chicago Press.

11 Human Development

"Now lift me onto the pillow," begged the frog. The Princess could hardly believe it, but she did as she was told. As she placed the frog on her silken pillow, an astonishing thing happened. Before her eyes the frog turned into a handsome Prince, who sat smiling at her. "I was bewitched by an evil enchantress," he explained. "Only the kindness of a Princess could release me from my spell."

Then the Princess was glad that she had kept her promise. For the Prince was very handsome indeed. Before many months had passed, the Prince and the Princess were married.

—THE STORY OF THE FROG PRINCE AS RELATED BY
NICOLA BAXTER IN "THE FROG PRINCE"

I must have read the story of the Frog Prince to my daughter hundreds of times by the time she was 5 years old, and now that my son is about that age I seem to be reading him fairy tales and nursery rhymes so often that I found myself humming his favorite rhymes to myself on the way to my office, in corridors, in elevators, while jogging, and even during duller moments in committee meetings. To catch oneself absent-mindedly giving a rendition of "Simple Simon" during a committee meeting is just a normal part of parenthood.

"Oh yes, you're at that stage; you've got 'parent of young children written' all over you," commented a colleague. "Learn to enjoy it. In the blink of an eye, the kids will go to college, start work, get married and have children, and you'll feel old like me. It's all very predictable, the stages of life."

Watching children grow up, struggle through the teenage years, complete formal schooling, become adults, form bonds with long-term partners and start families of their own, develop working careers, retire and grow old, one does get the impression that development takes place in predictable stages. Psychologists have attempted to formalize this process in models of stages, and such models have become highly influential in the mass media and popular culture.

Stage Models as Carriers

Stage models of human behavior are compatible with, and supportive of, the ideal of self-contained individualism that is so central to U.S. culture and, through that, becoming so influential around the world. Stage models typically depict development as primarily dependent on factors within the individual, with outcomes determined by individual characteristics. The environment plays a secondary role in stage models.

Observers have often wondered why certain European psychologists, such as the Swiss researcher Jean Piaget, have become so influential in the United States, while many others with equally or more innovative ideas have failed to make an impact. A major reason is that U.S. society is more receptive to accounts of behavior that correspond to the individualistic value system dominant in the United States, and Piaget's model fits this requirement very well. Despite references made to the context, Piaget's genetic epistemology ultimately maintains the focus on the individual rather than the environment.

Major Stage Models

The most important stage models of human development are those put forward by Sigmund Freud, Jean Piaget, Lawrence Kohlberg, and Erik Erikson. These models propose that progress to a higher stage of development is only possible after the lower stages have been successfully traversed—rather like climbing up a ladder on which each step has to be taken exactly in turn and no step can be skipped. The focus is on performance capacity, on how well individuals can perform tasks. Another important characteristic of these stage models is that they claim to encompass humankind, so that everyone is assumed to pass through the same developmental sequence.

■ Freud's Fiction of Psychosexual Development Freud sketched out five main stages of psychosexual development: oral, anal, phallic, latency, and genital. At each stage the individual's struggles are associated with particular regions of the body. In the first 18 months or so, the mouth is the center of experience and the main source of sensual pleasure. We come to know the world through our mouths, and we try to put everything we can get hold of into our mouths. In the second and third years we enter the anal stage, and a focus of our activities becomes toilet training. We gain more control over our own bodies, but we also feel increasing pressure to conform to societal norms, to use the newly achieved control over ourselves in socially acceptable ways. The phallic stage begins around the age of 3 and ends around age 6. Children learn more about their own bodies, as well as the physical differences between boys and girls. Associated with these changes is an internalization of societal morality, such that children learn to feel shame and guilt. The little boy of 6 now feels guilty about touching his penis, and the little girl feels shame in showing her naked body in public. Freud posits a latency period from around the age of 7 to puberty, a stage during which boys and girls repress their sexuality and prefer to keep company with peers of their own gender. Finally, with puberty begins the genital stage and the reemergence of sexual identity. Boys and girls develop an interest in the opposite sex.

Closely tied with psychosexual development is personality development. Freud's developmental model conceives of struggle between the instinctive desires of the individual and the normative system of society. In the first stage personality is centered on the *id* and driven by the pleasure principle, instant gratification being the goal. As the parents of any 6-month-old will confirm, babies are quick to express dissatisfaction when their needs are not instantly satisfied. But soon the infant learns that the external world has certain limitations, reality sets in, and an *ego* evolves, shaped by the reality principle. Finally, the normative system of the external world becomes internalized in the *superego*. A conscience develops, like a little police officer inside the person. Civilization has won.

Thus individuals begin life kicking, screaming, and demanding that their basic instinctive desires be instantly satisfied, but they are gradually socialized to control their urges and to conform to societal norms. Of course our self-centered urges and antisocial wishes do not just go away; they are pushed back from conscious experience to become part of the unconscious. Even though we are not conscious of such repressed urges and wishes, they continue to influence our behavior. Consequently, we are often not aware of what we are doing or why we behave the way we do, and in this sense humans develop into irrational beings.

Becoming civilized comes at a cost, but there are also benefits. The individual conforms to societal expectations about correct behavior but at the same time gains the support and companionship of others. In a sense, the process of development involves the negotiation of a social contract between each individual and society, personalized for each of us. The costs and benefits of this social contract can be different for each individual. In some cases the costs are extremely high and the benefits relatively little, as is the case when individuals fail to progress successfully through the psychosexual stages and consequently experience psychological problems as adults.

■ **Piaget's Construction of Universal Cognitive Stages** While Freud's main influence has been on the way we now perceive personality development, so with terms such as *ego* having become part of everyday language, modern ideas about cognitive development have been particularly influenced by the Swiss psychologist Jean Piaget. Like Freud's model, Piaget's posits a stepwise progression. However, whereas Freud's main focus is on the internal struggles of persons and the development of irrationality, Piaget's main concern is the quality of rational thinking, as well as the kind of knowledge, achieved at each developmental stage. The focus on performance capacity—how well tasks are carried out by independent individuals—is clearly evident in Piaget's model. During the sensorimotor stage, from birth to about 18 months, the world is experienced mostly through motor responses to sensory stimuli. According to Piaget, the infant is aware only of what is immediately visible. Lack of "object permanence" is assumed because infants typically do not look for objects that are placed out of sight. At around 18 months the infant enters the preoperational stage, which lasts until about age 7. Characteristic of this stage is a lack of the concept of conservation, the idea that objects can be rearranged and shaped differently but still retain certain essential properties such as weight and volume. For example, a piece of clay remains the same weight even when its shape is changed from round to flat. As suggested by the label for this stage, the preoperational child also lacks operations, the ability to reverse mental processes. For example, 5-year-old Jill reports that she has a brother, David, but when asked if David has a sister, she replies "no." From age 7 to 11, the child is in the stage of concrete operations, where the primary limiting characteristic is an inability to manipulate symbols and abstract concepts. This limitation is overcome in the final stage of formal operations, starting around age 11.

■ **Kohlberg's Construction of Universals in Moral Development** Piaget's model focuses on progress in cognitive ability, without specific concern for how well children reason about right and wrong. Lawrence Kohlberg proposes that development in moral thinking also progresses in stages. At the first and most basic level, the preconventional stage, individuals tend to reason in reference to punishments and rewards (e.g., "I will not steal because I will be caught and punished"). Individuals who move up to a second, conventional, stage reason morally in reference to societal norms (e.g., "I will not steal because it is against the law"). In the postconventional or principled stage, moral reasoning is guided by fundamental principles (e.g., "I will not steal because it is against my principles"). Not everyone advances to the highest, principled stage of moral thinking.

■ **Erikson's Construction of Stages Across the Life Span** Among the developmental models that have attempted to cover the entire life span and make distinctions between stages even in the adult years, Erik Erikson's has been the most influential. Erikson conceives of eight main stages in development, with each stage characterized by particular social and emotional struggles. The internal struggles of the infant center on trust and relate to a need for a stable, predictable social world. At ages 2 and 3, the main struggle is between autonomy and doubt, as the infant tries to do things independently but constantly requires the help of others. From age 3 to 6, the child struggles with initiative versus guilt, wanting to be good but feeling guilty about doing bad things. Between age 6 and 12, competitiveness becomes stronger and the main struggle is between industry and inferiority, as the child asks "How successful am I?" During the early teens, the struggle for identity takes center stage, as the individual tries to develop a satisfactory personal identity. In the late teens and early 20s, the young adult experiences conflicts between intimacy and isolation, wanting to be with a partner but fearing failure and isolation. In the middle adult years, from the late 20s to retirement, a struggle between generativity and stagnation dominates, as individuals strive to be successful at work and in family life. In the final stage of life, during the senior years, individuals experience conflict between ego integrity and despair, looking back on earlier successes and failures and asking themselves if they have fulfilled their potentials or been failures.

In conclusion, then, the main way of viewing development in contemporary Western societies has been as a stepwise progression. Freud, Erikson, Piaget, and Kohlberg, among others, have put forward different models, each claiming that the stages, the sequence, and the timing of their models are universal, with all humans going through the same developmental stages, in the same order, and in similar but not identical time periods. The search for universals has been associated with a neglect of context and culture, although their importance is often mentioned in passing by these and other developmental researchers.

Stage models have acquired the role of carriers, matching and supporting the ideal of self-contained individualism that is particularly pervasive in the United States. Such models, purportedly scientific and objective, are concerned with performance capacity. In actuality, they are themselves social constructions.

Rethinking the Stage Models

"And one man in his time plays many parts/His acts being seven ages . . ." So goes a famous speech in William Shakespeare's *As You Like It* (II, vii, 139) that puts forward what in modern terms is a stage model of life-span development.

The stages in Shakespeare's model are (1) infancy, with the infant "Mewling and puking in the nurse's arms"; (2) early childhood, when the schoolboy with "shining morning face" creeps "like snail/Unwillingly to school"; (3) the teenage years, with the adolescent preoccupied with romantic love and "Sighing like furnace"; (4) young adulthood, when the person is rash and hot-headed, "Jealous in honour, sudden and quick in quarrel/Seeking the bubble reputation"; (5) middle age, with the person "In fair round belly with good capon lin'd . . ./Full of wise saws and modern instances"; (6) old age, marked by "lean and slipper'd pantaloon/With spectacles on nose and pouch on side," a "shrunk shank," and voice "Turning again towards childish treble"; and (7) senility, "second childishness, and mere oblivion."

Shakespeare's "stage model" is every bit as convincing as those of Freud, Piaget, Kohlberg, or Erikson, and yet there is something importantly different about it: Shakespeare's model is not considered to be based on scientific studies or to represent a culture-free depiction of universal, hierarchical stages in human development.

Shakespeare is clearly a Western writer, and his work is part of the Western canon. When he discusses the "whining schoolboy" or the justice's "beard of formal cut," it is generally accepted that he is referring to culture-bound characteristics that belong to a particular time and place. Various other "stage models" are listed in *The Oxford Book of Aging,* from authors with ties to Chinese, Italian, Native American, and other cultural traditions. Like Shakespeare's model, these would not be claimed to be universal characteristics, but rather cultural constructions.

This is very different from claims made about the models of Freud, Piaget, Kohlberg, and Erikson. These models have been put forward as accurate for all humankind, and the assumption has been that they match "empirical" evidence gathered from different cultures around the world. But the developmental models of Freud and Erikson are in practice very difficult to test empirically, because they are too vague and nonspecific. They are what the philosopher of science Karl Popper would describe as nonfalsifiable. The models of Piaget and Kohlberg are more specific and easier to test, with the result that there is a more serious attempt to decide the merits of these models on the basis of empirical research. However, in order to properly assess the stage models, it is useful to take a step back and critically evaluate their assumptions.

The stage models explicitly or implicitly depict the individual as self-regulating and independent: self-regulating in the sense that the timing and nature of growth are assumed to be controlled by internal clocks, and independent because the causes of behavior are assumed to be within individuals. The image created is that of a plant or animal that grows in stages, with each stage predetermined by biological properties—rather like a caterpillar that eats and gets fat, spins itself into a cocoon, then emerges as a moth. The task of the researcher becomes one of studying the properties of the particular organism in order to recognize the exact timing of each stage of growth, as well as the possibilities and limitations of the organism at the different developmental stages.

The self-regulating, independent model of individuals has been further popularized by simplistic interpretations of research on the genetic basis of behavior. For example, the research of Jerome Kagan was interpreted, particularly in the 1970s and 1980s, as demonstrating that shyness and other personality characteristics are inherited. In following 500 children for several decades, Kagan found that by their second birthday about 15 to 20 percent were shy and wary of the unfamiliar, whereas about 25 to 30 percent were bold risk-takers. These differences were explained by reference to differences in neurochemistry, and animal research by Stephen Suomi and others at the National Institute of Child Health and Human Development put the spotlight more specifically on the role of serotonin. But by the 1990s, a more sober assessment was being made, with increased recognition that children are not locked into a genetic destiny and that the brain is shaped by experiences rather than being "fixed" at birth. Both human and animal research shows that the fate of a child "born shy" can change dramatically through different types of parenting—growing up to be an innovative leader if supported by especially sensitive parents or becoming poorly adjusted if burdened by poorly skilled parents. *The "biological destiny" of children can be dramatically altered by early experiences, such as parenting style and type of family interactions.*

In reading the latest research on the influence of the environment on brain and behavior, one has a strong sense that the pendulum is starting to swing back from simplistic genetic determinism and that in some ways the wheel is being reinvented. While the evidence demonstrating the impact of environmental conditions is novel, particularly that derived from neuroscience research, the basic message is well known. The pivotal role of the environment in development was demonstrated decades ago in classic animal research, such as Harry Harlow's studies demonstrating abnormalities and impairment in adult monkey behavior as a result of environmental deprivation in the early developmental years. Monkeys who had been deprived of social and emotional support as youngsters had severe difficulties in their relationships with other monkeys as adults. The role of the environment has also been demonstrated repeatedly by tragic real-life examples of environmental deprivation in humans, from historical cases, such as *The Wild Boy of Aveyron* discovered living in the woods and brought to Paris in 1800, to more contemporary cases, such as the severely deprived children discovered in orphanages after the collapse of Nicolae Ceausescu's dictatorship in Romania in 1989.

Although at least some stage theorists have acknowledged the role of the environment, in practice the environment has been almost completely neglected, with the entire focus of stage models remaining on the self-regulated, independent individual. In particular, the focus has been on performance capacity. This is most obvious when we consider how individuals have been tested to determine their developmental stage. Such testing has focused on *what individuals can do strictly on their own*, rather similar to the typical examination situation in schools.

Perhaps we should not be surprised that researchers have tried to measure developmental growth in the same way that individuals are tested in school examinations; after all, such researchers are themselves a product of an academic culture and take as normative the way of life of the academy. But what individuals can achieve on their own can be very different from what they can achieve through interactions with others, and in everyday life individuals do not live in isolation; they typically carry out tasks through interactions with others. Fortunately, some researchers have attended to this issue. Before turning to such research, however, it is useful to make more explicit the wider implications of the stage models.

Like all carriers, stage models of human development can perform a sustaining and stabilizing function in the context of the wider social order. Specifically, stage models help keep the focus on the characteristics of the individual child and away from the characteristics of the social and physical environment in which the child develops. For example, in debates about the quality of child care and the possible role of federal and local governments in providing high-quality care, stage models keep the focus on individual rather than environmental characteristics.

Even the stage models of Erikson and Piaget, which make some effort to take into consideration the context of development, ultimately depict development as progressing in a stepwise manner, with the sequence of steps being universal. The assumption of universality necessarily means that the environment becomes of secondary importance. Otherwise, how could we predict that individuals growing up in Bombay, Athens, San Francisco, and the jungles of northern Brazil will experience the same stages of development?

Beyond Stage Models

Despite lip service to environmental factors and social context, then, the developmental models most influential in Western societies have focused on the performance capacities of individuals, treating the person as a self-regulating and independent entity. Edward Sampson has pointed out that what he terms "self-contained individualism" is part and parcel of a wider ideology pervading important aspects of Western capitalist societies, including psychology and other knowledge domains. This ideology highlights self-help and individual responsibility, and it sees the causes of behavior as internal to individuals (e.g., "The reason a disproportionate number of African Americans are poor and without health insurance is because they are not talented and hardworking, and the reason why some people are rich is because they are talented and hardworking") rather than external to them (e.g., "The reason a disproportionate number of African Americans are poor and without health insurance has to do with the legacy of slavery and continued racial and economic discrimination").

Self-contained individualism, the model of humans as self-regulated and independent, has also fundamentally influenced the kinds of research that have thrived both in Western societies and, through exportation from the West, in most non-Western societies. For example, one reason that cognitive neuroscience, the study of the biology of the mind, has become increasingly influential in Western societies since the late 1970s is its perfect fit with the ideology of self-regulated and independent individuals. Cognitive neuroscience is based on *reductionism* coupled with *causal determinism*. The reducto-causal thesis asserts that, (1) human behavior is best explained by reference to the smallest unit possible, (2) human behavior is causally determined, and (3) the causes of human behavior are reducible to biological processes. The mind is treated as an encapsulated, self-contained entity that acts as an independent source of thoughts and cause of actions. In response to the question "What is the mind?" cognitive neuroscience points to isolated individuals and more specifically to their brain activity.

Certainly cognitive neuroscience can play a role in clarifying the minimal biological conditions for the development of thought and action. This enables us to make statements such as: "If section X of the brain is damaged, then Y-type thought and action are impaired. When section X is normal, then Y-type thought and action are possible." But in order to understand Y-type thought and action when they take place, it is necessary to examine social behavior and the *collaborative construction of meaning* in cultural context. This leads us to focus on what I have termed performance style: the meaning of behavior, rather than just performance capacity, the tasks isolated individuals are capable of performing by working on their own.

Similarly, the tremendous influence of Piaget on modern research in Europe and North America undoubtedly has to do with Piaget's adoption of the model of individuals as self-regulated and independent entities. In the Piagetian tradition, the focus is on what isolated persons can do by themselves and how individuals' internal, dispositional characteristics will move them from one level of thinking to another according to a timetable set by a universal biological clock. As with the other influential stage models of Freud, Kohlberg, Erikson, and others, the Piagetian tradition gives insufficient attention to how interactional processes involving the individual and others give rise to new individual capabilities as well as meaning construction.

The Zone of Proximal Development

A very useful concept in this connection is Lev Vygotsky's notion of a *zone of proximal development*, the difference between what a child can achieve on his or her own and what the child can achieve through collaboration with other children or adults. Typically, children can perform better on tasks though collaboration with others. For example, the 5-year-old child retelling the tale of the Frog Prince can do a lot better when an adult provides hints and reminders about the story. This is how a conversation with my 5-year-old daughter went:

Me: So now I told you a bedtime story. Will you tell me one?

Nikoo: Do I have to? I want you to tell me another story . . . another story, daddy.

Me: It's only fair you tell me a story now. I'm tired. I need a story to go to sleep.

Nikoo: All right, I'll tell you a story.

Me: The Frog Prince. You know that story, don't you?

Nikoo: I don't know that one.

Me: Oh yes you do. Remember this picture (I show her a book with pictures of the story).

Nikoo: A frog did something good for a princess, then she had to take him home.

Me: And did she want to do that?

Nikoo: No, she didn't. But her father and mother told her she had to.

Me: And did she take the frog to the dining table?

Nikoo: Yes, and she had to feed the frog and it was horrible.

Me: Then what?

Nikoo: She was very tired.

Me: Did she go to bed?

Nikoo: She went to bed and she had to take the frog.

Me: And where did she put the frog?

(Nikoo says nothing.)

Me: Did she put the frog on the floor?

Nikoo: The frog jumped on her bed.

Me: What happened next?

Nikoo: She had to kiss the frog goodnight and the frog changed into a prince.

Me: How did that happen?

Nikoo: A wicked witch had done it to him. A princess had to kiss the frog to save the prince.

In this kind of process, the child is able to do a lot better through the support of another person. Vygotsky likened this process to scaffolding, the temporary supports that are used in building construction. As a new building rises from the ground, scaffolding is used to support the structure; then when the building is complete, the scaffolding is removed. After relating the story of the Frog Prince with my collaboration, my daughter could tell it better on her own.

It is not just that children can do more through social interactions but that what they do through social interactions becomes different. For example, research shows that gender differences in behavior are often not revealed when girls and boys are studied in isolation. Individual girls and boys tend to behave in very similar ways. However, when boys and girls are together, their social behavior is markedly different. Girls tend to play with girls and boys with boys. Also, girls in their groups are more cooperative, more likely to take turns, less competitive, and physically less aggressive. Thus essential characteristics of male and female behavior are *collaboratively constructed* and have to be studied in social settings because they only arise in such settings.

Carriers, Activity, and Development

I have pointed out two limitations in the way we have construed development. First, despite lip service being given to the role of environment, individuals have been conceptualized as self-regulating and independent entities. This is in part because of the influence of the stage models and in part because of the more recent influence of a simplistic form of genetic determinism. Together, these factors have shaped a view of the developing individual as encapsulated, moving through developmental stages according to a preset genetic program. Only in the late 1990s and early 2000s did a corrective come about with the publication of more sophisticated biological accounts, such as Paul Ehrlich's *Human Natures.* Second, little attention has been given to children's collaborative construction of social life. When children interact with others, the result is something genuinely new. Studies of boys and girls in isolation do not tell us all that happens when boys and girls come to play together or when they interact with adults. In other words, the whole is more than the sum of its parts. This is particularly true because fundamentally important features of the larger social world, such as gender roles, ethnicity, social class, and the like, manifest themselves most clearly in collective life; they are less evident or even invisible when individuals are examined in isolation.

Let us now turn to an essential but neglected feature of socialization—the activities children learn to participate in and the carriers influencing them. In referring to activities, my concern is not so much the cognitive aspects— children's understanding and memorization of activities—as the taking on of activities as skilled performance; For example, learning to participate in singing the national anthem and respecting the flag. Of course, such activities involve memory and other aspects of cognition, but more than that, they involve becoming skilled performers in a set of behaviors—learning how to show respect for the flag by standing straight, looking up at the flag, singing with emotion, and so on. Moreover, these activities involve the appropriation of carriers—the incorporation of what a flag stands for, why it is something to fight for or even die for.

Childhood is a period when the carriers of a culture first become appropriated, and in this way the individual becomes "a person" according to the rules and norms of a particular culture. For example, in Islamic societies girls at the age of 9 start wearing a veil and learning the fundamentally important meaning of the veil in Islamic culture. During interviews with women about the veil, I discovered that most Western women interpret the Islamic veil using the rhetoric of rights, as in "It is the right of women to be free from such limitations." Indeed, more educated (and typically more Westernized) women in Islamic societies have a similar attitude, emphasizing the rights of individuals. However, many women who wear the veil in Islamic societies have learned to interpret the veil using the rhetoric of duties, as in "It is the duty of a woman to cover herself and be modest and dignified."

Such differences in interpretations are learned from a very early age, probably from the very first year of life. Just as little girls in Western societies tend to try on their mother's high-heeled shoes and apply lipstick, little girls in Islamic societies try on veils and imitate the mannerisms of their mothers and elder sisters. In each society, self-presentation in the public domain is learned in relation to carriers: The veil represents important values that majority powers want to uphold in some societies, just as a woman's wearing trousers represents important values that majority powers want to uphold in other societies.

One cannot overemphasize that these developmental processes, through which carriers are appropriated by the young, involve action as well as cognition, the learning of skilled behavior—"how to do things correctly"—not just abstract ideas. The rights and duties relating to the veil are not learned abstractly, but rather as part of a concrete set of skilled behaviors, with the veiled little girl learning through practice how to negotiate her way through her society, presenting herself in a manner deemed appropriate by others in her society. Of course, there are instances in which an individual knows how to behave correctly according to a set of rules and norms but chooses not to do so. For example, in Islamic societies some women have fully recognized the power of the veil as a carrier of certain traditional gender roles and attempted to reject it and the traditions it symbolizes.

Similarly, individuals who can articulate principles of morality and apply such principles in solving abstract dilemmas may in practice take very different courses of action. This highlights another major flaw in the Kohlbergian research tradition on moral development—the focus on abstract moral reasoning rather than actual behavior. A person may solve a moral dilemma one way in the abstract but behave very differently when actually faced with the same type of moral dilemma in practice. This was driven home for me recently when a female student I know who is strongly pro-life in principle decided in practice to have an abortion. Interestingly, even after having an abortion, she continued to argue for a pro-life position as being good for society in general. But I have also come across other individuals who are strongly pro-choice when the choice is to be made by others but admit that they would not have an abortion if it were their own unplanned child.

I now want to turn to another kind of gap, one between the socially constructed world of children and that of adults, which again highlights cultural rather than biological limitations in a purely top-down view of individual–society integration.

The Margin of Generational Development

The view that development is fundamentally shaped by social context and the larger culture has a danger associated with it, that of leading to a top-down view of individual–society integration, with individual behavior being viewed as causally determined by larger societal processes and the larger socially constructed world of adults. Obviously, we must avoid the lure of this overly simplistic top-down view.

But what prevents development from being shaped simply through a top-down process? Certainly, biological limitations and what I have termed performance capacity are influential. The performance capacities of 1-year-old children fundamentally limit the ways in which large-scale societal characteristics can shape them. One-year-olds do not have the minimum performance capacities required for abstract thinking, for example. No matter how the social context might be reorganized, it would not be possible for 1-year-olds to overcome this performance-capacity limitation and to think abstractly. But I want to highlight features of the socially constructed world of children that also serve as a limitation on top-down, societal-to-individual influences. It is useful at this point to introduce a concept I refer to as the *margin of generational development*, the extent of the difference between the cultural world of children, particularly the rules and norms regulating their behavior, and the cultural world of adults. The world of adults represents the practical limitations within which children must eventually conform and live, but childhood represents a period during which such practical limitations can to some extent be sidestepped.

There are two things we should first clarify about the cultural world of children, which consists not only of norms and rules appropriate for children but also children's games, stories, rituals, special rules, fantasies, and so on. First, this world has features that continue from generation to generation of children, separate and independent from the adult world There are rhymes and games that young children have passed on without the intervention of adults. Children who pass on these rhymes and games seldom remember them when they have themselves become adults. My 11-year-old daughter does not remember the rhymes and riddles that she knew as a 5-year-old and that she helped to pass on to the next generation of 5-year-olds. She will only come across these rhymes and games again if and when she herself has a 5-year-old daughter who tells her about these aspects of a child's culture.

A second point about the culture of children is that its rules and norms range from being very similar to to being very different from those applicable to adults. It is not the case that the intervention of adults makes this margin smaller and brings the cultures of children and adults closer together. Let me clarify this point through an example, one that concerns a pervasive practice in many Western and some non-Western cultures.

George and David are two 4-year-olds playing together in a playground. There is only one toy racing car, and George is playing with it. David grabs the car and wants to put Batman in it. George reacts by grabbing the car, and soon the boys are shouting at each other. The mothers of both boys intervene by telling them that they "have to share." This is a fairly common norm—that children should share toys when they are playing with one another. George protests to his mother, "But it's my car, I want to play with it!" His mother still insists that he share his car with David, or else she will take George back home.

In playgrounds, in day-care centers, in homes, in just about all contexts where young children play with one another, it is normative for adults to tell them they have to share toys, even if it is their own toy. Even when a visiting child wants to play with a favorite toy of a host, who is safely ensconced in his or her own home territory, the adult admonition to the protesting host is, "You have to share!"

Fast-forward to 20 years later, when George and David are 24-year-olds. Now the rules have changed very dramatically. George drives a sports car, but nobody around him suggests that he has to share his sports car with David. Quite the opposite; now the emphasis is on private ownership and the property rights of the individual. When we are told that "this car belongs to George," our expectation is *not* that he will share it with others his age. This is exactly the opposite of what happened when he was 4. Thus the margin of generational development in this domain is very wide, with the norms and rules for children being fundamentally different from those for adults.

The margin of generational development does not depend on biological performance-capacity features of children. On the contrary, it depends entirely on cultural performance-style features. We can imagine a very different type of social organization, however, one in which adults share cars and other goods but children have exclusive use of everything belonging to them personally.

Concluding Comment

The traditional stage models of development, together with simplistic genetic explanations, have acted as carriers, sustaining a view of individuals as self-regulated and independent. Such a viewpoint is also strengthened by experimental techniques that examine individuals in isolation and focus on performance capacity, the range of things isolated individuals can achieve. However, in recent years greater attention has been given to persons as cultural beings, collaboratively constructed through participation in collective life, and thus there is now more focus on performance style. This social perspective highlights the role of carriers as well as the co-construction and appropriation of meaning.

The larger world that the child enters is characterized by extreme inequalities of resources, and the major carriers that the child encounters act to sustain inequalities and strengthen the continuity of the existing social order. "Developmental science" has in large part helped maintain the status quo, endorsing an account of performance that views the individual and personal characteristics as the "causes" of life outcomes. This pervasive individualism undermines the influence of even those social scientists who do make greater efforts to strengthen intervention programs designed to improve the environmental conditions of economically deprived children. Even though we *know* that children born into poverty have *relatively* little chance of climbing up the ladder of success (of course, a much-glorified few do make it to the top), the larger cultural climate and value system insist that we consider each individual in isolation and apart from the environment.

Suggested Readings

Baxter, N. (Ed.). (1998). *My treasury of stories and rhymes*. New York: Barnes & Noble.

Blau, D. M. (1999). The effect of income on child development. *The Review of Economics and Statistics, 81*, 261–276.

Bronson, M. B. (2000). *Self-regulation in early childhood: Nature and nurture*. New York: Guilford.

Chase-Lansdale, P. L., & Brooks-Gunn, J. (1995). (Eds.). *Escape from poverty: What makes a difference for children?* New York: Cambridge University Press.

Cole, M., & Cole, S. R. (1996). *The development of children* (3rd. ed.). New York: Freeman.

Cole, T. R., & Winkler, M. G. (Eds.). (1994). *The Oxford book of aging.* Oxford, UK: Oxford University Press.

Duncan, G. J., Yeung, W. J., Brooks-Gunn, J., & Smith, J. (1998). How much does chilhood poverty affect the life chances of children? *American Sociological Review, 63,* 406–423.

Farran, D. C. (2000). Another decade of intervention for children who are low income or disabled: What do we do now? In J. P. Shonkoff & S. J. Meisels (Eds.), *Handbook of early childhood intervention* (2nd ed.) (pp. 510–548). New York: Cambridge University Press.

Lamb, M. E. (1999). *Parenting and child development in nontraditional families.* Mahwah, NJ: Erlbaum.

Lewis, M. L. (2000). The cultural context of infant mental health: The developmental niche of infant–caregiver relationships. In C. H. Zeanah (Ed.), *Handbook of infant mental health* (pp. 91–107). New York: Guilford.

Opie, P., & Opie, I. (1972). *The lore and language of schoolchildren.* Oxford, UK: Oxford University Press.

Reiss, D., Neiderhiser, J. M., Hetherington, M. E., & Plomin, R. (2000). *The relationship code: Deciphering genetic and social influences on adolescent development.* Cambridge, MA: Harvard University Press.

Shonkoff, J. P., & Phillips, D. A. (2000). *From neurons to neighborhoods: The science of early childhood development.* Washington, DC: National Academy Press.

Tomasello, M. (2000). Culture and cognitive development. *Current Directions in Psychological Sciences, 9,* 37–40.

Vygotsky, L. S. (1978). *Mind in society.* Cambridge, MA: Harvard University Press.

Watson, J. E., Kirby, R. S., Kelleher, K. J., & Bradley, R. H. (1996). Effects of poverty on home environment: An analysis of three-year outcome data for low birth weight premature infants. *Journal of Pediatric Psychology, 21,* 419–431.

12　Eating Disorders

Even as a little girl, Jill was unusual in always trying so hard to do the right thing. She was always neat and made sure to say "please" and "thank you" at the appropriate times. In first grade she got the prize for being "the most helpful person in the class," and often the boys teased her by calling her "teacher's pet" because she helped the teacher clean up the classroom. It was not just that she wanted to help—she wanted to do what she thought her teachers and parents wanted her to do.

One day when she was in second grade, her teacher read the class an Easter story about a little girl who wore yellow clothes and played with yellow chicks and looked after them when their mother hen died. Jill decided that she should go to school in yellow clothes the next day. She put on a yellow pair of pants and yellow socks but could not find a yellow shirt. She cried so much that her mother eventually went out and bought a yellow T-shirt so Jill could go to school in a completely yellow outfit. Everyone thought it amusing when Jill came to class wearing all yellow, but the teacher still did not recognize the huge influence she had exerted on Jill. Just by seeming to say that girls should wear yellow for Easter, the teacher had led Jill to go to a lot of trouble to do what she thought she was supposed to do. No matter how much Jill's parents tried to change her mind, the idea that she should wear yellow for Easter had sunk in and would not be dislodged easily.

Jill was pleasant and helpful around the house. Her parents were always surprised at how she did things without having to be told, at least directly. After the age of 8, she rarely had to be reminded to tidy up her room. She was also fairly good at keeping clean and brushing her teeth and hair. Her mother would say, "Jill is just naturally tidy. She was born different from her brother David. That's just the way it is. Jill likes dolls, and David likes cars and trucks and guns. They were born like that."

When Jill was 4 years old, her mother had entered her into a "talent and beauty pageant." The event was intended to raise money for worthy causes, and it was not supposed to be taken seriously. But as often happens in such situations, the parents became very competitive and the little girls came to understand that they really were supposed to be competing against one another and that the only thing that really mattered was to win. Jill did well in a number of the talent areas, particularly the painting, and when it came to the beauty parade she was doing fine until the announcer jokingly said she should lose some weight. Jill was actually of medium build and only a little above average weight, but her nickname in the family became "tubby." This nickname stuck to her right through elementary school and even in middle school.

Jill's mother was fairly heavily built. Although she did not carry much fat, her large frame and stocky looks meant that she was far removed from the long-legged, super-slim fashion models typically shown on the covers of glossy magazines since the late 1960s.

Jill's mother was always either on a diet, or planning to be on a diet, or intending to find out about a new "magic diet," or asking other people about their diets. She was constantly saying, "The last thing I want is to get fat like my mother." She would get into a bad mood if the scale showed she had gained a few pounds but would become elated when she lost a few pounds and one of her diets actually seemed to work for a while. To be around Jill's mother was to associate happiness with weight loss.

It was when Jill was a 7-year-old in second grade that she first consciously thought about dieting. A medical doctor, the mother of one of her classmates, made a presentation to her class about the food pyramid and the importance of eating the right kinds of things. She put a lot of stress on the importance of weight and how everyone should be careful to not gain too much weight. "It is never too early to start thinking about these things," the doctor had said at the end of her talk, "carrying too much fat is bad at any age." Jill looked around the class and noticed that other kids were looking at her. She became worried that the other kids saw her as fat. Being "overweight" was a kind of illness, the doctor seemed to be telling her class.

When she went home after school that day, she took even more note of her own mother's talk about her diet and her need to shed pounds. When Jill watched television or looked through magazines, she noticed that the heroines or models were almost always thin. Successful women, whether they were politicians, sports stars, television personalities, rock singers, or just about anything else, were slim. At school, the most popular kids were slim. There were very few fat people to look up to. Jill did not go out of her way to find out about these issues, and she seldom asked anybody about weight and eating and diets and related matters, but the information reached her nonetheless.

By the age of 14, Jill was five feet seven inches tall, and her weight had reached 130 pounds. She worried more and more about her weight, and several times she tried to follow a diet, using her mother's latest diet fad as a guide. She started to experience a cycle of eating a lot for a few days, then crash-dieting for a week or so. Her weight went up to 140 pounds, and when she reached age 15, her eating habits took a dramatic turn for the worse. For the first few months her family did not notice any change. Jill had for several years talked about "being on a diet," so there was nothing unusual in her being picky about food. But this time there was something different in that she actually did seem to be losing a lot of weight.

At first Jill's family were very supportive and talked about her new "slim figure" in glowing terms. Her nickname changed from "tubby" to "supermodel." But when her weight kept going down, they eventually became concerned that she should eat more. Jill insisted that she was eating, but because the family seldom had meals together, it was difficult to monitor her diet. By the time of her 16th birthday, Jill's weight had gone down to 80 pounds. She found it difficult to eat—or to even sit at a table when other people were eating. Although she was skin and bones, she still described herself as being "too fat." When her family finally persuaded her to submit to a medical checkup, her doctor diagnosed Jill as anorexic.

"Ideal Beauty" as a Carrier

Try the following exercise, which I did over a period of a week. As you proceed with your usual everyday activities, record the number of times images of ideal beauty reach you in one way or another. You will find such images in the newspapers and magazines you read, on television, on billboards around town, on news stands you pass by, on movie posters, in shops and supermarkets and malls—just about everywhere you go during the course of a normal day. In the course of only one week, I recorded being bombarded by 1,723 such images (1,451 of them were images of female beauty). In almost every case, the ideal of beauty confronting me was very slim, particularly in the case of women.

Whereas prior to the 1960s the ideal of feminine beauty tended to be described as "buxom" and "full-figured," since then the ideal has dramatically shifted toward thinness. This well-articulated image is being advertised by a highly powerful and international mass media. There is no escaping the message that "thin is beautiful," certainly not in Western societies and increasingly not even in non-Western societies. But this ideal of thinness exists in tension with two other trends: (1) More people now have access to more food, and (2) the mass media are also attempting to persuade people to consume more.

Consumers Should Be Thin, but They Should Also Eat More

To grow up in a Western society is to learn to want to control one's weight. Central to this desire for weight control is an ambivalence toward food. On the one hand, food is relatively cheap and easily available, and there is an enormous focus on the joys of cooking and eating. But on the other hand, food has become "dangerous" and "public enemy number one." Food is associated with poor health and even death.

At the same time as Western beauty ideals for women and increasingly for men turn toward a "waif" look, and as these ideals spread to different populations in the West and around the world, the focus on food and eating also increases. Associated with this seemingly paradoxical situation is a dramatic increase in eating disorders, particularly among women in societies that are either Western or strongly influenced by Western values. In the United States and other immigrant-receiving societies, eating disorders increase among immigrant groups as they become more integrated into the adopted societies.

"I need to lose weight" has become one of our most repeated phrases, and it is one of the first things immigrants learn. Dieting has become a collective obsession that is associated with an increasing dissatisfaction with our own physical appearance. In the United States in the early 1970s, about 75 percent of women and 85 percent of men reported being satisfied overall with their bodies, but by the late 1990s only 44 percent of women and 57 percent of men were satisfied. A similar decline in the number of people satisfied with their weight has occurred, so that now only about 34 percent of women and 48 percent of men are satisfied with their weight.

Even a cursory glance at magazine racks tells us that modern societies are obsessed with weight loss. Every glossy magazine has at least one section on weight, with headlines inviting us to be part of the weight-watch challenge: OPRAH LOSES 20 LBS! SPICE GIRLS ON SECRET DIET! ELVIS PUT ON 50 LBS IN HIS LAST MONTH OF LIFE! FANTASTIC NEW DIET CAN WORK WONDERS FOR YOU! Advertisements for different "new" diets jump at us from television screens and computer monitors, from radios and billboards, and from countless other sources, so even if we do not look at magazines there really is no escape. The weight-watch industry has grown to be all-encompassing, and its message of "give us your money and we will make you slim" is ever present.

But the weight-watch industry would not have become so phenomenally successful had it not been for the supportive role of the medical profession. In addition to the aesthetic advantage being slim has come to have since the

1960s, there has emerged a strong consensus among those in the health care industry to the effect that being slim is healthy. According to one set of "official statistics" on the matter, one out of every three U.S. adults over the age of 25 is overweight. Another estimate, produced by the National Institutes of Health in 1998, states that 55 percent of the U.S. adult population is overweight. When we look into the definition of *overweight,* it means being more than 20 percent over one's ideal body weight. This sounds like the last word, until we ask what exactly is meant by "ideal" body weight. On closer inspection, we discover that the term *ideal* is anything but scientific because the cutoff for what is "overweight" is a cultural one, based on contemporary taste rather than on any objective criteria. Despite this, the idea of "ideal weight" is very powerful; it moves people to try to change themselves, sometimes through drastic measures such as not eating, or eating and vomiting to purge oneself of food.

Eating disorders do not involve only decreasing food intake and losing weight. At the other extreme, some individuals eat such enormous amounts that it becomes impossible to burn off the calories taken into their bodies. They become obese, sometimes putting on hundreds of pounds! Given the contemporary focus on weight loss, how is it that some individuals eat far too much? This tends to occur much more in the United States than in other Western societies, such as France, pointing to a major role for cultural factors in weight issues. In order to unravel the mystery, a first step is to consider the evolutionary path humans have traveled.

Why Changing Weight Can Sometimes Seem as Difficult as Changing the Past

During almost all of our evolutionary past, our ancestors struggled to find sufficient food to keep themselves alive. Lacking efficient ways to store food, they had to eat whenever the opportunity arose. Fruit, berries, meat, and every other edible thing was devoured on the spot. Our ancestors had to develop fairly accurate ideas about what was good to eat, and along the way they learned to like sweet and fatty substances, which provided them with economical sources of energy. They could not afford to pass up the chance of eating the fat of an animal they had killed, because there was no telling when the next successful kill would take place. If they managed to find honey, sweet fruits, or any other sugary substance, they had to eat as much as they could and then move on. They might go weeks or even months without having access to meat or honey again. In the meantime, it was imperative for them to have enough energy to weather the harshness of outdoor life—to be ready to hunt again when the opportunity arose or to run away from dangerous animals and other threats in the environment.

Thus the life of our hunter-gatherer ancestors over the last 100,000 years for the most part involved a battle with hunger. Although some have argued that "Stone Age economics" was associated with less harsh living conditions than is popularly believed, the food supply tended to be unpredictable and often insufficient to feed everyone in the group adequately. One indication of the harsh conditions is that life expectancy 10,000 years ago was less than a third of what it is today in Western societies. In order to better understand this kind of experience, we need only consider the lives of villagers presently living in remote parts of North Korea or India, or in several dozen other Asian and African countries. For the vast majority of people in the world today, getting enough food is still a daily challenge. Farming methods in much of the world remain primitive, crops are not dependable, and droughts can lead to severe hardship or even starvation for millions. A major storm, such as the one that hit South America in 1998, can cause devastating damage and put the lives of millions of people at risk, because most people live with a very small margin of safety. They have very little food available as a reserve to get them through difficult periods. Thus people in these situations have a fundamentally different experience with food than that enjoyed by most Westerners today.

Like our ancestors, most people in the third world wake up every morning unsure whether they will have enough to eat that day. In such an environment, food is thought of as a necessity that must be grabbed when available, rather than a "problem" and a potential "danger" to health in the sense that Western dieters have come to view it. Travelers who have visited villages in developing countries can attest that dieting is not an issue for the natives there, who tend to be slim because it would be very difficult for them to find enough food to eat to become overweight. Indeed, obesity tends be rare in such villages.

Imagine if two of our ancestors from tens of thousands of years ago were put into a time machine and transported to the present. This couple—let us call them Dave and Pam—would no longer face uncertainty about finding food. They would suddenly find themselves in a world where food is always available—literally 24 hours a day. But perhaps even more important, they would find themselves in a cultural environment where people live by the motto "never satisfied." In most U.S. urban centers, Dave and Pam could walk into supermarkets that are open night and day and offer thousands of different food products. On every street corner they would find a McDonald's, Kentucky Fried Chicken, Burger King, or some other fast-food restaurant. Even if they did not have food on their minds for a while, there would be advertising all around to remind them of what they were missing. Even if Dave and Pam were super-thin when they stepped out of the time machine and into our era, the likelihood is that they would take advantage of the availability of food—and consequently gain weight. The abundance and variety of foods they find delicious, including fatty and sweet ones, would make it hard to resist eating.

A similar change is experienced by some people who move from third world societies to North America. Even among the middle classes in most parts of the world, food is not always plentiful. There simply is not as much affordable food on the market, in terms of both variety and volume. In practical terms, this means that when one walks into a shop or a market, the shelves look bare relative to what is offered in Western stores.

I still vividly remember how bewildered and shocked I felt when I came back to the West and shopped in Western supermarkets after spending almost six years in postrevolutionary Iran. Even though Iran is a relatively rich third world country because of enormous oil revenues, a series of events (revolutionary change, a long war with Iraq, the influx of millions of Afghan refugees, major earthquakes) meant that by the early 1980s most of the population was affected by severe food shortages and rationing. In poorer regions, such as Baluchistan, the shops did not have much to offer for sale. I left Iran in December 1983 and found myself in the West during the Christmas season. I remember gazing at the shop windows, feeling physically sick to see so much on display, such enormous opulence, with store shelves heaving under the weight of extravagant varieties of food.

Immigrants to the United States who come from places where obesity is extremely rare have the same weight problems as locals after a while. They, too, find themselves gaining weight, and obesity occurs among them at about the same rate as in the host population. Of course, not everyone becomes obese. Even when individuals take in the same number of calories and have similar levels of activity, their weight gain is not always the same. To understand such variations, we also need to consider biological factors that influence the rate at which our bodies burn up calories.

Weight as Performance Capacity and as Performance Style

The obsession with weight and the ideal of thinness do not arise from biology; they are a purely cultural phenomenon. However, biological factors do influence our control over weight, particularly the conditions in which we can gain and lose weight.

Biological Factors and Weight Change

In answer to the question, "Why is it so difficult for people to lose weight?" one plausible answer seems to be, "Because weight is largely determined by biological factors that are not controlled by the individual." There is some research evidence in support of this claim. First, two distinct "hunger-control" centers has been discovered in a small part of the brain, the hypothalamus. When the lateral hypothalamus is activated, through electrical stimulation using inserted microelectrodes, the research organism (usually a rat) feels hungry and eats if food is available. This happens even if the organism has eaten recently and, therefore, should not need to eat. The opposite happens if the lateral hypothalamus is destroyed; in this case the organism refuses to eat, even though if it has not eaten for some time prior to this event. When another part of the hypothalamus, the ventromedial hypothalamus, is stimulated, the organism stops eating. When this part is destroyed, the animal eats more and eventually becomes obese.

In addition to finding these "hunger centers" in the brain, researchers have discovered a number of chemicals that affect the hunger centers, signaling the animal to eat or to stop eating. One such chemical is glucagonlike peptide-1 (GLP-1), which acts as an appetite suppressant. When GLP-1 is injected into the brain of rats, it leads to reduced eating even though the animals had been starved by the experimenter. When GLP-1 is prevented from reaching the hypothalamus, the rats eat more. The same kind of role is probably played by GLP-1 in humans.

The discovery of hunger centers and chemicals that regulate them does not prove that weight is biologically determined. After all, it could be that hunger centers in the hypothalamus and chemicals such as GLP-1 are influenced by environmental factors. Something else was needed to give the biological explanation real credibility, and it came in the form of an influential proposition that each individual has a "weight set point" that is regulated by a built-in biological mechanism, rather like a thermostat. When we go above or below the set point, the thermostat triggers our bodies to respond in a way that brings our weight back to the "natural" level. The main ways in which this happens is that we increase or decrease food intake, or our metabolic rate changes so that we increase or decrease the rate at which we burn calories.

The set-point hypothesis suggests that when individuals diet, decreased food intake leads to a reduction of the *size* of their fat cells. However, the *number* of fat cells in their bodies does not decrease. The number of fat cells is mainly determined by a combination of early eating habits and genetic inheritance. Obese individuals have a greater number of fat cells. After an initial decrease in the size of fat cells through diet, there is a tendency for the size of fat cells to increase back to the set point—through less calories being burned, increased food intake, and so on. Thus there is a constant fluctuation of weight as individuals go on diets, lose some weight, then move slowly back to their set points.

The inability of most people to lose weight through dieting seems to support the set-point hypothesis. The vast majority of people who go on diets succeed in losing some weight, but only temporarily. After a while, they typically gain the weight back, returning to roughly their former weight. One reason is that when they eat less, their body adjusts by lowing its metabolic rate (the rate at which it uses up energy). Obese people tend to already have lower metabolic rates than people of normal weight.

Clearly genetic factors determine a certain range of *capacities* for weight. This explains why studies of identical (monozygotic) twins, who have the same genetic characteristics, show about a 60 percent to 70 percent likelihood that if one twin is overweight, then the other will be also. There is also a high chance that the location of weight gain will be similar for genetic kin. We can see this in families. If mom and dad both have pot bellies, then the chance of a pot belly for their offspring when they gain weight is high. This type of family resemblance persists even when children are raised by adoptive parents; such children have a tendency to put on weight in a way that is similar to their genetic parents.

Jill's mother is typical of millions of people who have tried various diets to lose weight but found that there is a rebound effect. She experienced a cycle of weight loss and weight gain, such that her weight moved up and down like a yo-yo around an apparent set point. This experience suggests that people have as much control of their weight as they do of their height. Surely it is all genetically determined? Surely environmental factors play no part in determining weight? As we shall see, the story is not so simple.

Weight and Cultural Values

The set-point explanation of weight is highly useful, as long as we keep in mind that a set point can be influenced by both genetic and environmental factors. It is both simplistic and wrong to assume that each person is born with a weight set point that is not at all influenced by environmental factors. This becomes obvious when we look at people who are genetic kin but have experienced very different environmental conditions. Consider immigrants to the United States from poorer parts of the third world. They gain weight and become heavy compared to their third world relatives. A much-cited example is the case of the Pima Native Americans who live in Mexico and their genetic kin, the Pima Native Americans who live in Arizona. The Pimas in Arizona have had much greater access to food, as well as better living conditions generally. Unfortunately, the Arizona Pimas have the highest recorded prevalence of obesity in the world. In contrast, the Mexican Pimas, living in conditions of less abundance and ease, have about an average rate of obesity. Clearly, the set-point explanation is useful only if we view set points as influenced by both genetic and environmental factors.

Similarly, it is simplistic to assume that twin studies necessarily isolate genetic and environmental influences. The fact that two people look alike may well lead others to treat them alike. Stereotypes about "lean and mean," "fat and cheerful," and the like are so pervasive in Western societies that it is difficult to imagine how people who look alike will not be treated in a similar manner. This leads us to consider the interaction between performance capacity and performance style in how weight changes over time.

Let me at this point recount some simple observations of life in non-Western cultures. Visitors to some parts of Asia will notice a number of intriguing social norms associated with eating. In Iran, for example, when food is offered to guests, the correct way to behave is for them to follow the norms of *taarof* and decline the offering at least for the first, second, and usually third and even fourth times. This norm is followed even when the people involved are very poor and have less access to food, and even when the guests are very hungry. After repeatedly declining and finally accepting some of the food offered after being repeatedly pressed by their hosts, the correct way for guests to behave is to eat modest portions. Behavior in such settings is regulated by norms and rules of correctness (which fall into the realm of performance style), rather than the appetites of the guests (which fall into the realm of performance capacity). Similarly, in some regions of South Asia guests are expected to leave a portion of their food on their plates at the end of the meal as a sign of appreciation for the hospitality they have received—even if they would enjoy eating more food. Whether food is or is not eaten, then, depends on the norms and rules about correct behavior, not on the appetites of individuals.

An example of rules and norms about correct behavior regulating eating in a Western context is the case of anorexics. Individuals suffering from anorexia nervosa come to believe that the correct way to behave is to eat less. They ignore their own sensations of hunger and act on the basis of subjectively defined rules and norms. They see themselves as "too fat," and this perception overrides their sensations of hunger.

In contrast to this, for the general population in the United States eating is regulated much more by rules and norms that encourage consumption and the satisfaction of individual desires. It is useful to consider this in the context of the larger economy, where increased consumption is seen to be good because it leads to increased demand, increased employment opportunities, and increased earnings, which in turn allow for increased consumption. For a significant portion of the U.S. population, eating habits are regulated by a general desire to seek pleasure through consumption, a desire that more and more is trained to be "never satisfied." Despite the environmental movement, the general principle of consumption in the United States has come to be "more is better." For some people, eating habits are influenced by the same principle.

Thus it is in the social arena, particularly through the continuity sustained by carriers, that eating habits are formed and behavior in the realm of "eating and not eating" occurs. The genetic characteristics of Americans have not changed to "cause" chronic weight increases over the last century. What has changed is the American capacity to purchase food as well as the increased focus on consumption in all areas—including food.

Concluding Comment

The carrier of thinness as ideal beauty has become all-powerful in Western and increasingly in non-Western societies, accompanied by a concern with weight control. The proposed means by which weight control is to be achieved is also characteristic of our time: Technical solutions are being sought for moral problems.

I have proposed that in exploring the issue of weight control, it is essential to consider interactions between performance capacity and performance style, since both have an influence. On the one hand, genetic factors, material wealth, and the availability of food—among other components of performance capacity—set certain limits to weight change. It is more difficult to become obese if one is born with a genetic tendency to burn calories efficiently or if one lives in an environment where food is scarce. On the other hand, norms, rules, and other components of performance style have a powerful influence on weight change. It is more difficult to become obese, or even to gain enough weight to become healthy, if one carries the belief system of a typical anorexic.

If we accept this view, then we must also accept the idea that to a large extent the issue of weight change concerns choices, both by individuals and by the larger society. When things go wrong, we must accept that they went wrong in large part because we made the wrong choices, by following unhealthy eating habits. This view is contrary to the modern, and particularly American, tendency to seek technical solutions to what are basically moral problems.

Thus far there has been a poverty of technical solutions to the problem of obesity. Until 1999, the obesity drugs approved for use in the United States were appetite suppressants, which typically enable users to lose about 10 percent of their initial body weight in six months. However, research trends suggests that in the next few decades we may have available a diet drug that enables people to eat essentially as much as they want without gaining weight. Imagine that we achieve such a goal and have available an effective diet drug with few side effects. Even in such a "no-weight-gain society," key choices will still have to be made: What to eat and how much? Would we consider it morally right to spend all our waking hours eating, just because it is pleasurable and we do not gain weight? Surely not! Technical solutions may eventually provide the means to control body weight to a far greater degree than we can today, but we will still face choices about what to eat and how much. Ultimately, these are moral choices, and they are closely tied to our desire for consumption in the wider sense.

Suggested Readings

Dolan, B. (1994). Cross-cultural aspects of anorexia nervosa and bulimia: A review. *Journal of the American Academy of Child and Adolescent Psychiatry, 37*, 802–809.

Gura, T. (1997). Obesity sheds its secrets. *Science, 275*, 751–753.

Hall, C., & Iijima, C. (1995). Asian eyes: Body image and eating disorders of Asian and Asian American Women. *Eating Disorders: The Journal of Treatment and Prevention, 3*, 8–19.

Ravussin, E., Valencia, M. E., Esparza, J., Bennett, P. H., & Schulz, L. O. (1994). Effects of a traditional lifestyle on obesity in Pima Indians. *Diabetes Care, 17*, 1067–1074.

Rawls, R. L. (1999). Weighing in on obesity: Increasingly complex array of chemicals that helps regulate body weight provides many targets for drugs. *Chemical & Engineering News, 77*(25), 35–44.

Rice, T., Perusse, L., Bouchard, C., & Rao, D. C. (1996). Familial clustering of abdominal visceral fat and total fat mass: The Quebec family study. *Obesity Research, 4*, 253–261.

Rosenblatt, R. (Ed.). (1999). *Consuming desires: Consumption, culture, and the pursuit of happiness.* Washington, DC: Island Press/Shearwater Books.

Thompson, J. K. (Ed.). (1996). *Body image, eating disorders, and obesity.* Washington, DC: American Psychological Association.

Turner, J. R., Cardon, L. R., & Hewitt, J. K. (Eds.). (1995). *Behavior genetic approaches to behavioral medicine.* New York: Plenum.

Wiseman, C. V. (1992). Cultural expectations of thinness in women: An update. *International Journal of Eating Disorders, 11*, 85–89.

13 Depression

"Everything looks dark. I don't have any energy. I can't get out of bed in the mornings." The speaker, a slim, dark-haired second-generation Italian-American woman in her mid-40s spoke slowly, with long pauses between each phrase. Every word seemed to require a great effort. "I can't help it. I'm not good for my children." She sat silent for a full five minutes, wringing her hands and seemingly in pain. "My husband," she continued even more slowly, "I've held him back. He could have got an executive position if I . . ." She broke off and just sat in silence.

The speaker, whom I shall call Mary, had been pushed by her family to take a psychology class over the summer, with the idea that the activity would do her good and that she might also come to understand her own problems better. From the very first day of class, I could see that Mary was finding the experience extremely difficult. Most days, she seemed to have little energy and was unable to concentrate on the class discussion. I tried very hard to communicate with her and finally convinced her to see me in my office. She started by talking about the semester paper and mid-term exam, but the discussion quickly turned to her own problems. I knew I had to persuade her to get professional clinical help.

The case of Mary proved to be particularly challenging because of the powerful carriers that operated in her everyday life, carriers that were personal in scope and interwoven with her family relationships. Families can develop particular behavioral styles of coping with life challenges, and such styles can be sustained by subtle carriers that become part of close relationships—between husband and wife, parents and children, among others.

Carriers and the Behavioral Styles of Families and Individuals

When Mary was only 8, her mother committed suicide. She was brought up by her father, a stern professional military man who ran the home like a small dictatorship. Mary and her younger brother were marched around like little soldiers, and things barely got better when her father remarried, to a frail, timid woman who obeyed his every command. Mary clung to memories of her mother but was never again allowed even to mention her by name or to keep a photograph of her. Mary had not seen much of the world when, at the age of 19, she married Marco, a traveling salesman at the time. Her husband proved to be in some ways like her father—ambitious, a strong believer in self-help and personal responsibility, but actually not at all hardworking or talented. Marco, 12 years older than Mary, did manage to land a few lower-level management jobs, but his dream of rising to executive positions was never realized. Similarly, their two sons left high school with poor records and showed little promise of having successful careers.

As I listened to Mary talk about her dark moods, it became clear that the relationship between husbands and wives had in some ways remained the same across at least two generations in her family. There were numerous "ways of doing things" in the family, some explicitly identified as "family tradition" and many others just taken to be part of the natural order of social life, that acted as carriers and sustained continuity in behavior. Mary's father blamed his own lack of success on his wives, particularly on Mary's mother, who, according to him, had "deserted her post," and Mary's husband blamed his lack of success on Mary. In both cases, blame was communicated in subtle and indirect ways, but it was effectively communicated nonetheless. During her childhood and teenage years, Mary was never allowed to talk about her mother in front of her father, but somehow she knew from an early age that her father's lack of progress and the family's poor conditions were the fault of her mother. After she married and had children, her husband never directly told her that she was holding him back, but she knew that he thought she was. If only she had been a better wife, a better mother, a better hostess, a better networker in the community, a better inspiration to their children, then the family would have made more progress.

One day when Mary was in my office, a former student, Liz, telephoned to tell me about her latest success. Having completed her M.B.A. degree and several years of managerial training, she had been offered a fast-track corporate job in New York. This was a remarkable achievement for a person with her background. Liz never knew her father, and her mother had six children with four different husbands. Liz spent much of her early life being moved between different foster homes; she saw little of her own mother, who had severe drug addiction problems. She was 12 by the time she found a more permanent home with her grandparents. But somehow, in the midst of all the instability, drugs, uncaring parents, siblings who showed little interest in books, and impoverished inner-city school conditions, she managed not only to survive but to thrive. As I sat listening to Liz on the phone telling me about her new job, I pondered the condition of Mary, sitting in my office. I was once again struck by the fact that individuals differ in how well they cope with challenging conditions. Liz was so full of energy and optimism, but Mary suffered crippling depression, even though the conditions suffered by Liz seemed just as bad or perhaps even worse than those suffered by Mary.

In this chapter I want to paint a broad picture of three types of factors associated with depression: biological processes, thinking styles, and social context. When individuals try to change their moods, either by their own efforts or through the help of professionals, they are confronted by the challenge of influencing these different sets of factors. Individuals such as Mary and Liz can be similar or different as regards any or all of these factors. The general practice in Western medical treatments has been to focus on the individual—and thus on biological processes and thinking styles—rather than on social context.

From the individualistic perspective of mainstream Western medicine, there seems little point in considering the larger issues of social context and the integration of individuals into society in order to better understand depression. Despite theoretical considerations of context by some writers, in practice in Western societies the main line of attack regarding illnesses remains drug therapy, and depression is no exception. This aggressive use of drugs is particularly high in the United States even compared to other Western countries. Lynn Payer and others have shown that a patient is far more likely to be given drugs for an illness, and to undergo major surgery, in the United States than in England, West Germany, or France. This drug-based approach ignores the role of social relationships and the larger social context; in at least some cases it tackles symptoms, not root causes.

In coming to understand depression, it is useful to consider the nature of social relationships and the collaboratively constructed social world within which the depressed person is enmeshed. The experience of depression is intimately connected with both actual social relationships and perceived possibilities for social relationships, that is, the social world in which the depressed person actually exists and the social world the depressed person sees as feasible for him- or herself. Such perceptions are fundamentally influenced by the larger society, as is the case for Mary. Of course, there are some aspects of Mary's experiences that are unique.

On Particular Cases and General Trends

On average, Bill Gates and I have a gloriously high income. But such a mythical "average income" does not actually exist (unfortunately for me); by computing such an average, one does not get a clear picture of my financial situation—or Bill Gates's. General statistical indicators tell us that women are more likely to experience depression than men, but this tells us nothing of value about specific men or women. If I knew that the next person coming into my office would be a woman, I could not use information about "women on average" to predict anything about this particular woman. At the same time, information about a specific individual might not yield a picture of general trends in a population.

The information gained from research on population trends is part of a *nomothetic* approach that tries to arrive at broad generalizations about behavior, whereas an individualistic approach that tries to unravel the particulars of specific cases, such as Mary's, is part of an *idiographic* approach.

Clearly, nomothetic and idiographic approaches each have their advantages. The nomothetic approach tells us about general trends among populations, such as the rise in reported depression in many different societies. This approach paints pictures with broad strokes and captures grand images that are best viewed from a distance, but it gives a very blurred image of individuals, so blurred that single persons are not identifiable. The idiographic approach provides detailed information about specific persons, but it gives only vague notions of general trends.

Both nomothetic and idiographic approaches provide invaluable information about effecting changes in moods, such as depression. Each depressed person, such as Mary, is in some ways like all other depressed persons and in some ways like no other depressed person. By changing things common to a population, such as the social role of women, we can influence many lives, but we also need to change things unique to particular individuals, such as Mary's family relationships and her particular style of coping with her situation.

Mary, Both Similar and Unique

Mary did finally seek professional help to treat her depression. Of course, we all experience mood swings and feel low on some days, but the kind of clinical depression suffered by people like Mary is very different. Clinically depressed individuals often lose energy and the motivation to do even routine things. Some days Mary found it impossible to get out of bed, wash, dress, and do the kinds of things people normally do to prepare for the day. Although she was bright, she could not apply herself to study or work hard. She just could not manage to energize herself. She was like a toy running very low on batteries.

Like most people who suffer depression, Mary experienced *unipolar depression*, meaning that her moods took only downward turns and pulled her through gloomy days and nights. She did not experience an upward turn to *mania*, the opposite of depression, involving frenzied activity associated with overconfidence and euphoria. *Bipolar mood swings*, involving mood shifts between depression and mania, are experienced by a small number of people compared to the numbers who suffer unipolar depression. Bipolar mood swings are more prevalent among economically more advantaged people—perhaps they are the only ones who enjoy the freedom to express such dramatic mood swings.

Although boys and girls are equally likely to experience depression, as people reach puberty and adulthood the rates for women become higher, so that about a quarter of all women are likely to experience sever unipolar depression sometime in their lives, with the rate for men being about half that for women. This gender difference is consistent across cultures. It does not matter whether we take samples from New York, New Delhi, or Nova Scotia—women have a higher rate of depression than men. Similarly, women have higher rates of depression among whites, African Americans, and other ethnic groups in North America.

Mary's case suggests a role for social context and carriers that helps explain why women experience depression more than men do. She felt she had little control over the events of her life, and even in her own home she had much less power and influence than her husband and sons. She had full responsibility for all the housework and sometimes took jobs outside the home to supplement the family income, but she got no credit for her efforts. Because her husband undermined her confidence, she almost always applied for jobs well below her level of ability and training. Such jobs were boring for her, and she found it difficult to motivate herself, which gave further ammunition to her husband to criticize her. But instead of blaming the boring job or some other aspect of her situation, she blamed herself and found yet another reason to see herself as worthless. Mary's depression seemed to become darker and lighter in cycles, perhaps as a result of hormonal fluctuations experienced by women, particularly at puberty and other critical periods, such as pregnancy.

It was apparent that her husband was also depressed about his situation, but he seemed to find a more active way of venting his frustrations. He was often angry, mostly at her but also sometimes at their two boys. Each time her husband felt depressed about his lack of success at work, he found ways of heaping blame on the rest of the family, and this worsened Mary's situation.

During the times that Mary's batteries got a recharge, she showed a genuine interest in the class topics and did research to find out more about depression. She was imaginative and would ask, "Would I have suffered this problem if I had been born in the eighteenth century or some other time in history?" She learned about one of the most mysterious trends uncovered by research—that depression rates are currently rising in many different societies around the world. Perhaps this is a result of rising expectations, of people's wrongly assuming that modernization and consumerism should make them happier and happier. Perhaps women are more affected because their political, economic, and social situation has changed more dramatically and their expectations of positive outcomes have risen faster than those of men.

Or perhaps people have now gotten used to talking about depression and expressing dissatisfaction with life, whereas before they put up with more and complained less. This may also explain the gender difference: Men are trained to talk less about their feelings and to keep things inside, whereas it is considered more appropriate for women to express their feelings and to tell others about their problems. On days when she was less depressed, Mary talked to me about these different possible explanations with genuine interest and insight. She also talked about her mother and the idea that depression might run in her family.

Research has shown that close relatives of people with clinical depression have as much as a 20 percent likelihood of developing the same disorder, compared to less than a 10 percent likelihood for the general population. If one identical twin suffers from depression, the other twin has almost a 50 percent chance of experiencing the same problem. But this rate drops to about 20 percent when the twin is fraternal. Mary reasoned that her mother must have suffered from depression, and she investigated other close family members and found several additional cases of what seemed like depression, although she could not be sure because people preferred to sweep such problems under the carpet. One older member of the family said to Mary, "Why are you digging up such shameful things from the past?"

Mary delved into the past in order to change things for the better. She felt guilty and anxious about the lack of progress in her family. More than anything, she wanted to change herself, to do better for her family. Her eagerness for change sometimes disappeared in the gloom of depression and inactivity, but it always came back again as the darkness receded. It was when she came out of a bout of depression and showed determination to move ahead that she became most like Liz, my former student. But Mary lacked Liz's sustained and consistent drive, in part because she lived in a family context in which it was not appropriate to display such behavior. Mary's family relationships kept her down, whereas Liz's family relationships pushed her ahead.

Performance Limitations and Depression

Part of the complexity in dealing with depression is the need to attend to limitations of both performance capacity and performance style, which circumscribe what can change physically and what can change socially in the life of the depressed person.

Performance-Capacity Limitations and Depression

It took tremendous effort for Mary to seek professional help for her depression. She actually tried to commit suicide before taking this step. Characteristically for her, after she recovered from her suicide attempt and came out of a depression swing, she used her renewed energy to investigate the topic of suicide. "I wonder why more women attempt suicide, but more men succeed in killing themselves?" she asked as she sat in my office one day, adding "I'm not sure about the idea that suicide is a cry for help. I meant to kill myself. I knew what I was doing."

Like millions of other patients diagnosed as suffering from depression, Mary was prescribed antidepressant drugs. Such drugs have become part of modern world culture. Most people have by now heard of Prozac, a leading antidepressant that first came onto the market in 1987. Mary was among the patients who responded favorably to Prozac. Like some of the patients described in Peter Kramer's book *Listening to Prozac*, Mary changed her low opinion of herself. She began to be more assertive and active on a continuous basis.

But how exactly did Prozac help her? The answer is that we are not sure. There is no doubt that some of the benefit comes from the placebo effect, which is always a headache for medical researchers. Hard evidence shows that administering a simple sugar pill to patients can alleviate symptoms simply because patients "expect to get better" now that they have taken medication. Reviews of the research literature on Prozac suggest that, in some cases at least, the placebo effect has as powerful an effect as the drug itself. In 1999 a major new antidepressant, a Merck invention known as MK-869, was withdrawn from the market because reanalysis of the clinical trials data showed that patients who had taken a dummy pill had improved just as much as those who had taken MK-869. At present, antidepressant drugs probably rely on the placebo effect for at least 50 percent, and perhaps a lot more in some cases, of their effectiveness. However, current research also suggests that antidepressants do have some real effect, and what we know about biological processes suggests some likely reasons.

Our search for an explanation for the biological effects of antidepressants begins at the brain, where information gathered by our senses is analyzed. The brain is not only the center of everything to do with thinking, including memory; it is also where our personality lies. All the personal experiences, aspirations, conscious and unconscious dreams, and so on of an individual take place in the brain. When people lose legs or have liver or heart transplants, they are still the same individuals, but a brain transplant (if and when it becomes medically possible) would mean the creation of a new person. Damage to the brain often detrimentally affects not only how efficiently we solve problems but also our personalities. One of the terrifying consequences of Alzheimer's disease is that the brain no longer does its job as the center of thinking and personality, and Alzheimer sufferers no longer recognize who they are (this topic is discussed in greater detail in Chapter 14).

The brain is able to house the complexities of "who we are" in large part because it is a miraculously efficient communications center. The human brain is made up of about a hundred billion *neurons*, tiny nerve cells, and an even greater number of *glia*, support cells. Brain messages are sent from neuron to neuron in the form of electrical impulses. There are hundreds of different types of neurons, with many different shapes and sizes. However, most neurons have the same basic characteristics. Each neuron has antennae, called *dendrites*, to receive messages from other neurons. These antennae are connected to the *cell body*, which contains the cell's genetic material in its nucleus. Received messages pass along a long fiber, an *axon*, extending from the cell body to nerve endings. The axon is covered with *myelin*, which acts as insulation and improves electrical conduction. From the nerve endings, the message is picked up by the antennae of other neurons. Thus there is a continuous flow of messages involving billions of neurons.

A message sent by a neuron will not have the same effect on all surrounding neurons. A message that fires off neuron A may not necessarily fire off neuron B or C—rather like a key that opens some doors but not others. The situation is much more complex, though, because at any given moment a single neuron could be receiving thousands of different messages. The combined effect of these messages determines whether a neuron will fire or not.

Neurons fire in an *all-or-none* manner. Either a message gets a neuron to fire, or it doesn't. This is rather like a finger pulling the trigger of a gun—either it is pulled hard enough to fire or it is not. A gun (or a neuron) does not fire less or more strongly. What, then, is the difference between the influence of a message that is just strong enough to get a neuron to fire and one that is much stronger? This difference shows in the number of times a neuron fires as a result of receiving a message. Some messages get neurons to fire often and rapidly, while others result in few and interspersed firings.

When a neuron is not firing, it carries a positive electrical charge on the outside and a negative electrical charge on the inside. The difference is tiny, only about 60 millivolts, but it is nonetheless important because this electrical charge has to be reversed for firing to occur. When a message is of the right kind and achieves firing, for a split second the poles of this batterylike system are reversed and the outside becomes negative and the inside becomes positive. Firing sends electrical impulses from a neuron's antennae to its nerve endings. There a message has to get across a very small gap, a *synapse*, that lies between these nerve endings and the antennae of other neurons.

Chemicals released by electrical stimulation at nerve endings travel across the synapse to reach antennae of other neurons. The kind of message sent from one neuron to another depends on these chemicals. Some chemicals get the next neuron to fire, while other chemicals are inhibitory and stop the next neuron from firing, while still others have no effect on the next neuron.

One way to understand depression, albeit in an all too limited manner, is to view it as things going wrong with the chemical changes taking place at the synapse. What could be going wrong? One possibility is too much or not enough of certain chemicals being released into the synapse. There are also other possibilities. The transmitter neuron could fail to reabsorb in a timely manner the chemicals it has released into the synapse, a process referred to as *reuptake*. If reuptake is not efficient, the released chemicals could linger at the synapse and interfere with normal functioning. Or the receiver neuron could take up too much or too little of the chemicals being released. If any of these kinds of problems arise, there will probably be communications problems across the nervous system, with possible detrimental consequences for moods and cognition, such as those associated with depression.

Antidepressant drugs work by effecting chemical processes at the synapse, so that communications across neurons can take place more efficiently. Research in the 1950s led to the first generation of modern antidepressant drugs—tricyclics and monoamine oxidase (MAO) inhibitors. On the positive side, these drugs have helped millions of people suffering from depression to feel better. Studies suggest that up to about 60 to 70 percent of depressed individuals can be helped using these types of drugs (of course, some of the benefits of drug therapy, as discussed earlier, may be placebo-related). On the negative side, tricyclics can have serious side effects, including blurred vision, dry mouth, and even weak heartbeats (arrhythmia). Patients on MAO inhibitors have to observe very strict diets to limit the intake of tyramine; otherwise they risk dangerously high blood pressure, which can be lethal.

But what chemical processes do tricyclics and MAO inhibitors influence? The most likely explanation is that they help to normalize the availability of the neurotransmitters norepinephrine and serotonin at the synapse. A second generation of antidepressants now available do a much better job of targeting the specific link among norepinephrine, serotonin, and depression, with far less serious side effects for most patients. These more advanced drugs have trade names such as Prozac, Paxil, and Zoloft. Although in most cases doctors have to test the suitability of these drugs for particular patients in a trial-and-error manner, the decreased side effects as well as the better ability to focus on specific neurotransmitter activities have led to their far more widespread use.

Performance Style and Depression

When Mary finally agreed to get professional help, she took a step toward trying to change her mood patterns and thus to end the crippling depression she suffered. The fact that she took this initiative suggests that she was motivated to recover. To help bring about this desired change, her therapist started her treatment with drug therapy. In addition to the usual benefits of the placebo effect, the second-generation antidepressants change moods by changing chemical processes at the synapse. In many cases the chemical changes they bring about are fairly speedy. More than half the depressives who have been given these drugs have shown marked improvement within a few weeks. This is a much faster change than that achieved by traditional talk therapies alone. In the long run, drug therapy and talk therapies are both able to improve the lives of most depressives. However, talk therapies are more costly and take a longer time to have an effect. The most successful treatment for depressed persons is a combination of drug therapy and talk therapy.

After several weeks of drug therapy, Mary's condition improved to such a degree that the therapist was now able to treat her through talk therapy as well. The therapist focused on teaching Mary new thinking skills, so that she could control her moods better. In our everyday lives we often try to change our moods by recalling past events or thinking of future ones. We cheer ourselves up by reminding ourselves of a past success or of things we have to look forward to, or we might purposefully make ourselves feel angry by recalling how we were mistreated by somebody or by thinking about ordeals we have to go through in the future. We also use these kinds of mental strategies to change the moods of other people. "Cheer up," we tell our friends, "you're going on vacation next week." Or "You didn't get a bonus this year, but at least you have a job. Think of poor Jack, who got fired." Depressed individuals such as Mary tend not to use such strategies; instead, they have thinking styles that highlight the negative rather than the positive, that lead to bad rather than good moods.

Instead of seeing the glass as "half full," Mary had always seen it as "half empty." Instead of saying, "I have done well, raised two children, helped my family financially by working outside the home when needed and encouraging my husband and sons in their careers," she tended to focus on things she had failed to do. All of us have failed to take up countless challenges, and if we focused on the mountains we have failed to climb we could become depressed. Everyone has missed opportunities and failed to rise to some occasions. A major difference between depressed and nondepressed individuals is that the former focus exclusively on the negative.

But the therapist's challenge is far greater than to lead a depressed person to see things accurately, because in many instances it is a matter of teaching depressed persons to see the world in a more rather than less biased way. Depressed persons often perceive the world more accurately than do the nondepressed. Depressed persons are more likely to see their own shortcomings and to acknowledge them realistically ("I am not a good driver"; "Some people dislike me"; "I made the wrong choice in marriage"; "Many people are better than I in my line of work"), while nondepressed persons tend to have a more biased view, one that glorifies their positive features and denies the negative ("The other driver caused the accident"; "Most people like me, and the few who dislike me are weird"; "My partner is the right choice"; "I am among the best in my line of work"). Particularly in North America, everyone is "better than average." But depressed persons are more likely to see themselves as below average.

By a stroke of good fortune, Mary's therapy moved ahead at a time when her husband and sons were away from home a great deal. Within six months, the combination of drug therapy and cognitive talk therapy had turned things around for Mary. She volunteered her time as a research assistant in one of my research projects, so I met with her every week and observed her improvement. It was a joyous experience, seeing a fragile, withdrawn, inactive person transform into an energetic, active, and articulate personality. It was like seeing a different, new person come to life.

But after about a year, I began to see Mary withdraw and slip back into former ways of thinking. She was still on drug therapy and meeting once a month with her therapist, but clearly something was going wrong. After some probing, I discovered that her husband had lost his job again and was spending a lot more time at home, as was their older son. The home environment was pulling Mary back to her former way of thinking, one that highlighted her feelings of guilt and all those opportunities her family had missed (supposedly) because of her.

The therapist had brought about change at the chemical level within a few weeks and at the level of Mary's personal thinking style within a few months. He had transformed her in isolation, and this was an impressive achievement. However, much more difficult to change was the larger social context in which Mary lived and which contributed in substantial ways to her behavior. Mary's style of thought and behavior was not independent of her social environment; it was part of a larger social world. To change her and help her out of depression, it was also necessary to change the social relationships and the larger context in which she lived.

Part of the challenge was to change Mary's attitudes toward her own situation and to help her recognize that she was not personally to blame for her family's problems—and also that she need not feel guilty when she experienced mood swings. Mary was plagued by feelings of guilt, particularly about not being able to stay happy, not being a "fun" mother and wife for her family. In the North American context in which Mary lives, negative emotions are not valued and can even be a source of shame.

Cultural Context and Depression

A serious consideration of the relationship between culture and emotional experiences leads to the conclusion that depression as it is medically recognized and treated in Western societies is fundamentally a cultural construct. This is not to say that people in other historical eras and in other societies have not experienced the same biological processes as do depressed people in Western societies today, but that the meanings and implications of experiences arising from such processes have been different in major ways. A first issue is to consider current attitudes toward happiness and sadness; a second is to consider such attitudes in cross-cultural perspective.

■ **Self-Presentation and Happiness in the United States** A first point is that in modern Western societies, particularly in the United States, greater and greater emphasis is being placed on presenting the self in a positive and happy way. This bias manifests itself even in the ways in which people are supposed to greet one another. When asked "How are you?" the respondent in America is not supposed to say anything as low-key as "Not bad" or "Okay," but to exuberantly declare "I'm great!" or "Wonderful." During a period in the 1990s when I was frequently traveling back and forth between Europe and the United States, I recorded responses to my greeting "How are you doing?" from different people I met on the two sides of the Atlantic. After I had recorded responses from 250 different people in Europe and another 250 in the United States, I found that whereas 82 percent of the American responses were of the "I'm great!" and "Wonderful" variety, 64 percent of the European responses were of the "Can't complain" and "Not bad" type. Asian greetings tend to be even more subdued. In Farsi a typical response to "How are you?" is "Thank God, it passes."

Whereas it is normative to present the self as successful and positive, and to make declarations such as "I'm great!" in response to a greeting in the United States, such a self-presentational style would not be normative in most Eastern cultures, and a person displaying such a style would be regarded in a negative light. Reflecting this difference, most American students tend to evaluate themselves as above average in their class, whereas only about half of Japanese students do so. This more positive self-presentational style of Americans is also associated with the high value placed on happy moods and a depreciation of negative moods. To be sad, melancholic, gloomy, and the like is regarded as bad, as "sick," as something to be avoided if at all possible.

An alternative view is that sadness and other such "negative" emotions are a normal part of life and should be valued as an essential feature of human experience. This point is further clarified when we consider the cultural and historical context of emotional experiences.

■ Contemporary Attitudes Toward "Negative" Emotions in Cross-Cultural Perspective

Even in the Western tradition, "negative" emotions—sadness, melancholy, depression—have not always been shunned. For example, a cult of melancholy existed from about the mid-eighteenth to the late nineteenth century, a cult in which melancholic moods were valued as a rich and essential aspect of human experience. This is reflected, for example, in John Keats's (1795–1821) highly praised poem "Ode on Melancholy," which celebrates the melancholic mood and encourages the reader to cling to melancholy when it comes "sudden from heaven like a weeping cloud." Consider also the enormous success of Edward Fitzgerald's (1809–1883) translation of Persian poetry that he titled *The Rubaiya of Omar Khayyam* (1048–1131), with its "defeatist," fatalistic, even gloomy mood:

> Oh, come with old Khayyam, and
> Leave the wise
> To talk; one thing is certain, that life
> Flies;
> One thing is certain, and the Rest
> Is Lies;
> The Flower that once has blown for
> ever dies.

The theme of melancholy and sadness is still highly prominent in Farsi-speaking culture, a theme that is sustained by powerful religious carriers. In Shiite Islam (the religion of over 96 percent of Iranians and about 45 percent of Iraqis) a number of important religious ceremonies are specifically designed to lead participants to feel sad and melancholic, to weep and hit themselves, and in general to experience and express misery. One such ceremony is *rowzeh-khani*, during which a chanter retells well-known stories from the lives of Islamic martyrs and saints; the ceremony is considered a success only if participants weep and engage in self-flagellation. It is not unusual for such ceremonies to end with mass weeping, involving hundreds or even thousands of people shedding tears, wailing, and hitting themselves on the head and chest. Despite globalization and creeping Westernization, in Islamic societies and most other traditional Eastern societies, there is still a tendency to see a constructive and even necessary role for moods akin to sadness, melancholy, depression, and other experiences that in the Western context would typically be shunned, stigmatized and treated as illness.

Even studies conducted by Western-trained researchers, using instruments geared to identify depression in the Western model and focusing on participants (typically university students) who are part of the modern Westernized sections of non-Western societies, have uncovered cross-cultural differences in the domain of depression. A consistent finding has been that depressed individuals in Western societies report feelings of guilt and self-blame, as well as mood states such as loneliness and anxiety, whereas guilt does not seem to be part of the experiences akin to depression in non-Western societies, where the focus is less on internal mood states and more on somatic symptoms, such as bodily pain and fatigue. Even when researchers translate the term *depression* into other languages, in which often there is no direct translation, and squeeze the experiences of non-Western people into the Western mold, it is clear that depressed individuals in the West tend to focus on internal mood states and their independent experiences, whereas individuals in non-Western cultures typically look outside and refer to rain, seasons, fate, and numerous phenomena outside the self to explain their experiences.

Concluding Comment

From the perspective of Western medical models, depression is an illness with specific dispositional causes, and the treatment of depression in practice focuses on changing aspects of the individual. Practical and particularly economic limitations mean that drug therapy is at the heart of treatment, and sometimes actually the only treatment, and so Prozac and other drugs are in danger of taking on the role that soma plays in Aldous Huxley's *Brave New World*. There is a real possibility that anyone unable to conform to the norm of a positive self-presentational style will increasingly come under pressure to use drugs to "make themselves better," just as people in *Brave New World* were expected to use soma to avoid negative moods. Not surprisingly, in this normative system those who slip back into feeling "bad" also experience guilt; after all, they are doing something wrong because they are not presenting themselves as happy.

This focus on the individual completely misses an essential point: Depression can be sustained through carriers that are interwoven in family and personal relationships, a style of small-group life that often transcends generations and impacts the lives of different age groups. The case of Mary is not atypical. Drug therapy could help Mary improve if she were left alone, but no person is an island, and the web of personal and family relationships in which Mary was enmeshed pulled her back into depression again. This is not to suggest that therapy should focus exclusively on family and personal relationships, but that it should seriously attend to them.

There is also a need to reconsider the treatment of varieties of emotions in the larger society. In the United States in particular, far too high a priority is now given to positive self-presentation, leaving too little room for a whole variety of emotions that do not fit in with the "I'm great!" image. Sadness, gloominess, and various negative emotions are part of the natural range of human experiences. They allow human beings to feel deeply and differently, to become more creative and original, and just because they are not "fun" does not mean they should be a cause for taking "happy pills." The growing literature on depression and creativity suggests that there is great value in negative moods. Humanity would be a lot poorer culturally if we all opted for sustained fun and happiness: One wonders what Van Gogh would have painted if he had been on Prozac.

Suggested Readings

Davies, K. E., & Tilghman, S. M. (Eds.). (1993). *Genome maps and neurological disorders*. Plainview, NY: Cold Spring Harbor Laboratory Press.

Enserink, M. (1999). Can the placebo be the cure? *Science, 284*, 238–240.

Fitzgerald, E. (Trans.). (1993). *The Rubaiyat of Omar Khayyam*. Ware, UK: Wordsworth Classics. (Original work published 1859.)

Goodwin, F. K., & Jamison, K. R. (1990). *Manic depressive illness*. New York: Oxford University Press.

Hedaya, R. J. (1996). *Understanding biological psychiatry*. New York: Norton.

Hrobjartsson, A., & Gtzche, P. (2001). Is the placebo powerless? An analysis of clinical trials comparing placebo with no treatment. *The New England Journal of Medicine, 344*, 1594–1602.

Ingram, R. E., Miranda, J., & Segal, Z. V. (1998). *Cognitive vulnerability to depression*. New York: Guilford.

Jablow, H. D., & Lieb, J. (1998). *Manic depression and creativity*. Amherst, NY: Prometheus.

Kato, P. M., & Mann, T. (Eds.). (1996). *Handbook of diversity issues in health psychology*. New York: Plenum.

Kleinman, A., & Good, B. (Eds.). (1986). *Culture and depression: Studies in anthropology and cross-cultural psychiatry of affect and disorder.* Berkeley: University of California Press.

Koslow, S. H., Meinecke, D. L., Lederhendler, I. I., Khachaturian, H., Nakamura, R. K., Karp, D., Vitkovic, L., Glanzman, D. L., & Zaleman, S. (Eds.). (1995). *The neuroscience of mental health II: A report on neuroscience research, status and potential for mental health and mental illness.* Rockville, MD.: National Institute of Mental Health/National Institutes of Health.

Kramer, P. D. (1993). *Listening to Prozac.* New York: Viking.

Marsella, T. (1998). Toward a "global community psychology": Meeting the needs of a changing world. *American Psychologist, 53,* 1282–1291.

Mezzich, J. E., Kleinman, A., Horacio, F., Jr., & Parron, D. L. (Eds.). (1996). *Culture and psychiatric diagnosis: A DSM-IV perspective.* Washington, DC: American Psychiatric Press.

Payer, L. (1988). *Medicine and culture.* New York: Penguin.

Ryan, R. M., & Deci, E. L. (2001). On happiness and human potentials: A review of research on hedonic and eudaimonic well-being. *Annual Review of Psychology, 52,* 141–166.

Schildkraut, J. J., & Otero, A. (Eds.). (1996). *Depression and the spiritual in modern art.* New York: Wiley.

Tanaka-Matsumi, J., & Draguns, J. (1997). Culture and psychopathology. In J. W. Berry, M. H. Segal., & C. Kagitcibasi (Eds.), *Handbook of cross-cultural psychology* (Vol. 3; pp. 449–491). Needham Heights, MA.: Allyn & Bacon.

14

Alzheimer's Disease and the "Margin of Performance Expectations"

Dr. M, a woman living in a major U.S. urban center, has two advanced degrees and had been a professor for decades. She had enjoyed the role of teacher and the opportunity to use her finely tuned communications skills with students. It was particularly painful for her when she began to experience word-finding and memory problems. By the age of 75, standard psychological tests revealed her to have decreased ability in a number of cognitive areas, consistent with dementia. Dr. M had built a successful academic career and achieved high social status through her memory, verbal abilities, and intellect generally, but she was now cruelly being deprived of just these assets.

Aging brings with it biological changes that influence performance capacity: how well we do on traditional tests of abilities, which typically assess us in isolation in examlike situations. Our capacities for hearing, seeing, sensing touch, and so on are diminished once we reach adulthood and the years march on. Accompanying this are changes in performance style, so that the meaning of behavior is transformed as we get older. Even when we behave in the same manner as we did when we were younger, *others now have different expectations of us and interpret our behavior differently.* When a 35-year-old professor forgets where she put her keys, this event is likely to be taken as just another indication that she is an absent-minded professor. Students, friends, and family will jokingly recount such incidents as evidence that she really *does* fit the stereotype. However, a 65-year-old professor who forgets where she put her keys is more likely to be seen as suffering from dementia. "Her mind is going," people will say.

In this chapter we explore the *margin of performance expectations,* the difference between the actual performance capacity of individuals and the expectations that others have about their performance. Using the example of seniors with a particular degenerative disorder, I shall argue that there is a strong tendency for the expectations of others to influence the behavior of individuals.

All things being equal, *the larger the margin of performance expectations, the poorer will be the performance of individuals compared to their actual performance capacities.* For example, if Joe is a 75-year-old who has the capacity to score 90 out of a 100 on a particular language test, he will score closer to 90 if the expectation is that he will score 89 than if the expectation is that he will score 19.

The margin of performance expectations is sustained by carriers, such as the physical carrier represented by an "old body." Biological aging has clearly visible signs, such as wrinkled skin, white hair, and the like, and the physically aged body is a carrier of specific stereotypes—"Old people have poor memories," "Old people are not technologically sophisticated," and so on. Just the physical appearance of an old person can trigger in the mind of observers stereotypes about seniors, leading to a huge margin between what that senior can actually do and what the holder of the stereotype expects him or her to be able to do. Expectations can put pressure on a senior to underpreform, to do what is expected rather than what he or she is actually capable of doing.

While the biological process of aging is gradual, the social process of changed expectations for correct behavior can be sudden and rapid. In the case of Dr. M, the shift in social expectations was even more dramatic because (1) she was now seen as old and (2) she was diagnosed as having Alzheimer's disease. *Alzheimer's disease*—named after Alois Alzheimer, the German physician who first identified it in 1907—is a degenerative disorder that destroys the brain, robbing victims of memory, sense of identity, and decision-making abilities, leaving them dependent on others. Dr. M was now labeled in such a way that her remaining abilities suddenly went unrecognized.

Although Alzheimer's is a progressive disease, often taking years and sometimes even decades to have severe effects, the shift in social relations for those suffering from Alzheimer's disease can be sudden and swift, a matter of days or even hours or minutes. Once labeled as having Alzheimer's disease, an individual quickly becomes enmeshed in dramatically changed social relationships, with the individual expected to play the role of a dependent, ill person. There is pressure to conform to the changed social expectations, and by conforming and taking on the role of a dependent, ill person, the Alzheimer's sufferer participates in the collaborative construction and objectification of the new social context. The expectations of others with respect to the performance of the person with Alzheimer's disease become fulfilled.

Consequently, although Alzheimer's is a disease affecting biological processes within individuals, to understand the actual deterioration of the Alzheimer's sufferer it is often necessary to consider the larger social context and societal characteristics. To better appreciate the urgency of attending to this situation, it is useful to consider the demographic changes taking place and the prevalence of Alzheimer's disease.

Demographic Trends and the Performance Capacity of Persons with Alzheimer's Disease

Why is it important to attend to the problems of Alzheimer's sufferers? What do we know about the biological causes of the disease? By addressing these two questions, I shall prepare the way for an exploration of the social and cultural aspects of Alzheimer's disease.

The Aging Population and Alzheimer's Disease

Alzheimer's disease represents a major challenge to modern societies because of the aging population and the prevalence of this disease among the aged. Since the beginning of the twentieth century, life expectancy has increased markedly, particularly in the United States (see Fig 14.1) and other Western societies, leading to a sharp rise in the number of elderly people and therefore

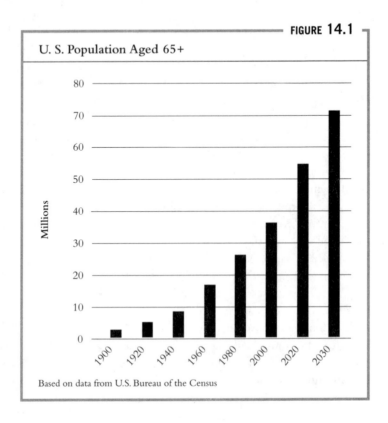

FIGURE **14.1**

U. S. Population Aged 65+

Based on data from U.S. Bureau of the Census

the incidence of dementia associated with aging. Alzheimer's disease accounts for about half of all dementia cases in the United States.

But Alzheimer's is not just a challenge for industrial societies. In 1975, about half the world population over 60 years of age lived in lower income countries. By 2000, more than 60 percent of people over age 60 lived in lower income countries, and by 2025 this figure will have reached almost 75 percent (see Table 14.1). How this aged population will be affected by Alzheimer's disease is suggested by trends in the United States, where the affliction rate is 2 percent of people aged 65, 4 percent by age 70, 8 percent by age 75, 16 percent by age 80, 32 percent by age 85, and almost 50 percent of people over 85. However, there are indications that the rate of increase drops off for the very old. In sum, the number of Alzheimer's sufferers increases exponentially every five years after the age of 60 and plateaus sometime after the age of 90. In the United States the number of Alzheimer's sufferers is already over half a million.

At the personal level, Alzheimer's disease is the cause of considerable suffering for both victims and their families and friends. The disease progressively worsens over a course of anywhere from 2 to more than 20 years. It starts to manifest itself when victims have difficulty keeping focused on a task and have lapses of memory. Eventually, the afflicted person cannot concentrate even on important things and forgets essential bits of information, such as the names and telephone numbers of close family members. As the disease robs victims of basic cognitive abilities, including the ability to recall simple events, persons, and places, normal functioning as an independent person becomes increasingly difficult—and eventually impossible. Social relationships break down. The victim eventually becomes completely dependent on others.

This deterioration is extremely painful for both victims and their loved ones. The victim may at first deny that any change has taken place, explaining away memory lapses as simple "forgetfulness." However, as memory deteriorates and decision making gets poorer, the victim reaches a point where even close family members, such as a spouse or children, are not recognized. Even

TABLE 14.1

Population aged 65 and over (in millions)

	1980s	2000	2020
Higher income countries	128	166	230
Lower income countries	132	237	530

Based on data from the United Nations

when reminded that "this is your wife, who has lived with you for 40 years," a victim may ask "Who is this?" when his wife returns to the room after an absence of just a few minutes.

At the economic level, Alzheimer's disease is contributing substantially to the increased costs of health care. In the United States alone, the disease is estimated to cost over $100 billion annually. The health care crisis confronting the United States and other Western societies is associated with the ballooning cost of caring for Alzheimer's sufferers. Clearly, on both humanitarian and economic grounds there is a need to try to meet the challenge of Alzheimer's disease.

Performance Capacity and Alzheimer's Disease

Physical change is part of normal aging. Our bodies change a great deal when we develop as youngsters, and change is just as dramatic during old age. But not all parts of our body change at the same rate. Age-related changes in the central nervous system—the spinal cord and the brain—are selective. Although we experience substantial neuronal loss in some parts of the brain, other regions remain relatively unimpaired.

As people age, neurofibrillary tangles, made up of twisted protein fibers, develop within the cells of those parts of the brain associated with memory and other vital cognitive functions. In addition, increased numbers of senile plaques appear in parts of the brain. This is a normal change experienced by most or all older people, but it occurs to a much greater degree among persons with Alzheimer's disease. At the same time, these individuals experience particularly marked abnormalities of certain neurotransmitters. Neurofibrillary tangles, senile plaques, and neurotransmitter abnormalities all contribute to impairment of communication between neurons, and this in turn may cause loss of memory and other cognitive functioning. Over the next few decades, medical research is expected to arrive at a better understanding of what causes these problems and also to develop more effective medical responses. But we have a long way to go on this front.

Given that some level of neurofibrillary tangles and other such changes are a normal feature of aging, why is it that some people age without suffering from Alzheimer's disease but others fall victim to it? Studies have established that one group of Alzheimer's sufferers are from families with a higher than normal prevalence of the disease, which suggests a genetic basis (although it does not exclude the possibility that environmental factors, such as family climate, play an important role). Even if some cases of Alzheimer's disease prove to be caused by infectious agents, as proposed by some researchers, this raises the likelihood that some individuals are genetically more predisposed to this disease. Comparisons of positron emission tomography (PET) scans of the brain and genetic tests of members of families prone to the disease suggest it may be possible to predict *the likelihood of* Alzheimer's years, perhaps decades, before the symptoms appear.

However, another substantial group of Alzheimer's sufferers do not have a family history of the disease. This suggests an important role for environmental factors, as well as for complex interactions between genetic and environmental factors. Among the more obvious environmental risk factors is that of head injury; for example, through involvement in certain types of employment and sports. But a more subtle environmental factor is suggested by the relationship between education and Alzheimer's disease: There is the strong probability that individuals who remain mentally active in old age will be more likely to postpone or even evade Alzheimer's disease.

Carriers, Performance Style, and Alzheimer's Disease

In the search for solutions, it is important to go beyond issues of performance capacity and to attend with care to issues of performance style, the meaning of behavior, and the carriers that sustain meanings. This approach requires closer attention to culture and the details of everyday social interactions.

Searching for Solutions

Ours is the age of science and technology. We tend to see all human health problems from a medical perspective and to place our faith in technical solutions. Not surprisingly, the main focus in the search for solutions to Alzheimer's disease has been biological research. Some progress is being made in discovering biological changes associated with Alzheimer's disease, in identifying and predicting susceptibility to the disease, and even in finding possible remedies. For example, cell repair may provide practical solutions to at least some cases of Alzheimer's disease in the next few decades. But like other biological solutions to Alzheimer's disease, there are a lot of uncertainties in this approach. We cannot be sure as to when research projects will yield practical solutions or which research avenues will ultimately prove successful.

The urgent need for more immediate solutions is underlined by the suffering of the increasing number of people afflicted by Alzheimer's disease in both Western and non-Western societies, as well as by purely practical economic challenges. In the United States alone, if the onset of Alzheimer's could be delayed in individuals by five years, there would be an estimated annual savings of more than $50 billion in health care costs. Western nations are finding it difficult to bear the heavy health care costs of Alzheimer's disease, but the costs are an even greater challenge for third world societies already struggling to make any real economic progress. Clearly, we cannot wait for the far-off solutions promised by biological research; immediate solutions are needed.

A very promising path to solutions *is* at hand. This path has been opened up by researchers looking at the social relationships of Alzheimer's sufferers. By contrasting change at the biological level and change at the level of social relations, an important insight has been gained. Although Alzheimer's disease typically involves biological change that spans many years and even decades, change in social relations for Alzheimer's sufferers is often very rapid and dramatic. Change in social relations can occur instantly, as soon as psychological tests are completed and a person is labeled an "Alzheimer's sufferer." In one moment, perceptions change and the still-intact abilities of Alzheimer's sufferers are overlooked.

The dramatic and powerful impact of this kind of labeling has been demonstrated in numerous different settings, including the classroom. Research shows that when children are given a positive label, such as "gifted," their academic performance can improve markedly, in large part because of the changed expectations of not only themselves but also of teachers and other key people in the social environment. This happens even when the tests on which such labels are based have no objective merit and the children labeled "gifted" are selected purely on a chance basis.

At least since the 1950s, sociologists have demonstrated the powerful impact of labeling and stigmatization on individuals and groups. Study after study has demonstrated that those who are labeled come under tremendous pressure to adapt their self-conceptions, such that they come to think of themselves in the way that they are labeled. Of course, this does not mean that all minorities have low self-esteem and feel stigmatized. The ghettoization and marginalization of minority groups can serve as mechanism for self-protection under certain conditions. The redefinition of "Black as Beautiful" was no doubt influenced by such processes. But in situations in which a single individual, such as an Alzheimer's sufferer, comes under pressure from powerful medical, professional, and familial forces, it is more likely that labeling will have a negative and major effect on the target.

Stereotypes as Carriers

Imagine that a huge publicity campaign is launched by government security forces with the purpose of catching a group of terrorists suspected of planning a bomb attack. Photographs and descriptions of the suspected terrorists are published in all newspapers and broadcast on television, and all your friends notice a striking resemblance between a picture of one of the terrorists and you. For a while you laugh about the "joke," but after being stopped and searched several times by police, the situation stops being funny. Each time you go out in public, to shop or to go to a movie or restaurant or for some other reason, you are anxious that people might see you as a terrorist. This threat in the air begins to make your life uncomfortable. After a week, the real terrorists are captured and the threat evaporates for you. However, for many seniors the threat of being stereotyped as an "Alzheimer's type" is real and very difficult to shake off.

Being social constructions themselves, stereotypes are well adapted to survive through numerous carriers. For example, plays, songs, and jokes and "humorous" stories with ethnic characters serve as powerful carriers for stereotypes about ethnic minorities in Western societies. Even at the turn of the twenty-first century, one can find demeaning sculptures of African Americans in the gardens of some houses in the southern parts of the United States. All kinds of artistic works serve as carriers for stereotypes, many of which are about groups of people deemed to be mentally ill.

Fortunately, there are many effective strategies for dealing with such "threats." Individuals diagnosed as suffering from Alzheimer's disease do not just passively conform to the stereotype of what an Alzheimer's sufferer is supposed to be like. Other people may assume them to have no memory or cognitive or social abilities left, but they often try to find opportunities to use and demonstrate their abilities that are still intact. Such opportunities may not arise in many contexts, but when they are available they are often snatched. The following cases illustrates this point.

Mrs. D had been diagnosed with Alzheimer's disease when she was 65 years old. By the time she was 70, standard tests assessed her as moderately to severely afflicted. She experienced frequent word-finding problems, she failed to remember some basic things (such as her age, the day of the week, and the year), and she could not coordinate her movements to accomplish some everyday tasks (such as getting food to her mouth). According to her husband, she might have suffered from delusions. For example, when her husband drove her to a day-care center, she would urge him to hurry so that she would not be late "for work."

The label "Alzheimer's sufferer" could easily have led others, even her husband, to view Mrs. D's behavior as "delusional." However, a more careful and detailed investigation into her situation revealed that her concern for not being late "for work" made good sense. Mrs. D's "job" was to serve as a morale raiser, to be the "life of the party," at the day-care center she attended. She had been brought up in a show business family, and she still knew numerous songs and jokes. She would sing and tell jokes and get people singing and laughing along with her. Although her husband reported that she did nothing around their home, Mrs. D did a lot around the day-care center. She helped set tables for meals, moved furniture around for different activities, helped people in wheelchairs get around, alerted staff to people needing attention, directed people to bathrooms. She would strike up conversations with people who seemed isolated, and the staff at the center began to rely on her to help them lift the spirits of individuals doing poorly. She even cheered up staff members.

Although Mrs. D was not officially employed at the day-care center, the work she had taken on was important, both for her personally and for the rest of the people at the center. She served a highly useful function. She also made herself useful in other ways, such as by volunteering as a participant in research projects at the National Institutes of Health. Clearly, this kind of "job" gave a great deal of satisfaction, because she was willing to expose herself to psychological test batteries on which she knew she performed poorly. It was more important for her to do the job of being useful than it was to "look good" on tests in front of psychologists and others.

Mrs. D seemed to have developed two separate existences. At home, she was passive and did not seem able to participate in activities. She showed little initiative and was more dependent. In the day-care center, however, she had a "job" and performed her "duties" conscientiously. She showed initiative and seemed to get satisfaction from participation. One explanation for this is that after she was diagnosed with Alzheimer's disease, her intact abilities were overlooked in the home environment. She could not do a lot of routine things and she could not remember many routine bits of information, and this seemed to conform to the idea that she was completely dependent. It was overlooked, by her husband and others, that there was still a great deal she could do. Her intact abilities had an opportunity to blossom in the day-care center. One of the interesting things this points to is the positive role some types of day institutions can perform in caring for Alzheimer's sufferers.

A great deal of criticism has been leveled at total institutions as a solution for the aged, and for the most part rightly so. Total institutions have typically restricted old people and robbed them of opportunities to remain active. However, some part-time day-care centers have been much more successful—economically because of their lower costs and in terms of health because they often allow participants to remain more active.

The Margin-of-Performance Expectations and Scaffolding

Despite the shortcomings of Western societies in coping with the challenge of old age and Alzheimer's disease, the actual coping strategies of individual Alzheimer's sufferers provides some hope. As Steven Sabat and others have recently documented through detailed case studies, Alzheimer's sufferers adopt a variety of different coping styles, many of which are aimed at influencing change rather than just remaining passive in the face of it. The cases of Dr. M, briefly discussed earlier in this chapter, and Mrs. D represent contrasting coping styles. Dr. M tried to cope by withdrawing from the activities of the day-care center, by simply avoiding all social interactions that threatened her status and showed what she *could not do*. She made a point of having minimal exposure to psychological-testing situations. As she put it, she did not want her life to be one of "always going to see people to see what's wrong with me." She withdrew from an Alzheimer's support group because she did not want to embarrass herself in a group setting, where she found her level of speech very limited compared to what it had been previously. From one perspective, Dr. M's strategy seems passive, because she withdrew from activities. But from an alternative viewpoint, her strategy was active and intended to maintain greater control of change, to not allow herself to be pushed along by forces she could not influence.

Mrs. D also adopted a combination of coping styles. In the home setting, she coped with change by retreating, by doing very little, and by allowing her husband to direct activities. But her behavior changed dramatically in the day-care center, where she was continually diving into social situations in order to initiate change, exert influence, help others, and thus gain status in this new social context. Mrs. D was interested in changing her own label from "patient" to "helper," from receiver of help to giver of help to others. Unlike Dr. M, she went out of her way to be a participant in psychological research. It mattered so much to her to be seen as a "helper," "volunteer," and "active" that she was willing to take tests that she knew revealed her inabilities on even simple tasks. Also, it was exactly because she could have said "no" to the opportunity to participate in research that it was more attractive to her to demonstrate her active and participatory nature by saying "yes." Such cases underline the strong role of social context and societal expectations in the development of even those aspects of experience, such as suffering from Alzheimer's disease, that may at first appear to be based purely on performance capacity and biological processes.

But the individual with Alzheimer's disease needs effective professional support to cope with the enormous challenges confronting him or her. One way in which such support can be provided is by training professionals and family caregivers to use a method akin to scaffolding, a Vygotskian strategy we discussed earlier in Chapter 11. In the following, Steven Sabat (S.R.S) demonstrates this method while interacting with "B," an Alzheimer's sufferer:

S.R.S: The other day you mentioned that you had some problem with (name of the program director). Does that strike any familiar notes?

B.: Every so often I, I get uh, frustrated with him.

S.R.S: This is (name)—with the moustache?

B.: Yeah, yeah. I like him very much. Um, he, he goes to a, let's see how could I do it? I'm certy not nasty with him at all whatsoever, and but uh, every so often, uh, uh, the uh, Barnum and Bailey—it's the Barnum and Bailey that I don't like.

S.R.S: You mean it's like a circus around here?

B.: Oh yeah. It's a big, tremendously big circus . . .

S.R.S: All of the chaos becomes very difficult for you to deal with?

B.: Yeah . . .

—Sabat, 1994, p. 337

In this interaction, Sabat makes the connection between what the Alzheimer's sufferer says and a circus, and directly asks: "You mean it's like a circus around here?" Next, Sabat asks if it is the chaos that is difficult to deal with, and the Alzheimer's sufferer confirms this. What we have here, then, is a collaborative process, whereby a scaffolding is constructed to help the person with Alzheimer's disease express his intended meaning. Because the margin of performance expectations is minimal, and because of scaffolding support, the Alzheimer's sufferer is able to communicate better than his individual performance capacity alone would allow.

Concluding Comment

Over the next few decades there will be enormous moral and economic pressures to find effective solutions to the problems of the rapidly increasing population of Alzheimer's sufferers. Effective and affordable medical treatment in the form of drug therapy does not seem to be at hand in the immediate future and may not be available for many years to come. But the detailed, innovative, and truly insightful research of a small handful of scholars, as discussed above, suggests that the situation can be alleviated in major ways. Such research can help to better educate both professionals and family caregivers.

Negative stereotypes about old people generally, and Alzheimer's sufferers specifically, mean that the margin of performance expectations is often very wide: Caregivers and even professionals, as well as the general lay public, tend to expect a person labeled as an Alzheimer's sufferer to communicate poorly or not at all and to be cognitively impaired in serious ways. But this expectation can often be wrong, particularly in the early stages of the disease.

Although the biological changes associated with Alzheimer's disease can take many years to have a serious impact, the labeling of a person as an Alzheimer's sufferer can have an immediate and terrible impact. Standardized tests on an isolated individual, assessed out of social context, can in a matter of minutes negatively label a person and lead to dramatically changed expectations for behavior. As long as standardized tests focus exclusively on performance capacity and ignore performance style and the carriers that sustain meaning systems, they will continue to be part of the problem rather than the solution to the plight of individuals with Alzheimer's disease.

On the other hand, appropriate training for caregivers and professionals can allow a person who is identified as being in an early stage of Alzheimer's disease to function adequately and at least semi-independently for many years. Part of such training should be the use of scaffolding—providing support to Alzheimer's sufferers so that they can communicate more fully in order to express their intentions more clearly.

Suggested Readings

American Federation for Aging Research (AFAR) and the Alliance for Aging Research. (1995). *Putting aging on hold: Delaying the diseases of old age* (Report to the White House Conference on Aging). Washington, DC: Alliance for Aging Research.

Cole, T. R., & Winkler, M. G. (Eds.). (1994). *The Oxford book of aging: Reflections on the journey of life*. Oxford: Oxford University Press.

Goffman, E. (1963). *Stigma: Notes on the management of spoiled identity*. Englewood Cliffs, NJ: Prentice-Hall.

Jorm, A. F. (1990). *The epidemiology of Alzheimer's disease and related disorders*. London: Chapman & Hall.

Kitwood, T. (1990). The dialetics of dementia: With particular reference to Alzheimer's disease. *Ageing and Society, 10,* 177–196.

Rosenthal, R. (1991). Teacher expectancy effects: A brief update 25 years after the Pygmalian experiment. *Journal of Research in Education, 1,* 3–12.

Sabat, S. R. (1994). Language function in Alzheimer's disease: A critical review of selected literature. *Language & Communication, 14,* 331–351.

Sabat, S. R. (2001). *The experience of Alzheimer's disease: Life through a tangled web.* Oxford: Blackwell.

Sabat, S. R., Fath, H., Moghaddam, F. M., & Harré, R. (1999). The maintenance of self-esteem: Lessons from the culture of Alzheimer's sufferers. *Culture and Psychology, 5,* 5–31.

Sidorenko, A. (1993). The UN program on aging: Towards a practical strategy 1992–2001. In J. L. C. Dall, M. Ermani., P. L. Herrling, U. Lehr, W. Meier-Ruge, & H. B. Stahelin, *Prospects in aging* (pp. xxi–xxvii). New York: Academic Press.

Steele, C. (1997). A threat in the air: How stereotypes shape intellectual identity and performance. *American Psychologist, 52,* 613–629.

Van Duijn, C. M., Stijnen, T., & Hofman, A. (1991). Risk factors for Alzheimer's disease: Overview of the EURODEM collaborative re-analysis of case-control studies. *International Journal of Epidemiology, 20,* S4–S11.

15

Carriers: The Individual in Society and Society in the Individual

She's become a lot more poised and confident since she started ballet. Both my husband and I noticed it. Of course it's good exercise, but besides that we want her to be elegant. We don't like a lot of the new trends in education; all this political correctness has gone too far. Of course, women have to have equal rights, go as far as they can in education. I have a law degree, but at the same time I think women should have grace, be elegant, be feminine. There are some things worth keeping. A lot of traditions are wonderful, and we want to keep them. Modern dance and jazz and all that is fine, I like some of it, but it doesn't give a woman poise and elegance the way ballet does. Even if my daughter never practices ballet again after this year, for the rest of her life when she walks across a room, anyone with an eye for these things will recognize her poise.

While interviewing the parents of young girls attending ballet classes, such as the mother quoted above, it became clear to me and my student collaborators that many such parents think of ballet as much more than dance and a lot more than just exercise. For many, ballet serves as a powerful carrier, sustaining key values associated with gender roles. Ballet, they assume, can help girls gain the poise needed to be "ladylike"—to sit, stand, walk, talk, and generally behave in a feminine manner. Ballet is part of a tradition that many of them strive to maintain.

The same themes of tradition and continuity can be found in the literature designed to teach children about ballet. In an authoritative book for young readers, the ballet dancer Anton Dolin declares, "I deplore the changing of the great classics, whether by the young who know no better or by the older who certainly should. Who would dare change a note of a Beethoven or Tchaikovsky symphony or change the colour or figures of a Goya or Raphael masterpiece?" (quoted in Gregory, p. 7). In a more recent book for *The Young Dancer*, the ballerina Darcey Bussell stresses the same theme of tradition in advice to the newest generation of children in ballet classes: "You need to feel and understand the tradition of ballet. Try to learn and appreciate it for yourself and feel that you are part of it. Your dancing will grow and develop in feeling if you know about other arts, too, such as music and painting" (p.7). Such instruction books stress tradition, grace, poise, discipline, proper dress, and proper communications, such as how to bow or curtsy at the end of a class.

Moreover, the decision to send a young child to ballet class is intended, sometimes explicitly, to influence more than just the life of that particular child. By training their children in ballet, some parents see themselves as sustaining a larger tradition, one that runs counter to some more recent trends, such as those associated with popular culture (rap music and so on) and sometimes also with political correctness in education. This, then, is an example of individuals intentionally making decisions in their everyday lives in a way that aims to influence some aspects of the larger society that are of high value to them personally.

Far from behaving like helpless pawns, individuals often intentionally make choices in their everyday lives with the goal of impacting the larger society around them. The exploration of carriers enables us to better unravel how even seemingly "trivial" choices, such as deciding between ballet and modern dance classes for a child, are sometimes made with very important and large-scale issues in mind. A number of parents we interviewed argued that if sufficiently large enough numbers of parents chose ballet and the values associated with ballet, they would be able to influence the climate of educational institutions thus change the culture of schools. All this is attempted through first training a child in ballet; in other words, using ballet as a gateway for the child to enter into society and, after entering, to influence society.

The vast majority of individuals exert whatever power they can by sustaining or rejecting existing carriers, such as ballet, through choices in their everyday lives, but they do not enjoy the power to construct new carriers *and* to make them widely effective. However, a very small elite do enjoy such power; examples are routinely reported in the media. This morning I came across the following example reported in a story appearing on the front page of my daily newspaper:

> About two years ago, newspaper, magazine and television news stories began popping up across the country about a little-known malady called social anxiety disorder. Psychiatrists and patient advocates appeared on television shows and in articles explaining that the debilitating form of bashfulness was extremely widespread and easily treatable. The stories and appearances were part of a campaign, coordinated by a New York public relations agency, that included pitches to

newspapers, radio and TV, satellite and Internet communications, and testimonials from advocates and doctors who said social anxiety was America's third most common mental disorder with more than 10 million sufferers.

—*Washington Post,* July 16, 2001, p.1

According to this report, the advertising campaign was so successful that media accounts of social anxiety increased from just 50 stories in 1997 and 1998 to more than 1 billion references in 1999. The vast majority of these stories informed the audience that "Paxil is the first and only FDA-approved medication for the treatment of social anxiety disorder." The public relations agency and the entire "educational campaign" were funded by the pharmaceutical company that manufactures the antidepressant Paxil.

The case of "social anxiety disorder" is one of many that illustrate the power of elites to construct effective new carriers. (For another example of such cases "hyped" in the mass media, see Mary Egan's article on so-called Syndrome X in *Forbes* magazine, listed in the Suggested Readings at the end of this chapter. We are asked to believe that one in four Americans has a mysterious and potentially fatal condition known as Syndrome X.) Through the newly created carrier "social anxiety disorder," millions of people have been persuaded to interpret their bashfulness as a "disorder," as something that is abnormal and must be *assessed through a medical model and treated through drug therapy.* Once again, the focus is on the search for causes within isolated individuals, with complete disregard for the context of their lives. This is particularly ironic in this case, because so-called social anxiety disorder has been manufactured by the context—it is purely a cultural construct, created for marketing purposes. Out of the millions of individuals influenced by this carrier, perhaps several hundred actually need medical help through drug therapy. For the rest, there is no need for drug therapy, profitable though it is for shareholders in pharmaceutical companies, because so-called social anxiety disorder is not a chemical problem with the brain but rather a carrier that sustains particular ways of interpreting the world.

The case of this newly manufactured carrier also illustrates the process of society entering the individual. Through the accumulated influence of psychiatrists, psychologists, and other "experts," as well as countless media talk shows and other outlets, the new carrier becomes widely known and easily available for appropriation by individuals. It "enters into" individuals by becoming part of their everyday knowledge about the world, by becoming something they, too, can talk about and act on. The "problem," social anxiety disorder, and the "solution," the drug, become part of the common sense of the culture.

Carriers, then, are numerous and pervasive in the lives of both elites and nonelites. In this final chapter, I want to explore the dynamic picture of human behavior we arrive at through the concept of carriers. To begin, I examine the implications of carriers for how we go about examining the individual and society.

Implications of Carriers

Carriers act as transporters of meaning; they are containers into which people load values, beliefs, faith, and the like. The most important carriers are "out there" in public space, and they are shared by many, sometimes millions of, different people. Many such carriers span generations, helping to sustain ways of doing and thinking, sometimes over thousands of years. Well-known examples are carriers that support continuity in religious activities, such as the Christian cross.

Carriers are at once public and collective, private and individual. They are public and collective in the sense that they are present in public space and are collaboratively constructed through the contributions of many people over many generations. For example, in some countries a military uniform acts as a carrier of honor and patriotism, and this has been so for centuries. But carriers are at the same time private and individual in the sense that each individual has a personal representation of a military uniform in her or his mind, and some aspects of this representation may be unique. For example, while a military uniform generally is a carrier of honor and patriotism for Janet, she feels particular pride in being a female officer in the army. The uniform has a special meaning for her that is not shared by Wendy, who is a civilian.

The concept of carrier guides us to look to the larger, shared, collaboratively constructed social world for explanations of human behavior. Although representations of carriers exist inside private minds, carriers are effective through being "out there" in the external world. This has a number of important implications, as discussed below.

Beyond Reductionism

Reductionism, the tendency to analyze phenomena by focusing on smaller and smaller units, is a fundamental and pervasive shortcoming of contemporary research on human behavior. Reductionism has led to an almost complete neglect of the context and the larger world of meaning in which human behavior takes place. Researchers have turned inward to focus on isolated "mental mechanisms" or biological processes as explanations of how humans behave. This strong bias in favor of reductionism arises from the cultural characteristics of the dominant society in the world, the United States.

The ideology of self-help and individual responsibility, reflecting the pervasive individualism of U.S. culture, in large part explains the prominence of reductionist research strategies in the twenty-first century. The rise of research areas such as cognitive psychology, neuroscience, and sociobiology—and their influence on psychology, sociology, anthropology, economics, and political science—has a lot more to do with the cultural biases of the United States than with the scientific merit of such approaches. Cognitive psychology, neuroscience, and sociobiology keep the focus on smaller, nonsocial units, such as assumed cognitive processes, neurons, and genes; they are part of a reductionist tradition.

Of course, this is not to suggest that cognitive psychology, neuroscience, and sociobiology do not have valuable contributions to make to human knowledge. Rather, my claim is that the enormous and *disproportional* resources and attention allocated to these research areas—and their very great prominence in the contemporary world—arises from their perfect fit with the individualism of U.S. culture. It is not difficult to imagine that in a different world order—one headed by India or China, for example—the areas of research given greatest prominence would be different. In particular, the role of context and community might be taken more seriously, particularly in attempts to change behavior. Therapeutic techniques, for example, would focus more on changing relationships and the social context, rather than focusing almost exclusively on processes inside a person.

Thus, I am interpreting reductionism as a direct product of strong cultural biases in the United States, biases that depict behavior as causally determined by intraindividual characteristics, things inside persons. I am also pointing out that far from being unbiased and objective, research fields such as cognitive psychology, neuroscience, and sociobiology are the areas *most* influenced by this cultural bias.

Beyond Performance Capacity and the Causal Model

Perhaps the greatest mistake of students of human behavior since the mid-nineteenth century has been to try to copy the physical sciences, such as chemistry and physics. Of course, it is not difficult to see why students of human behavior took this path: They wanted to emulate the "real" sciences and thus to enjoy the high status of science rather than be branded "soft" and similar to the arts and humanities. They, too, wanted to be able to put forward "scientific facts" and to have their findings interpreted as objective.

One way to achieve this, it has been assumed, is to study the internal characteristics of isolated individuals under controlled conditions, just as a biochemist might isolate an enzyme and study its characteristics in laboratory conditions.

Undoubtedly, some concepts and ideas are transferable from the physical sciences to the study of human behavior; broadly, these are the ones most appropriate for studying performance capacity (as discussed in Chapter 1). But certain fundamental differences exist between studying human beings and studying nonhuman phenomena, and in traditional research no more than lip service is given to this fundamental difference. An obvious point is that students of human behavior share the same characteristics as the object of their study, one such characteristic being the tendency both to be influenced by and to contribute to the shaping of cultural surroundings. Human beings reflect on, and intentionally change, their own surroundings; and the surroundings in turn influence human behavior, a process Anthony Giddens terms "double structuration" and discusses with much insight. One of the most important features of the context is carriers, particularly their collaboratively constructed and collectively sustained nature.

I have introduced the concepts of performance capacity and performance style to clarify the domains in which it is, and is not, appropriate to transfer methods of study from the physical sciences to the study of human behavior. Performance capacity concerns human abilities that are determined by physical characteristics, such as how well a person can see or hear. Such capacities are causally determined by the physical characteristics of persons, just as the activities of an enzyme are determined by its physical properties. For example, when David is in an automobile accident and suffers an eye injury, the physical disability causes him to see less well.

But how David interprets what he sees—the meaning he ascribes to the world around him—is a matter of performance style, and this is not explained by the kind of causal relationship found in the physical sciences. For David, an activist in the growing anti-globalization movement, the World Bank serves as a carrier of pro-globalization values. A first issue is how well David can see the World Bank building as he stands across the street from it in Washington, D.C., but a second issue is the meanings this building carries for him. Through social interactions with numerous others in the anti-globalization movement, David has participated in the collaborative construction of the carrier "World Bank," and this carrier sustains values and meanings central to his life as a citizen of the world.

Thus, in order to emulate the physical sciences, students of human behavior have seen it as appropriate to treat all human behavior as capacities that can be measured on a low–high continuum. What is being measured is assumed to be dependent on characteristics internal to the individual. For example, personality is reduced to scores on a low–high continuum on each of five factors (Chapter 8), and intelligence is reduced to a score on a low–high continuum on an IQ scale (Chapter 9)—all on the assumption that factors internal to individuals determine such scores. But as Michael Cole and others have demonstrated, the results produced by such research are highly dependent on the nature of the research instruments being used. When Cole used traditional Western measures of intelligence, his non-Western test-takers scored very low. But when he assessed the same individuals using tests more appropriate for their cultures, they scored much higher. Studies by Fanny Cheung and others in China have shown that even if the standard personality-measurement procedures are used, results would look very different if Chinese rather than U.S. researchers dominated the field of personality assessment.

The concept of carriers highlights the importance of the collaboratively constructed world outside the individual: the shared culture into which individuals enter and which they help to shape. Another implication of carriers concerns continuities in culture and behavior, in both collective and individual life.

Toward Understanding Continuity

Paris's Crillon Ball is a debutante dance with a fashion accent. Twenty-four young women, chosen from the international crème de la crème, are presented in haute couture gowns by renowned designers . . . the tenth edition included four princesses and the daughter of an English marquess. But all eyes were on American Lauren Bush, granddaughter of the first President Bush, niece of the present President Bush. . . . She was escorted by Prince Louis de Bourbon . . . direct descendent of the Bourbon kings of France.

—*Town & Country*, April 2001, p. 31

"Faster! Faster!" And they went so fast that at last they seemed to skim through the air, hardly touching the ground with their feet, till suddenly, just as Alice was getting quite exhausted, they stopped, and she found herself sitting on the ground, breathless and giddy.

The Queen propped her up against a tree, and said kindly, "You may rest a little, now."

Alice looked around her in great surprise. "Why, I do believe we've been under this tree the whole time! Everything's just as it was!"

"Of course it is," said the Queen, "What would you have it?"

"Well, in *our* country," said Alice, still panting a little, "you'd generally get to somewhere else—if you ran very fast for a long time as we've been doing."

"A slow sort of country!" said the Queen. "Now, *here*, you see, it takes all the running you can do, to keep in the same place. If *you* want to get somewhere else, you must run at least twice as fast as that."

—Lewis Carroll, *Alice's Adventures in Wonderland*, pp. 209–210

An important contribution of carriers is in highlighting processes of continuity in human societies. The identification of continuity is of particular value in our era, when there is so much talk of the increasingly fast pace of life. The rapid speed of technological change and shifts in certain aspects of lifestyles such as changes in family structure and the decline of the traditional family, can lead to the impression that everything is changing and that modern societies have little in common with societies 50 or 100 or 1,000 years ago. Indeed, in twenty-first-century North America people often feel like Alice when she finds herself in a country where "it takes all the running you can do, to keep in the same place." Carriers such as "American exceptionalism," discussed in Chapter 4, underline this idea of the United States being a different kind of place, a society that changes rapidly and is not hindered by the inequalities and social-class markers characteristic of the Old World of Europe, with its (assumed) class system and inherited inequalities.

But through carriers we can gain a different perspective on continuity and change, one that allows us to identify processes through which people *intentionally* sustain certain activities, values, beliefs—and a way of life more generally—both in the United States and elsewhere. One example is the debutante ball, referred to above in the quotation from the magazine *Town & Country*. The debutante ball had its origins in England, where aristocratic families took up the tradition of presenting their daughters of marriageable age at the Court of St. James (the title given to the court of the kings and queens of England). After a young lady was presented at court and completed the ceremonial bow to the queen, she was considered as being officially "out" in society. The rest of the "season" consisted of balls given by different aristocratic families, in which marriageable young men and women would meet. The main purpose of the debutante ball, then, was to ensure that young men and women from "the right kind of" families married into other such families.

The debutante ball might have disappeared in England in the latter part of the nineteenth century, when the power and wealth of the landed gentry declined and that of the newly emerging manufacturing class increased. The entrepreneurs who made up the "new rich" could have set aside archaic traditions, such as having their daughters do the "St. James Bow" at court. However, rather than doing away with debutante balls, the new rich bought into them and made them even more extravagant.

Similarly, the people in the New World of North America, avowedly opposed to the elitism and the prejudices of Old World Europe, might have turned away from the debutante ball. But far from it! There were already early forms of the debutante ball in Philadelphia in the eighteenth century, and in the twenty-first century just about every major region of the United States has its own "deb season," and this is in addition to the national and international seasons. The new world order and the global economy have been very kind to the debutante ball.

The debutante ball is a carrier that sustains fundamentally important values associated with distinctions between the elite and the nonelite. The separateness and superiority of the elite is endorsed, in part by the exclusiveness of the event and in part by the highlighting of historical "aristocratic" links. For example, in the case of Paris's Crillon Ball, not only are the debutantes chosen from an international crème de la crème but genuine princesses and other aristocrats attend. Their escorts are similarly "superior," with several princes among them.

The theme of continuity becomes particularly intriguing in the case of the star couple at the ball, the debutante Lauren Bush and her escort Prince Louis de Bourbon. Prince Louis is legitimized by being a descendant of the Bourbon kings, and Lauren Bush is legitimized by being a descendant of an elite American family, living members of which are the former President Bush and his son, the current President Bush. The debutante ball serves as a carrier in both New and Old Worlds, illuminating *normative distance*: the distance between the formal system and the informal system, what is formally presented as taking place and what actually takes place. There are many examples of this in daily life. For example, Americans experienced a dramatic reminder of normative distance in the 2000 presidential election. The crafting of the formal picture of what took place was dominated by the Republican party and led to the presidency of George Bush, while the informal picture of events was experienced and constructed very differently by the opposition, particularly by some African-American voters in Florida.

The continuity of normative distance is sustained through carriers, anchored as they are to everyday social practices. Because the informal normative system is mostly implicit and integrated tightly into the fabric of everyday social practices, it is extremely difficult to change by relying only on top-down solutions. For example, the disenfranchisement of some African-American voters in Florida in the 2000 presidential election is intimately connected with everyday social practices and relations between blacks and whites—the details of discriminatory practices ingrained in U.S. culture and social life—and will not be causally affected through top-down efforts alone. The persistence of such challenges is obvious not only in the "dirty" world of politics but also in academia, where numerous carriers sustain continuity of inequalities.

An example of such carriers is science, which continues to be anchored in everyday social practices that still work against some female academics in fields such as physics, mathematics, and chemistry (interestingly, there is growing concern that an anti-male bias is becoming institutionalized in some humanities and social science fields). A 2001 report in the journal *Science* reflects this state of affairs, which is perplexing if viewed from a traditional perspective that ignores the role of normative distance and the details of informal daily practices. Although 31 percent of the Ph.D. pool of chemists is now female, only 7 percent of full professors, 16 percent of associate professors, and 14 percent of assistant professors in chemistry departments at nine top U.S. research universities are females. This is decades after antidiscrimination legislation changed the official context for hiring in academia. It is only through attending to the fine details of everyday practices, such as subtle communication cues and networking styles, that it becomes apparent how carriers such as science serve to uphold an informal normative system that perpetuates inequalities (as discussed in the case of gender relations in Chapter 6).

Future Directions

Further explorations of carriers must begin by dealing with a "straw man" criticism concerning the so-called group-mind fallacy, and it is to this that I turn next.

The Group-Mind Straw Man

I have criticized reductionism and the tendency to focus on assumed causal factors within individuals. As an alternative approach, I have drawn attention to carriers and the collaboratively constructed social world *outside* the individual. This orientation may lead some critics to accuse me of assuming that a "group mind" exists. As Gustav Jahoda has shown, this line of attack has been well known at least since Wilhelm Wundt (1832–1920) produced his 10-volume treatise on *Volkerpsychologie*, typically translated as "Folk Psychology," in the latter part of the nineteenth century.

Critics of the idea that more attention needs to be given to context and collective processes outside the individual often drag out the straw man of group mind, on the assumption that attention to collective processes (and concepts such as carriers) must necessarily assume a group mind. These critics then set about knocking down the straw man of group mind by using variations of the following argument: Thoughts exist only in individual minds, and actions are taken by individual persons. There is no such thing as a collective brain or a group mind. Even when a large group of individuals act in unison, and agree with one another in their thoughts, each mind is still a separate entity. Minds do not merge to make a collectivity. Thus the unit of analysis and the focus of study must remain the individual person.

The above analysis misses a major point made by Wundt in his monumental *Volkerpsychologie*, as well as by Lev Vygotsky and various modern cultural and discursive researchers, such as Jerome Bruner, Rom Harré, Michael Cole, and

Richard Shweder: It is not necessary to, and indeed one should not, assume a group mind, in order to give adequate attention to the collaboratively constructed social world of which the individual is a part. The focus on social life outside individuals highlights the features of the human world that stand apart from single persons, that do not depend on any particular individual for their existence. These features come to be appropriated by individuals and shared among groups of persons, but this in no way implies the existence of a group-mind.

Individuals tend to appropriate carriers in conformity with others in their group. Thus most people adopt the national flag of their country as a carrier, but not everyone does so. Also, a carrier that is adopted today may be abandoned tomorrow. This underlines flexibility in the use made of carriers.

Flexibility in the Use of Carriers

> Here is something material, something I can see, feel and understand. This means victory. This *is* victory.
> —Abraham Lincoln, upon receiving a captured Confederate battle flag (quoted in the *Washington Post,* April 23, 2000, p. F1)

The Confederate flag, once hailed by President Lincoln as a tangible indication of victory, continues to play an important role as a carrier in the United States, as shown by the high visibility of the flag in and around numerous American homes, particularly in the South, and the continued controversies about the official role of the flag in a number of southern states. The Confederate flag reflects continuity and stability as central features of carriers. But carriers are adopted by individuals and groups to serve particular purposes; they are first and foremost functional, a means to an end rather than an end in themselves. In order to serve their purposes, carriers have also to be flexible, in the sense that they could be set aside and taken up again as the need arises.

Consider, for example, the case of the veil worn by women (by force or otherwise, as discussed in Chapter 6) in many Islamic countries. The veil is used as a carrier of the traditional female role. In the case of Islamic women living in Western countries, conflicts often arise between the veil and the requirements of working outside the home in a modern Western society. The following is a report in a local Maryland paper showing how such conflicts can be resolved:

> A Montgomery County firefighter who converted to Islam has reached a compromise with her bosses on wearing a head scarf required by her religion . . . [she] can wear the hijab while on the job as a paramedic. She has agreed to switch to a fire-retardant hood when she's pressed into firefighting duties.
> —Associated Press, July 13, 2001

In the above case, although the veil continues to be retained as an important carrier by the new convert to Islam, she sets it aside and takes it up again as the situation demands (unfortunately, women in some Islamic countries, such as Iran and Afghanistan, do not have a choice in this matter; they have to wear the veil at all times). In other cases, a carrier can decline in importance but still be used in a ceremonial sense. For example, consider the following case of a bride and groom, a cadet at the U.S. Naval Academy in Annapolis, Maryland:

> [The] groom removes his bride's garter, a traditional symbol of virginity. By pub-
> licly removing her garter, [the] groom employs a Civil-War ritual to claim his
> bride in front of other young men in his community—in this case, fellow cadets.
> —David Cohen, *The Circle of Life*, p. 160.

On the surface, it may appear that this modern bride and groom are engaged in a ritual with little meaning; after all, mainstream modern America is far removed from societies in which the virginity of the bride is prized and considered essential for marriage. Although virginity has lost its traditional role in modern Western so-cieties, fidelity, loyalty, and honesty continue to be among the important character-istics prized in marriage partners. The ceremony of garter removal can still act as a carrier, but in a situation where there has been a reinterpretation of duties (as dis-cussed in Chapter 3). The bride is no longer expected to be a virgin, but she is ex-pected to be faithful to her husband. Thus her duty to be faithful has not changed, although how she should carry out this duty has changed.

The above cases reflect the functional aspect of carriers, which is primary. Carriers serve a purpose, and when they fail to do so they can be adapted or completely discarded. Consider, for example, bra burning as a carrier incorpo-rated into the women's movement in the 1960s, or the Afro haircut that served as a carrier in the African-American movement in that era. Both of these have been abandoned, because they are no longer effective today.

The flexibility of carriers—the ability of people to abandon some carriers and take up others—shows that the cause sustained by the carrier, rather than the carrier itself, is the most important element. Collective movements have shown again and again that they will strive to maintain carriers that are effec-tive and useful for their causes but will adopt new carriers when and if it serves their purpose to do so. The exploration of carriers highlights the fluid, dynamic, and evolving nature of the collaboratively constructed social world outside the individual. The study of carriers is part of a cultural turn in research.

Carriers and the Cultural Turn in Research on Human Behavior

Research on human behavior began to take a dramatic cultural turn in the last few decades of the twentieth century. This has largely been a result of the political influence of ethnic mobilization, involving the collective movement of African-Americans, Native Americans, and other minorities in North America. Other contributing factors have been increasing globalization and the growing populations of ethnic minorities in Western European countries (South Asians in England, North Africans in France, Turks in Germany, and so on). Ethnic-minority movements and increased contact between Westerners and non-Westerners have led to heightened awareness of cultural diversity both within nations and internationally as well as to a need for more research that takes culture into consideration.

A related dramatic shift has involved sharp criticisms of the traditional research methods employed to study human behavior. The major hallmarks of such traditional methods are (1) a focus on testing isolated individuals divorced from their cultural contexts and, (2) an exclusive reliance on quantitative methods. This line of criticism is associated with calls for more research using qualitative and mixed methods; that is, methods that combine a variety of quantitative and qualitative approaches. As Jaber Gubrium and James Holstein have pointed out, this movement has led to a new language of qualitative research methods; the entire discourse used to evaluate and conduct research is changing.

Another development has been the call for a more multidisciplinary approach to understanding the individual and society. Academics from many different disciplines have lamented the impact of rigid disciplinary boundaries and increasing specialization, as well as limitations of what I have discussed as *the specialized society*—social worlds characterized by increasing specialization and fragmentation. Greater efforts are being made to reach across specialty boundaries, as demonstrated by the rapid growth of multidisciplinary majors and minors on numerous university campuses. Perhaps as part of this same trend, a "holistic" liberal arts education is once again receiving strong support.

The exploration of carriers and the call for more attention to the relationship between individuals and the collaboratively constructed world outside individuals is in line with these three major developments: the cultural turn, more focus on qualitative and mixed methods, and a push toward multidiscipliary understanding. There is also a fourth trend, one that is not yet very explicit; it is indicated by the distinction I have drawn between performance capacity and performance style.

This fourth trend is toward a split between research that focuses on performance capacity (how well the human organism does on various tasks when tested in isolation) and research that focuses on performance style (the meaning various things have for people). For example, in the tradition of research on performance capacity, researchers address questions such as "How many bits of information can Jim remember after a week when tested under controlled laboratory conditions?" or "How has damage to part X of Jim's brain impacted on his ability to remember?" In the tradition of research on performance style, researchers address such questions as "How do Jim and his friends collaboratively construct the events of last week?" or "What carriers are used by Jim to sustain the memories of last week?" This split between research on performance capacity and on performance style will influence the ongoing reorganization of research and academic disciplines over the next century, breaking old boundaries and highlighting multidisciplicary studies.

Suggested Readings

Associated Press. (2001, July 13). Compromise reached to allow Muslim firefighter to wear scarf. *Montgomery Journal*, p. A3.

Bussell, D. (1994). *The young dancer.* London: Dorling Kindersley.

Carroll, L. (1998). *The annotated Alice: Alice's adventures in wonderland; Through the looking glass.* New York: Randon House. (Original work published 1871.)

Cheung, F. M., Leung, K., Zhang, J., Sun, H., Gan, Y., Song, W., & Xie, D. (2001). Indigenous Chinese personality constructs: Is the five-factor model complete? *Journal of Cross-Cultural Psychology, 32,* 407–433.

Cohen, D. (Ed.). (1991). *The circle of life: Rituals from the human family album.* New York: HarperCollins.

Cole, M. (1996). *Cultural psychology: A once and future science.* Cambridge, MA: Harvard University Press.

Egen, M. E. (2001, August 6). The unknown epidemic. *Forbes*, pp. 110–111.

Gregory, J. (1972). *Understanding ballet: The steps of dance from classroom to stage.* London: Octopus.

Gubrium, J. F., & Holstein, J. A. (1997). *The new language of qualitative method.* New York: Oxford University Press.

Jahoda, G. (1993). *Crossroads between culture and mind: Continuities and change in theories of human nature.* Cambridge, MA: Harvard University Press.

Lawler, A. (2001). College heads pledge to remove barriers. *Science, 291,* 806.

Moghaddam, F. M. (1997). *The specialized society: The plight of the individual in an age of individualism.* Westport, CT: Praeger.

Vedantam, S. (2001, July 16). Drug ads hyping anxiety make some uneasy. *Washington Post*, pp. A1, A6.

Name
Index

Subject Index